Veterinary Forensic Pathology, Volume 2

Jason W. Brooks

Editor

Veterinary Forensic Pathology, Volume 2

 Springer

Editor
Jason W. Brooks
Department of Veterinary and Biomedical Sciences
The Pennsylvania State University
University Park
Pennsylvania
USA

ISBN 978-3-319-67173-4   ISBN 978-3-319-67175-8   (eBook)
https://doi.org/10.1007/978-3-319-67175-8

Library of Congress Control Number: 2018930341

Printed on acid-free paper

This Springer imprint is published by Springer Nature
The registered company is Springer International Publishing AG
The registered company address is: Gewerbestrasse 11, 6330 Cham, Switzerland

For my Family, and for those who cannot speak for themselves
Speravit anima mea…exaudi vocem meam

Preface

What is truth? This fundamental concept has inspired me since childhood. The quest for truth has been a continual motivation through a lifelong journey in search of answers to questions that others would not ask. Truth, at times, can be humbling, unwelcome, and disconcerting to the unprepared mind. Truth can be foul and offensive, surprising and spectacular, dirty and horrific, but it remains truth nonetheless. Both liberating and incriminating, it cannot be defiled or adulterated. Truth is what is. This is its simple elegant beauty.

Forensic pathology is, at its core, a quest for the discovery of truth. The recognition and development of the subdiscipline of veterinary forensic pathology within the broader field of veterinary pathology seemed almost an impossibility only a decade ago. Yet today there is more interest and demand than ever for such expertise, and requests for forensic necropsy are increasing at an unprecedented rate. Yet, despite the apparent need and the interest of a small passionate segment of veterinary pathologists, there is a paucity of training courses and reference materials in the field. This textbook is an earnest effort to not only fill the void in reference materials but also pioneer a new era in veterinary medicine and pathology—an era in which the truth can be brought to light through science, and the voices of the victims may finally speak through those who understand.

I am proud to be breaking new ground with the publication of the first textbook solely dedicated to veterinary forensic pathology. With expertise ranging from animal fighting and hoarding to ballistics, toxicology, thanatology, entomology, and a variety of traumatic injuries, this group of contributing authors represents a veritable force in the quest for truth through the investigation of animal crimes. These contributors are among the most talented and seasoned experts in the discipline, and I am honored and humbled to have each of them as a part of this team.

While no single resource alone can transform a professional into a competent veterinary forensic pathologist, this textbook will assist the properly trained veterinary pathologist, forensic veterinarian, or other veterinary professional as they attempt to interpret the tangled web of clues left among the dead. It is my sincere hope that this textbook will serve as a useful and practical reference for the forensic necropsy of the many unfortunate animal victims and that within its pages will be found some wisdom that will aid in the investigation and resolution of animal crimes.

The truth remains to be told to us if we are only wise enough to know how to listen.

Quid est veritas?

University Park, PA, USA   Jason W. Brooks

Contents

Drowning and Bodies Recovered from Water

Beverly J. McEwen and Jodie A. Gerdin

1.1 Introduction

Determining the cause of death in animals recovered from bodies of water, swimming pools, or other water-containing vessels is challenging. The key question is "Was the animal alive when it entered the water?" [1]. Animals recovered from water may had drowned, died from other causes in water, died on land, and either have fallen into water or have been disposed of in water (Fig. 1.1). Animals that have drowned may be translocated to other sites, including land, by tides, currents, people, or other animals (Fig. 1.1). Postmortem changes due to submersion, injuries, or scavengers introduce artifacts and obscure lesions. The diagnosis of drowning in animals and people is usually one of exclusion, requiring information from the crime scene, recovery scene, the medical history, or reliable witness accounts [2–5].

The definition and terminology associated with drowning, as with other types of asphyxia, are varied [6, 7]. Submersion signifies that the entire body is under water, whereas immersion refers to the body being partly covered with water, although the airway must be immersed for drowning to occur [8]. Terminology prior to 2002 was confusing: "near-drowning" was used if the person survived even temporarily and "drowning" if it was fatal; both were then divided into those cases in which aspiration of water was present or absent [7]. The following adjectives describing drowning outcomes are no longer recommended: passive, silent, wet, dry, active, secondary drowning [7, 8] or near-drowning [9]. In 2002, the definitions of drowning and its possible outcomes were decided by an international group of experts: "Drowning is the process of experiencing respiratory impairment from submersion/immersion in liquid" with outcomes of "death, morbidity or no morbidity" [7]. The revised terminology is used in at least one review of canine drowning [10], and we recommend that it be adopted by veterinarians [11].

An estimated 388,000 people drown annually, and it is the third leading cause of accidental death worldwide [12]. The frequency of drowning in animals is unknown, although a website that tracks animal abuse (pet-abuse.com) listed 205 drowning cases out of 19,464 cases (1.05%) in its database (October 20, 2016). The accuracy of this statistic is not known as there is no mandatory reporting of animal drowning or cruelty in most jurisdictions, although databases such as the newly implemented National Incident-Based Reporting System at the

B.J. McEwen, DVM, MSc, PhD, DACVP (✉)
Animal Health Laboratory, Ontario Veterinary College, University of Guelph, 419 Gordon Street, Building 89, Guelph, ON, Canada, N1G 2W1
e-mail: bmcewen@uoguelph.ca

J.A. Gerdin, DVM, DACVP
Antech Diagnostics, 9 Schilling Road, Suite 211, Hunt Valley, MD 21031, USA
e-mail: Jodie.gerdin@antechmail.com

© Springer International Publishing AG 2018
J.W. Brooks (ed.), *Veterinary Forensic Pathology, Volume 2*,
https://doi.org/10.1007/978-3-319-67175-8_1

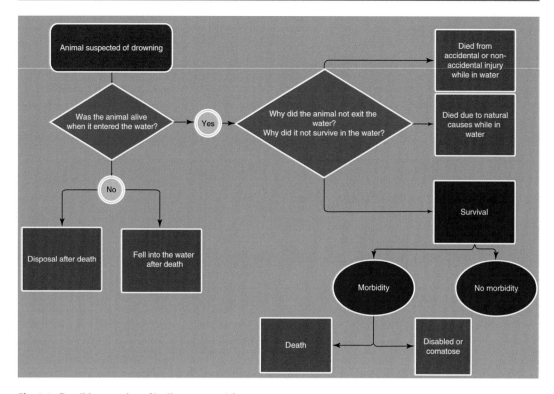

Fig. 1.1 Possible scenarios of bodies recovered from water

Federal Bureau of Investigation should provide improved estimates [13].

The peer-reviewed veterinary literature on accidental and non-accidental drowning in animals is scarce [1, 10, 14–17], although the topic is covered briefly in several veterinary forensic textbooks [18–20]. Reports of accidental drowning in animals include situations involving electrical shock, entrapment, entanglement, or victims with pre-existent medical conditions such as ataxia and epilepsy [14, 21]. Experiments in which dogs or other animals were drowned to determine physiological and biochemical responses to various volumes, temperatures, and salinity of water or other liquids provide information into the drowning process [22–35]. The lack of consideration for the welfare of animals used in these experiments, performed between 20–200 years ago, is disturbing. We recognize, however, useful information can be gained from these experiments and applied to veterinary forensic pathology for the benefit of animals today [1, 11]. The objective of this paper is to review the mechanisms, lesions, and diagnostic issues associated with drowning in nonaquatic companion animals.

1.2 The Process and Mechanism of Drowning

The central mechanism of drowning is rapid and persistent hypoxemia following the introduction of liquid at the entrance of the airway [23, 25, 34, 36–38]. The drowning process (Fig. 1.2), reviewed extensively in the medical literature [2, 3, 5, 7, 8, 36, 37, 39, 40], is largely based on experiments in dogs and incorporates behavioral and biological responses to drowning [23, 29, 30, 34, 38, 41]. This has been categorized into the five phases of drowning (Fig. 1.3) [42].

The drowning process is complex, involving sequential and overlapping cardiorespiratory reflexes, electrolyte and blood gas abnormalities, aspiration and swallowing of liquid, vomition, struggling, involuntary movements, physical exhaustion,

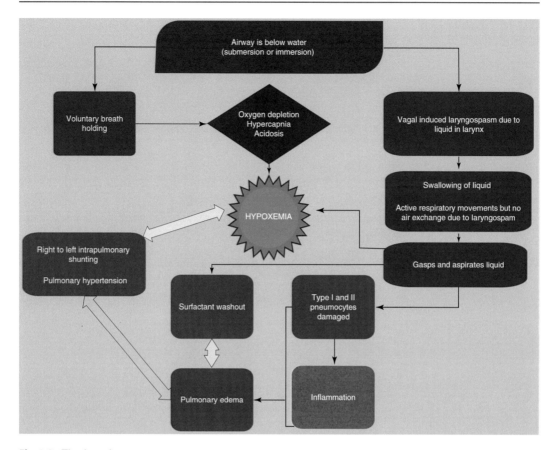

Fig. 1.2 The drowning process

and breathlessness or "air hunger" [43] eventually culminating in death [44] (Fig. 1.2). Survival time is inversely proportional to the volume of water rather than the temperature or salinity [23, 38].

Upon immersion, there may be a few deep respirations, although breath holding and vagal-mediated laryngospasm usually occur upon submersion [26, 41] and arterial oxygen decreases abruptly. As little as 2 mL of water contacting the larynx or aspirated into the lung causes laryngospasm in dogs, and aspiration of only 5 mL of salt- or freshwater in dogs causes rapid and persistent hypoxia without significant hypercarbia [23, 30, 38]. Laryngospasm may last 1.5–2 min during which arterial CO_2 increases [25] and acidosis develops [21, 34, 36]. Bradycardia [23, 30, 45] occurs immediately following submersion [26, 33] or after brief tachycardia [32, 34]. Blood pressure immediately increases and then progressively decreases [23, 32].

Submerged, non-anesthetized dogs struggle violently for 1.5 min [41, 42]. Thoracic inspiratory movements caused liquid to be swallowed, but because the glottis is closed [9, 30, 45], ventilation and gas exchange does not occur. Aspiration will occur with continued submersion whether the animal is conscious or not; if unconsciousness occurs due to hypoxemia, the larynx relaxes and water is aspirated [46]. If the animal is conscious, water is aspirated and swallowed due to deep inspiratory gasping that lasts up to 3.5 minutes [41, 47]. After 3 minutes, spasmodic convulsions and seizures occur [32, 41], and overdistension of the stomach with water causes violent vomition [41]. Electroencephalograph (EEG) activity varies with the duration of initial apnea [45]: cardiac asystole or observed death occurs usually within 5 min but occasionally up to 10 min following submersion [25, 26, 32, 38, 41, 42, 47]. The initial hypoxemia in fresh- and

Fig. 1.3 The five
phases of drowning

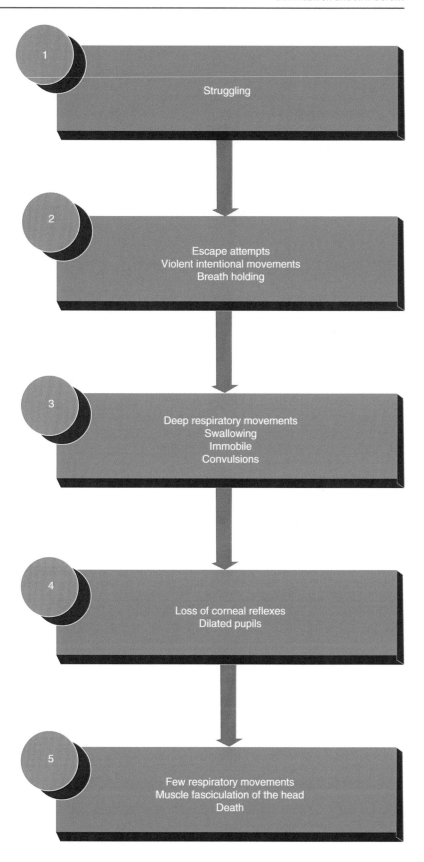

saltwater drowning is intensified by pulmonary edema and is exacerbated by exponential catecholamine release, subsequent vasoconstriction, cardiac arrhythmias [34], pulmonary hypertension, and right to left intrapulmonary shunting [34, 37, 48].

Electrolyte and intravascular volumetric changes in drowning depend on the salinity and/or volume of water aspirated. The biochemical effect of water salinity is primarily osmotic [23, 24, 28, 29] and not temperature related [34]. Distinguishing between saltwater and freshwater drowning is given little clinical significance in people [9, 37], although some think that it does impact the likelihood of successful resuscitation and survival [34]. The location of drowning, however, is critical to the forensic investigation [49].

In dogs, aspirated freshwater enters the circulation within 3 minutes [23, 46], and an estimated 10% of the body weight can be absorbed by the lungs during freshwater immersion [34]. The changes are transient due to redistribution of fluids within the body [23, 25], and dilutional hyponatremia was not present in a case series of dogs and cats resuscitated following submersion in freshwater. However, hemodilution and electrolyte alterations may persist if the volume of water aspirated is 22 mL/kg or greater [25, 28]. Volume-dependent ventricular fibrillation is common, occurring in many, but not all dogs drowned by 9.1 mL/kg but not by 4.5 mL/kg [23]. The ionic charges responsible for the surface-tension properties of surfactant are altered by freshwater which results in alveolar instability and pulmonary atelectasis [23, 40]. Atelectatic alveoli are perfused but not ventilated, resulting in right to

left intrapulmonary shunting [40], further exacerbating the hypoxemia.

Death due to saltwater aspiration requires half the aspirated volume as for freshwater (Table 1.1) [23, 26, 34, 38, 50, 51]. The aspirated hypertonic water pulls fluid from the circulation into the alveoli, leading to the damage of the basement membrane, washout of surfactant, and reduced lung compliance [52]. Ensuing pulmonary edema decreases the ventilation-to-perfusion ratio, and right to left intrapulmonary shunts develop [37]. Type I and II pneumocytes [53–55] and alveolar-capillary endothelium [50, 53] are damaged by both fresh- and saltwater. Neither hemolysis nor ventricular fibrillation are features of experimental seawater drowning [28, 29].

Drowning ultimately results in progressive cerebral hypoxia [37] and death. In people, irreversible injury occurs in the selective regions of the brain within 4–10 min, and persistent coma develops within a few minutes after that time period [56, 57]. The precise outcome of hypoxic injury due to drowning is difficult to predict even if the individual is resuscitated [58].

1.2.1 Autonomic Conflict: The Diving Response and Cold Shock Responses in Cold Water Immersion

People suddenly submersed in water 5 °C below body temperature may become unconscious and develop cardiac arrhythmia, possibly due to vagal stimulation and/or catecholamine release [9, 34, 59–62]. The parasympathetic and sympathetic responses following rapid submersion and breath

Table 1.1 Volumetric and electrolyte changes in saltwater compared to freshwater drowning [24–26, 28, 34, 38, 50, 51]

Variable	Freshwater	Saltwater
Blood volume	Hemodilution	Hemoconcentration
Serum sodium	Decreased	Increased
Serum chloride	Decreased	Increased
Serum potassium	Increased	Increased
Serum osmolality	Decreased	Increased
Hemolysis	Occurs with aspiration of >2.3 mL/kg	Not reported
Experimental lethal volumes of aspirated water	9.1 mL/kg	4.5 mL/kg

holding are the diving response and cold shock response, respectively [61]. These responses are often discussed as isolated physiologic reflexes but in reality are concurrent reflex reactions that produce a predictable, often opposing complement of physiological events (Table 1.2) [62, 63]. The diving response is postulated to be protective if the animal is suddenly immersed in water by inhibiting respiration and producing bradycardia; however, it is frequently exacerbated by anxiety and/or antagonized by the cold shock response.

The diving reflex response of apnea and bradycardia, presumed present in all vertebrates [61, 62], is activated by the receptors of the face via the ophthalmic and maxillary divisions of the trigeminal nerve, which cause reflex inhibition of the medullary respiratory center [4]. Vagal receptors in the pharynx and larynx produce similar responses [61]. The response is enhanced as the water temperature decreases [4]. Cold thermoreceptors of the skin mediate the sympathetic-associated cold shock response which causes tachycardia, hyperventilation, peripheral vasoconstriction, and hypertension [60, 61]. Both responses can cause cardiac arrhythmias independently or together by issuing conflicting, simultaneous signals to the heart [61, 63, 66–68].

Within 2 min of submersion in cold water, core body temperature decreases more rapidly and deeply than with immersion [34], due to the aspiration of larger quantities of water and contact with the large surface area of the pulmonary circulation. Primary hypothermia due to submersion causing rectal temperatures to drop to 20 °C or below [69] is fatal. The onset and duration of cardiorespiratory and cerebral responses were similar in dogs which were submerged in 0–1 °C and had their tracheas clamped [47] to those submerged in normothermic or cold water but allowed to aspirate water [28–30, 41]. The absolute and relative decreases in rectal and cerebral temperatures were proportional to the submersion time.

1.3 Morbidity

A case series of 25 dogs and 3 cats resuscitated following submersion in freshwater concluded that the prognosis for survival is good if respiratory tract failure and cardiac arrhythmias do not develop [21]. Level of consciousness upon presentation, even coma, was not associated with outcome [21]. Complications in animals that survive drowning include reduced mentation or neurological deficits [50], non-cardiogenic pulmonary edema [70], septic pneumonia [15], and acute respiratory distress syndrome [21].

1.4 Macroscopic and Microscopic Lesions of Drowning

Tables 1.3 and 1.4 list macroscopic and microscopic lesions in drowned animals. In individual cases, these lesions may or may not be present. *Emphysema aquosum*, a term used in medical forensic pathology describing overinflated, waterlogged lungs and alveolar dilation, thinning

Table 1.2 Diving and cold shock responses [4, 60–65]

	Diving response	Cold shock response
Autonomic system	Parasympathetic	Sympathetic
Activation	Cold receptors of the face via maxillary and ophthalmic branches of the trigeminal nerve	Integumentary cold thermoreceptors
Similar response can be initiated by	Vagal receptors in pharynx and larynx	
Physiological responses	Bradycardia	Tachycardia
	Apnea	Hyperventilation
		Vasoconstriction
		Increased blood pressure

Table 1.3 Macroscopic lesions of drowning documented in animals [1, 11, 17, 18, 33, 39, 71, 73–75]

Lesion
Hair coat is wet, damp, or dry hair and is aggregated in spikes or clumps
Froth emanating from nostrils or oral cavity
Froth in larynx or airways
Lungs distended and fail to collapse
Pulmonary congestion and edema
Pulmonary hemorrhages ranging in size from pinpoint to locally extensive
Pulmonary emphysema
Right ventricular distension
Water and/or foreign material in stomach
Aspirated stomach contents or other foreign material in upper or lower airway
Mucus at the base of the tongue or in larynx
Fluid in the frontal or paranasal sinuses
Traumatic lesions including dermal or subcutaneous contusions and fractures with forced submersion

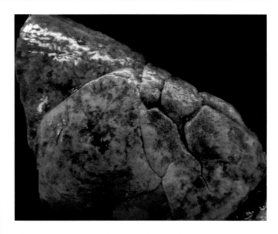

Fig. 1.4 Lung, canine, aspirated foreign material in drowning. Abundant foreign material is present in an airway (Courtesy of Dr. M. Hazlett)

Table 1.4 Microscopic lesions of drowning documented in animals [11, 18]

Lesion
Intra-alveolar hemorrhage
Flooding of alveoli with pale eosinophilic proteinaceous fluid
Alveolar overdistension
Attenuation of alveolar septa
Aspirated stomach contents, bacteria or foreign material in upper or lower airways

Fig. 1.5 Lung, canine. Same lung as in Fig. 1.4, adjacent to area with foreign body demonstrating only mild congestion and hemorrhage (Courtesy of Dr. M. Hazlett)

of alveolar septa, and compression of alveolar capillaries histologically [4, 71], should be avoided in veterinary pathology. Instead, lesions should be appropriately and fully described for clarity. The presence, severity, and type of pulmonary macroscopic and microscopic lesions are frequently not uniform and often vary within a single histological section (Figs. 1.4 and 1.5).

In cases of suspected drowning, the appearance of the fur should be recorded as wet or dry or if the hair is dried in clumps or spikes, indicating recent wetness. Distended, heavy, edematous lungs that fail to collapse and stable froth in the upper airway including the mouth and nasal passages are characteristic of drowning (Fig. 1.6) but not specific, as these may be due to other causes [37, 71].

A small to moderate amount of watery, colorless to pale pink-brown tracheal foam is a fairly common postmortem artifact in a variety of species, especially in the setting of barbiturate euthanasia, and may be especially prominent in horses [72]. Stable froth in the tracheobronchial tree (Fig. 1.7), larynx, and nostrils can only be produced by a live animal [18] and may also arise with other causes of pulmonary edema [37]. Blood-tinged froth is produced by hemolysis of red blood cells within the edema fluid [42]. A mare that initially survived drowning had stable red froth at the nares and continued to expectorate this material by paroxysmal coughing for a few hours after treatment

Fig. 1.6 Lung, canine, drowning. The lungs are distended, edematous with emphysema, petechiae, random atelectatic foci, and subpleural hemorrhages (Courtesy of Dr. S. McDonough)

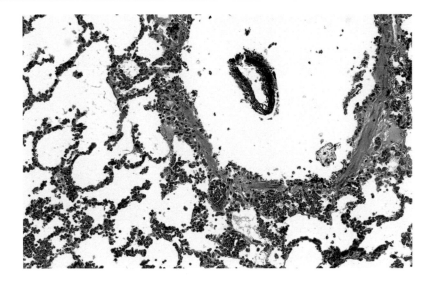

Fig. 1.7 Trachea, canine, drowning. Abundant stable froth and red-tinged fluid are present in the trachea (Courtesy of Dr. S. McDonough)

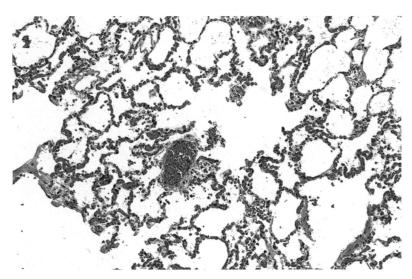

was initiated [14]. Macroscopic or microscopic foreign material deep within the tracheobronchial tree and lungs is compatible with aspiration (Fig. 1.4) [18]. In people, the external foam and stable airway froth may persist for several days, even with the onset of putrefaction [37]. Both features may disappear or be altered by the effects of time, handling, storage, and freezing of the body prior to the postmortem examination [11]. This is another reason why investigators should provide, and pathologists should request, photographs and documentation of the animal at the recovery scene.

The amount of liquid penetrating the lungs depends upon the respiratory efforts, laryngo-spasm, and time of cardiac arrest [46]. Most people die with typical pulmonary lesions of marked edema and abundant tracheal froth ("wet drowning"), whereas 2–15% is classified as drowning without discernible evidence of aspiration ("dry drowning") [46]. "Dry" lungs in human victims attributed to sudden cardiac arrhythmias including channelopathies [61, 76], cardiac arrest, or laryngospasm following submersion [46]. "Dry drowning" may represent not only one end of the spectrum of drowning lesions but also deaths in water due to natural causes and bodies that were disposed of in water [9, 42, 46]. The significance and pathophysiology of "dry drowning" is debated in medical forensic pathology [46], and as stated previously, this term should be avoided. In dogs, even low volumes of aspirated water caused hypoxemia and decreased lung compliance [24, 38]. Lungs lacking evidence of aspiration are documented in experimental drownings of muskrat and beavers that had a mucus plug in the trachea [33]. In dogs, lack of significant fluid aspiration was attributed to laryngospasm [41] or the failure to gasp [30] although the latter seems unlikely.

Pleural effusion, subdural discoloration of the petrous temporal bone due to congestion, or hemorrhage in the mastoid process and middle ear, hemorrhage in the neck muscles, a contracted spleen [3, 4, 37], subpleural intra-alveolar hemorrhages with blurred margins (Paltauf's or Rasskazov-Lukomskij spots) [77], and hemolytic red staining of the aortic intima [78, 79] and left heart [80] are additional findings in people that may support a diagnosis of drowning. Subpleural hemorrhages were present in lungs from a drowned dog (Fig. 1.6).

Weights such as blocks, tires, or chains bound to the animal indicate intentional submersion of the body but do not indicate if the animal was alive or dead at the time of submersion [11]. Lesions of blunt force trauma of the head, neck, or limbs may be present in animals that were forcibly immersed or submerged in water [18, 20, 81].

The appearance and approximate volume of gastric contents should be documented, as swallowing water is common during drowning [11, 30, 41]. Gastric mucosal lacerations due to overdistension of the stomach with water are sporadically reported in human drowning victims [37]. Elevated liver enzymes in animals resuscitated following submersion were attributed to hepatic hypoxia and necrosis, but this cannot be confirmed as histopathological examination of the liver has not been described [21] Hepatocellular necrosis was confirmed in one dog that aspirated water from a drainage ditch, but it cannot be determined if this was due to the initial drowning or sequelae such as heart failure [15]. Myocardial lesions of contraction bands and rupture of intercalated discs in the cardiac myocytes of rats drowned in either salt- or freshwater may be due to excessive catecholamine release [82].

A thorough postmortem examination will aid in determining if significant intercurrent diseases are present [21], and a medical history of conditions such as epilepsy will also be useful particularly in determining why an animal was unable to extricate itself from the drowning medium [11, 18]. Hyponatremic encephalopathy due to excessive intake of freshwater (water intoxication) should also be considered as a contributing or alternative cause of death, particularly in animals that play or train in freshwater [83].

1.5 Postmortem Changes

The postmortem submersion interval (PMSI) and postmortem changes that occur while in water and following retrieval may make examination and determination of the cause of death even more challenging [11]. Early changes are skin maceration, lividity, rigor mortis, and algor mortis, and late changes include initial putrefaction, advanced putrefaction including adipocere formation, and skeletonization [37, 84]. Adipocere is a waxy material on bodies submersed in water produced by degradation of adipose tissue by endogenous and bacterial enzymes [85]. Postmortem changes in the water, as on land, are time and temperature dependent [37]. The lower temperatures of bodies of water usually retard rigor mortis and accelerate body cooling [37, 84]. Decomposition while in water is slower than on land; however, once a body is removed from the water, it rapidly accelerates. The body initially sinks and then rises to the surface once putrefactive gases increase buoyancy [85]. If the water is cold enough, putrefaction may not occur and the body may never resurface. Depending on the duration and conditions of submersion, hair may slip from the skin, and the entire body may be waterlogged [37]. Scavenging by aquatic animals and trauma inflicted by natural and man-made elements of the aquatic environment may create postmortem lesions or may alter or destroy antemortem lesions [37]. Water may dilute antemortem hemorrhages, and projectile, sharp force or blunt force injuries may be obscured or effaced by maceration and hemolysis.

Fig. 1.8 Photograph of the scene with a dead dog at the edge of the wet cement patio and a plastic portable swimming pool partially filled with murky water (Courtesy Dr. N. Bradley-Siemens)

Fig. 1.9 Dog from Fig. 1.8 at the edge of the patio. Note the wet hair and the wet cement patio (Courtesy Dr. N. Bradley-Siemens)

1.6   Case Report of Drowning [81][1]

Law enforcement arrived at a premise following a telephone call about a disturbance. Two dead dogs were found in the backyard and other dogs present appeared to be in good health. The dogs

were seized and submitted for postmortem examination. The photographs from the scene showed children's plastic wading pool approximately two thirds full of murky water, located on a wet cement patio and a dead dog with wet hair at the edge of the patio (Figs. 1.8 and 1.9). The dog was a 2-year-old female pit bull that weighed 25 kg. Radiographs revealed gaseous distension of the

---

[1] Courtesy of Dr. Nancy Bradley-Siemens.

stomach and intestinal loops and a diffuse interstitial pattern in the lungs. Multifocal to coalescent subcutaneous and intramuscular contusions were present around the right eye and nasal bone. The lungs were distended, diffusely and markedly edematous with multifocal random subpleural petechiae and ecchymoses. Abundant red froth present throughout the entire tracheal lumen extended into the primary bronchi. The stomach contained abundant fluid. Diffuse severe pulmonary edema and periocular hemorrhage were confirmed histologically.

Although the pulmonary lesions were suggestive of drowning, this could not have been confirmed without the documentation at the scene: the pool, the wet patio cement, and the wet dogs were corroborative evidence that permitted the investigators convict the perpetrator for animal cruelty.

1.7   Ancillary Tests and Methods Used in Determination of Drowning

1.7.1   Lung Weights

The increased weight of lungs and pleural fluid used to support the diagnosis of drowning in people is unreliable as many variables influence the result [8, 9, 46, 86]. Lung weights of 1000 [4]–1400 g [86] used to confirm drowning in people are misleading as there is no agreement in the medical literature regarding normal lung weights [46]. Similarly, reference values for postmortem lung weights are not available for most species and breeds, and application of allometrically determined lung weights [73, 74] requires further validation if applied in a forensic context. A drowning index of the weight ratio of the lungs and pleural effusion to the spleen has been proposed in people to be more accurate than absolute lung weights [87], although it is affected by postmortem interval and has a relatively low sensitivity and specificity of 66% and 77.5%, respectively [75]. It remains to be determined if this measurement is applicable to or accurate in animals and could be confounded by barbiturate euthanasia.

1.7.2   Diatoms

Perhaps no other ancillary test in the diagnosis of drowning in people has received as much attention, scrutiny, and debate as the use of diatoms [2, 4, 5, 37, 46, 88–95]. Diatoms are unicellular algae with a silica cell wall (frustule) that makes them inert to acids, high temperatures, and enzymatic digestion [96]. The use of diatoms as a diagnostic test for drowning is based on the assumption that the individual must be alive for them to be aspirated, penetrate the alveolar-capillary membrane, enter the circulation, and enter tissues including marrow [15, 85]. If meticulous techniques are used to retrieve diatoms from the marrow, their presence in large numbers may corroborate a diagnosis of drowning, and their unique characteristics may identify the location and drowning medium of the victim [93, 94]. The sensitivity of the method is relatively low and depends upon the time of year when the algae bloom [93]. The specificity may be high with the appropriate techniques; however, the prospect of contamination during the postmortem submersion interval and sample preparation is high, resulting in false-positive results [84]. Because diatoms are found in bodies not recovered from water and in living people, the possibility that they enter the circulation from ingested food must be considered [96]. Although diatoms were identified in the tracheal wash of a dog that aspirated during a seizure in a water-filled drainage ditch [15], application of the diatom test to confirm drowning in animals requires additional rigorous validation studies.

1.7.3   Electrolyte Tests

Differentiation between saltwater and freshwater drownings using electrolyte levels in blood or vitreous humor has not been widely accepted. The Gettler test comparing chloride levels in right and left ventricular blood [4] has been shown to be unreliable. Elevated vitreous humor sodium levels in cases of saltwater drowning and decreased levels in freshwater drowning proposed as a marker of the drowning medium [49] may be useful but requires further validation.

1.8   Summary

Diagnosis of drowning is difficult in both human and animals [11, 18, 20, 37, 71, 97]. Additionally, bodies recovered from water may or may not have drowned [11, 18]. A thorough postmortem examination is necessary to:

- Identify and document the presence and absence of lesions that may corroborate or rule out death due to drowning.
- Identify intercurrent disease that may have influenced the animal's behavior in or around the water.
- Identify traumatic injuries consistent with non-accidental injuries of forced submersion or immersion.

While there are characteristic macroscopic and microscopic lesions of drowning, none are specific. Additional information from the crime scene investigators, including witness accounts, an accurate history, previous medical conditions of the animal, and disposition of the body when retrieved from the drowning medium are often needed to provide the pathologist with the context of the postmortem findings.

References

1. Munro R, Munro HMC. Some challenges in forensic veterinary pathology: a review. J Comp Pathol. 2013;149:57–73. https://doi.org/10.1016/j.jcpa.2012.10.001.
2. Byard RW. Immersion deaths and drowning: issues arising in the investigation of bodies recovered from water. Forensic Sci Med Pathol. 2015;11:323–5. https://doi.org/10.1007/s12024-014-9564-5.
3. Prahlow JA, Byard RW. An Atlas of forensic pathology. New York: Springer; 2012.
4. Shkrum M, Ramsay D. Bodies recovered from water. In: Forensic science, medicine, forensic pathology of trauma: common problems for the in pathologist. Totowa, NJ: Humana Press Inc.; 2007. p. 243–92.
5. MH a P, De LE a. Drowning: still a difficult autopsy diagnosis. Forensic Sci Int. 2006;163:1–9. https://doi.org/10.1016/j.forsciint.2004.10.027.
6. Sauvageau A, Boghossian E. Classification of asphyxia: the need for standardization. J Forensic Sci. 2010;55:1259–67. https://doi.org/10.1111/j.1556-4029.2010.01459.x.
7. Van BEF, Branche CM, Szpilman D, et al. A new definition of drowning: towards documentation and prevention of a global public health problem. World Heal Organ. 2005;83:853–6.
8. Idris AH, Berg RA, Bierens J, et al. Recommended guidelines for uniform reporting of data from drowning the "Utstein style". Circulation. 2003;108:2565–74. https://doi.org/10.1161/01.CIR.0000099581.70012.68.
9. Orlowski JP, Szpilman D. Drowning. Pediatr Clin N Am. 2001;48:627–46. https://doi.org/10.1016/S0031-3955(05)70331-X.
10. Goldkamp CE, Schaer M. Canine drowning. Compend Contin Educ Vet. 2008;30:340–52.
11. McEwen BJ, Gerdin J. Veterinary forensic pathology: drowning and bodies recovered from water. Vet Pathol. 2016;53:1049–56. https://doi.org/10.1177/0300985815625757.
12. Peden M, Oyegbite K, Ozanne-Smith J, et al. World report on child injury prevention. Geneva; 2008.
13. Tracking animal cruelty. In: Fed. Bueau Investig. https://www.fbi.gov/news/stories/-tracking-animal-cruelty. Accessed 17 Sep 2016.
14. Austin SM, Foreman JH, Goetz TE. Aspiration pneumonia following near-drowning in a mare: a case report. J Equine Vet Sci. 1988;8:313–6. https://doi.org/10.1016/S0737-0806(88)80058-3.
15. Benson CJ, Edlund MB, Gray S, et al. The presence of diatom algae in a tracheal wash from a German wirehaired pointer with aspiration pneumonia. Vet Clin Pathol. 2013;42:221–6. https://doi.org/10.1111/vcp.12037 ER.
16. Humber KA. Near drowning of a gelding. J Am Vet Med Assoc. 1988;192:377–8.
17. Munro HMC, Thrusfield MV. Battered pets: non-accidental physical injuries found in dogs and cats. J Small Anim Pract. 2001;42:279–90.
18. Munro R, Munro HMC. Animal abuse and unlawful killing. Anim Abus Unlawful Kill. 2008. https://doi.org/10.1016/B978-0-7020-2878-6.50018-0.
19. Cooper JE, Cooper ME. Wildlife forensic investigation principles and practice. Boca Raton: CRC Press; 2013.
20. Merck M, Miller D. Asphyxia. In: Merck M, editor. Veterinary forensics: animal cruelty investigations. 2nd ed. Oxford: Wiley; 2013. p. 169–84.
21. Heffner GG, E a R, Beal MW, et al. Evaluation of freshwater submersion in small animals: 28 cases (1996–2006). J Am Vet Med Assoc. 2008;232:244–8. https://doi.org/10.2460/javma.232.2.244.
22. Ives A. An experimental inquiry into the proximate cause of death from suspended respiration in drowning and hanging with the means of resuscitation. New York State: College of Physicians and Surgeons; 1814.
23. Modell JH, Gaub M, Moya F, et al. Physiological effect of near drowning with chlorinated fresh water, distilled water and isotonic saline. Anesthesiology. 1966;27:33–41.
24. Modell JH, Moya F. Effects of volume of aspirated fluid during chlorinated fresh water drown-

ing. Anesthesiology. 1966;27:662–72. https://doi.org/10.1097/00000542-196609000-00018.

25. Rai UC, Bhardwaj PK, Mohan M. Effects of aspirated and swallowed water in mongrel dogs subjected to fresh-water drowning. Indian J Physiol Pharmacol. 1980;24:197–204.

26. Bhardwaj W, Mohan M, Rai UC. Electrocardiographic changes in experimental drowning. Indian J Physiol Pharmacol. 1982;26:85–9.

27. Redding JS, Cozine RA, Voigt GC, Safar P. Resuscitation from drowning. J Am Med Assoc. 1961;178:1136–9.

28. Swann HG, Brucer M, Moore C, Vezien BL. Fresh water and sea water drowning: a study of the terminal cardiac and biochemical events. Texas Rep Biol Med. 1947;5:423–537.

29. Swann HG, Spafford N. Body salt and water changes during fresh and sea water drowning. Texas Rep Biol Med. 1951;9:356–62.

30. Banting FG, Hall GE, Janes JM, et al. Physiological studies in experimental drowning (a preliminary report). Can Med Assoc J. 1938;39:226–8.

31. Moritz AR. Chemical methods for the determination of death by drowning. Physiol Rev. 1944;24:70–88.

32. Gilbertson L, Safar P, Stezoski W, Bircher N. Pattern of dying during cold water drowning in dogs. Crit Care Med. 1982;10:216.

33. Gilbert FF, Gofton N. Terminal dives in mink, muskrat and beaver. Physiol Behav. 1982;28:835–40. https://doi.org/10.1016/0031-9384(82)90200-1.

34. Conn AW, Miyasaka K, Katayama M, et al. A canine study of cold water drowning in fresh versus salt water. Crit Care Med. 1995;23:2029–37. https://doi.org/10.1097/00003246-199512000-00012.

35. Brouardel PCH (1897) La pendaison, la strangulation, la suffocation, la submersion. Librairie J.B. Baillier et fils, Paris.

36. Layon AJ, Modell JH. Drowning update 2009. Anesthesiology. 2009;110:1390–401.

37. Lunetta P, Modell JH. Macroscopical, microscopical, and laboratory findings in drowning victims a comprehensive review. In: Tsokos M, editor. Forensic pathology reviews. Totowa, NJ: Humana Press; 2005. p. 3–77.

38. Modell JH, Moya F, Newby EJ, et al. The effects of fluid volume in seawater drowning. Ann Intern Med. 1967;67:68–80.

39. Szpilman D, Bierens JJLM, Handley AJ, Orlowski JP. Drowning. N Engl J Med. 2012;366:2102–10. https://doi.org/10.1056/NEJMra1013317.

40. Modell JH. Biology of drowning. Annu Rev Med. 1978;29:1–8. https://doi.org/10.1146/annurev.me.29.020178.000245.

41. Lougheed DW, Janes JM, Hall GE. Physiological studies in experimental asphyxia and drowning. Can Med Assoc J. 1939;40:423–8.

42. Modell JH, Bellefleur M, Davis JH. Drowning without aspiration: is this an appropriate diagnosis? J Forensic Sci. 1999;44:1119–23.

43. Beausoleil N, Mellor D. Introducing breathlessness as a significant animal welfare issue. N Z Vet J. 2015;63:44–51. https://doi.org/10.1080/00480169.2014.940410.

44. Beynon J. Not waving, not drowning. Asphyxia Torture. 2012;22:25–9.

45. Suzuki T. Suffocation and related problems. Forensic Sci Int. 1996;80:71–8.

46. Lunetta P, Modell JH, Sajantila A. What is the incidence and significance of "dry-lungs" in bodies found in water? Am J Forensic Med Pathol. 2004;25:291–301. https://doi.org/10.1097/01.paf.0000146240.92905.7e.

47. Tisherman S, Chabal C, Safar P, Stezoski W. Resuscitation of dogs from cold-water submersion using cardiopulmonary bypass. Ann Emerg Med. 1985;14:389–96. https://doi.org/10.1016/S0196-0644(85)80279-1.

48. Irwin DC, Subudhi AW, Klopp L, et al. Pulmonary edema induced by cerebral hypoxic insult in a canine model. Aviat Sp Environ Med. 2008;79:472–8. https://doi.org/10.3357/ASEM.2217.2008.

49. Byard RW, Summersides G. Vitreous humor sodium levels in immersion deaths. J Forensic Sci. 2011;56:643–4. https://doi.org/10.1111/j.1556-4029.2011.01735.x.

50. Karch SB. Pathology of the lung in near-drowning. Am J Emerg Med. 1986;4:4–9. https://doi.org/10.1016/0735-6757(86)90240-8.

51. de Boer J, Biewenga TJ, Kuipers HA, den Otter G. The effects of aspirated and swallowed water in drowning: sea-water and fresh-water experiments on rats and dogs. Anesthesiology. 1970;32:51–9. https://doi.org/10.1097/00000542-197001000-00012.

52. Giammona ST, Modell JH. Drowning by total immersion. Effects on pulmonary surfactant of distilled water, isotonic saline, and sea water. Am J Dis Child. 1967;114:612–6.

53. Brinkmann B, Fechner G, Püschel K. Ultrastructural pathology of the alveolar apparatus in experimental drowning. Z Rechtsmed. 1983;91:47–60.

54. Torre C, Varetto L. Scanning electron microscope study of the lung in drowning. J Forensic Sci. 1985;30:456–61.

55. Torre C, Varetto L, Tappi E. Scanning electron microscopic ultrastructural alterations of the pulmonary alveolus in experimental drowning. J Forensic Sci. 1983;28:1008–12.

56. Finnie JW. Pathology of traumatic brain injury. Vet Res Commun. 2014;38:297–305. https://doi.org/10.1007/s11259-014-9616-z.

57. Oechmichen M, Meissner C. Cerebral hypoxia and ischemia: the forensic point of view: a review. J Forensic Sci. 2006;51:880–7. https://doi.org/10.1111/j.1556-4029.2006.00174.x.

58. Topjian AA, Berg RA, Bierens JJLM, et al. Brain resuscitation in the drowning victim. Neurocrit Care. 2012;17:441–67. https://doi.org/10.1007/s12028-012-9747-4.

59. Marabotti C, Scalzini A, Cialoni D, et al. Cardiac changes induced by immersion and breath-hold diving in humans. J Appl Physiol. 2009;106:293–7. https://doi.org/10.1152/japplphysiol.00126.2008.

60. Datta A, Tipton M. Respiratory responses to cold water immersion: neural pathways, interactions, and clinical consequences awake and asleep. J Appl Physiol. 2005;100:2057–64. https://doi.org/10.1152/japplphysiol.01201.2005.

61. Shattock MJ, Tipton MJ. "Autonomic conflict": a different way to die during cold water immersion? J Physiol. 2012;590:3219–30. https://doi.org/10.1113/jphysiol.2012.229864.

62. Lindholm P, Lundgren CEG. The physiology and pathophysiology of human breath-hold diving. J Appl Physiol. 2009;106:284–92. https://doi.org/10.1152/japplphysiol.90991.2008.

63. Elsner R, Gooden B. Diving and asphyxia: a comparative study of animals and man. Cambridge: Cambridge University Press; 1983.

64. Elsner R. Comparative circulation studies of diving and asphyxia. Adv Exp Med Biol. 1972;22:69–80.

65. Elsner R, Franklin DL, Van Citters RL, Kenney DW. Cardiovascular defense against asphyxia. Science. 1966;153:941–9.

66. Koizumi K, Terui N, Kollai M. Effect of cardiac vagal and sympathetic nerve activity on heart rate in rhythmic fluctuations. J Auton Nerv Syst. 1985;12:25125–9.

67. Shen MJ, Zipes DP. Role of the autonomic nervous system in modulating cardiac arrhythmias. Circ Res. 2014;114:1004–21. https://doi.org/10.1161/CIRCRESAHA.113.302549.

68. Hooser SB, Van Alstine W, Kiupel M, Sojka J. Acute pit gas (hydrogen sulfide) poisoning in confinement cattle. J Vet Diagn Investig. 2000;12:272–5. https://doi.org/10.1177/104063870001200315.

69. Oncken A, Kirby R, Rudloff E. Hypothermia in critically ill dogs and cats. Compendium. 2001;23:506–21.

70. Haldane S, Marks SL, Raffe M. Noncardiogenic pulmonary edema. Stand Care Emerg Crit Care Med. 2002;4:1–7.

71. Lunetta P, Penttila A, Sajantila A. Circumstances and macropathologic findings in 1590 consecutive cases of bodies found in water. Am J Forensic Med Pathol. 2002;23:371–6. https://doi.org/10.1097/00000433-200212000-00015.

72. Bonagura JD, Reef VB, Schwarzwald CC (2010) Cardiovascular diseases. In: Reed SM, Bayly WM, Sellon DC (eds) Equine internal medicine, 3rd ed. Saunders, St. Louis, pp 372–487.

73. Lindstedt SL, Schaeffer PJ. Use of allometry in predicting anatomical and physiological parameters of mammals. Lab Anim. 2002;36:1–19. https://doi.org/10.1258/0023677021911731.

74. Stahl WR. Scaling of respiratory variables in mammals. J Appl Physiol. 1967;22:453–60.

75. Sugimura T, Kashiwagi M, Matsusue A, et al. Application of the drowning index to actual drowning cases. Legal Med. 2010;12:68–72. https://doi.org/10.1016/j.legalmed.2009.11.006.

76. Tester DJ, Medeiros-Domingo A, Will ML, Ackerman MJ. Unexplained drownings and the cardiac channelopathies: a molecular autopsy series. Mayo Clin Proc. 2011;86:941–7. https://doi.org/10.4065/mcp.2011.0373.

77. Nečas P, Hejna P. Eponyms in forensic pathology. Forensic Sci Med Pathol. 2012;8:395–401. https://doi.org/10.1007/s12024-012-9328-z.

78. Byard RW, Cains G, Simpson E, et al. Drowning, haemodilution, haemolysis and staining of the intima of the aortic root-- preliminary observations. J Clin Forensic Med. 2006;13:121–4. https://doi.org/10.1016/j.jcfm.2006.01.003.

79. Byard RW. Aortic intimal staining in drowning. Forensic Sci Med Pathol. 2015;11:442–4. https://doi.org/10.1007/s12024-014-9563-6.

80. Zátopková L, Hejna P, Janík M. Hemolytic staining of the endocardium of the left heart chambers: a new sign for autopsy diagnosis of freshwater drowning. Forensic Sci Med Pathol. 2015;11:65–8.

81. Bradley-Siemens N. Asphyxia : the unusual tale of two cases. In: N Am Vet Conf; 2016. p. 353–5.

82. Karch SB. Pathology of the heart in drowning. Arch Pathol Lab Med. 1985;109:176–8.

83. Toll J, Barr SC, Hickford FH. Acute water intoxication in a dog. J Vet Emerg Crit Care. 1999;9: 19–22.

84. Di Giancamillo A, Giudici E, Andreola S, et al. Immersion of piglet carcasses in water—the applicability of microscopic analysis and limits of diatom testing on an animal model. Legal Med. 2010;12:13–8. https://doi.org/10.1016/j.legalmed.2009.09.007.

85. Saukko P, Knight BH. Knight's forensic pathology. 3rd ed. London: CRC Press; 2004.

86. Kringsholm B, Filskov A, Kock K. Autopsied cases of drowning in December 1987–1989. Forensic Sci Int. 1991;52:85–92. https://doi.org/10.1016/0379-0738(91)90099-5.

87. Nishitani Y, Fujii K, Okazaki S, et al. Weight ratio of the lungs and pleural effusion to the spleen in the diagnosis of drowning. Legal Med. 2006;8:22–7. https://doi.org/10.1016/j.legalmed.2005.08.001.

88. Peabody AJ. Diatoms and drowning—a review. Med Sci Law. 2000;20:254–61.

89. Verma K. Role of diatoms in the world of forensic science. J Forensic Res. 2013;4:2–5. https://doi.org/10.4172/2157-7145.1000181.

90. Kakizaki E, Yukawa N. Simple protocol for extracting diatoms from lung tissues of suspected drowning cases within 3h: first practical application. Forensic Sci Int. 2015;251:179–85. https://doi.org/10.1016/j.forsciint.2015.03.025.

91. Lin C-Y, Yen W-C, Hsieh H-M, et al. Diatomological investigation in sphenoid sinus fluid and lung tissue from cases of suspected drowning. Forensic Sci Int. 2014;244:111–5. https://doi.org/10.1016/j.forsciint.2014.08.023.

92. Dettmeyer RB. Forensic histopathology. Berlin, Heidelberg: Springer-Verlag; 2011. https://doi.org/10.1007/978-3-642-20659-7.

93. Pollanen MS. Diatoms and homicide. Forensic Sci Int. 1998;91:29–34.

94. Pollanen M. The diagnostic value of the diatom test for drowning II. Validity: analysis of diatoms in bone marrow and drowning medium. J Forensic Sci. 1997;42:286–90.

95. Pollanen M. The diagnostic value of the diatom test for drowning I. Utility: a retrospective analysis of 771 cases of drowning in Ontario, Canada. Can J Forensic Sci. 1997;42:281–5.

96. Yen LY, Jayaprakash PT. Prevalence of diatom frustules in non-vegetarian foodstuffs and its implications in interpreting identification of diatom frustules in drowning cases. Forensic Sci Int. 2007;170:1–7. https://doi.org/10.1016/j.forsciint.2006.08.020.

97. Byard R. Issues in the classification and pathological diagnosis of asphyxia. Aust J Forensic Sci. 2011;43:27–38. https://doi.org/10.1080/00450618.2010.482107.

Thermal/Electrical Injuries

2

Tabitha C. Viner

2.1 Burns

Burns to the skin are described by addressing the depth and size, most often described as total body surface area (TBSA) affected. In the human literature, size and depth of a burn are prognostic indicators for survival or post-burn sequelae. The location and shape of a burn or scald may also provide evidence of intentional or unintentional injury.

The morphology of a burn varies depending on the agent of heat and the duration of contact. An open fire burning at 600 °C may produce burns of different depths depending on how close and how long an animal is exposed to it. Prolonged contact at a distance from the flame may produce pathologic changes similar to direct contact and quick exposure. Similarly, water at a sub-boiling temperature of 65 °C can produce deep burns if exposure or submersion is prolonged.

Burns to the skin have been classically described as first, second, third, or fourth degree based on gross characteristics and the depth of affected tissue. However, because heat is not evenly distributed across the skin surface, gross manifestations of heat injury may range from simple erythema to full-thickness necrosis of the skin. Full gross and microscopic descriptions of

the lesions seen in a thermal injury case can help dispel any confusion that may arise with the use of classical monikers.

The gross and microscopic appearance of the different depths of burns is described by Tintinalli et al. [1] and shown in Table 2.1. Superficial burns affect only the upper epidermis. They appear hyperemic and are sensitive to the touch. The classic example of a superficial burn is sunburn, in which the skin appears pink and the animal exhibits withdrawal or avoidance when the area is touched. Superficial partial-thickness burns affect the epidermis and the dermal papilla, while sparing deeper layers. The adnexa remain intact and the skin is very painful. Blisters are the hallmark of this depth of burn and the area appears moist and red. Hot, water-based liquids often cause superficial partial-thickness burns.

Deep partial-thickness burns extend into the dermis, affecting adnexa, but spare the panniculus. These burns appear white or pale yellow. Because the nerves in a deep partial-thickness burn have been affected, the area is not painful to the touch. Similarly, blood vessels in the area are cauterized and the skin does not blanch when pressed. These lesions may be caused by exposure to hot objects, such as cigarettes and flames or hot, oil-based liquids.

Full-thickness burns extend into the panniculus adiposus and carnosus. All adnexa in the area become necrotic or are destroyed, depending on the agent of the burn. These wounds may be

T.C. Viner, D.V.M., D.A.C.V.P.
Clark R. Bavin National Fish and Wildlife Forensics
Laboratory, Ashland, OR, USA
e-mail: tabitha_viner@fws.gov

© Springer International Publishing AG 2018
J.W. Brooks (ed.), *Veterinary Forensic Pathology, Volume 2*,
https://doi.org/10.1007/978-3-319-67175-8_2

Table 2.1 Burns of the skin may be classified by the level to which the thermal agent has an effect. Each classification is associated with clinical, gross, and histological characteristics that may overlap or differ based on the portion of the burn that is examined

	Superficial burn	Superficial partial-thickness burn	Deep partial-thickness burn	Full-thickness burn
Depth	Epithelium only	Upper dermis sparing adnexa	Deep dermis affecting some parts of adnexa	Panniculus affecting the entire depth of adnexa
Clinical presentation	Painful to the touch	Very painful to the touch	Discolored area is painless	Painless
Gross appearance	Smooth, erythematous skin that blanches with pressure	Moist, erythematous skin with blisters that blanches with pressure	Erythema with central, static area of white or yellow discoloration (zone of coagulation)	Charred, leathery skin may be black or pale
Histological appearance	Capillary and lymphatic ectasia with cutaneous edema	Separation of the epithelium from the dermis with proteinaceous fluid or cellular infiltrate within the void. Elongation of basilar cell nuclei in intact skin	Coagulative necrosis and smudging of dermal collagen. Loss of differential staining and nuclear pyknosis	Possible tissue loss or metal deposition (depending on thermal agent)
Causes	Radiant heat (sun)	Hot water scalds	Hot water, oil, or grease, steam, flame	Contact with fire, hot metal, hot oil

blackened, leathery, or pale and are painless. Common agents of full-thickness burns include high-voltage electrocution; hot objects, such as soldering irons; or prolonged contact with steam or oil-based liquids.

Heat dissipates with distance from the injurious agent, and the gross and histologic alterations in the skin reflect this temperature differential. In 1953, Jackson described three zones of tissue alteration that result from a deep partial-thickness or full-thickness burn [2]. At and directly surrounding the point of contact with the hot object or electrical current is the zone of coagulation. In this area, the tissue is necrotic and damage is irreversible. In a live animal, the skin appears blanched and the coloring is not responsive to pressure. Surrounding the zone of coagulation is the zone of stasis, which is characterized initially by vasoconstriction and ischemia. Immediately after the burn event, tissue in this zone remains viable, though subject to the effects of inflammatory mediators. Without local and systemic treatment of the burn victim, tissue in the zone of stasis may become necrotic. Between the zone of stasis and unaffected tissue is the zone of hyperemia. Vessels in this area are dilated due to local

release of inflammatory mediators. Unless subject to additional insults—such as infection—tissue in the zone of hyperemia remains viable and heals with little to no scarring.

The estimation of the body area affected by burns is well established in the human literature by the "rule of 9 s." In this schema, the arms each represent 9% of a human's surface area; the legs, 18%; the head, 9%; the trunk, 36%; and the genitalia, 1% of the total body area. Because of obvious physical differences between quadrupeds and humans, this rule cannot be directly applied to animals. Additionally, variations in conformation between breeds make a single rule difficult to formulate. A rough estimation of the surface area of different body parts can be made based on a generic dog schematic (Fig. 2.1). In this diagram, the forelimbs represent 10% of the surface area; the hind limbs, 15%; the head and neck, 25%; and the trunk, 50%. Animal tails vary widely in surface area and pelage character, and a description of the effects of thermal damage should be included in the narrative on affected surface area.

The skin reacts to heat consistently, whether the injurious agent is a flame, hot liquid, heating pad, or electric current. The patterns of injury

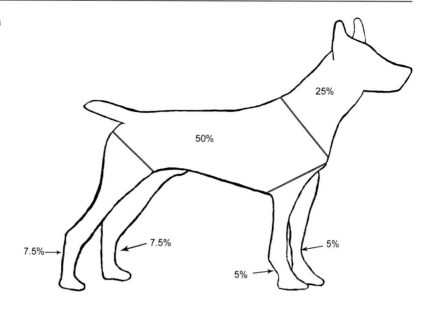

Fig. 2.1 Approximation of body surface area represented in a schematic of a generic dog. In this model, the forelimbs collectively represent 10% of the body surface area; the hind limbs, 15%; the trunk, 50%; and the head and neck, 25%. Estimation of the body surface area affected by thermal or chemical burns can inform predictions for healing and survival

vary depending on the electrothermal cause. Despite the source, protein degeneration begins to occur when the cell temperature reaches approximately 45 °C [1]. Coagulation necrosis is the norm. Additional histologic changes include intraepidermal or epidermal-dermal separation (blisters). Intraepidermal separation is much more common in electrocution events than in thermal burns [3]. The presence of concurrent intraepidermal and subepidermal separation is also more common in electrocuted skin than in flame-damaged skin. Other electrothermal changes in the skin include dermal smudging or homogenization, darkening of the epidermal cell nuclei, and elongation of the nuclei in the basal and hair follicle epidermis.

In animals, the primary barrier to exogenous heat or electricity is the hair or feathers. Often, the effects of heat exposure are limited to this barrier only. As keratin melts, it curls and discolors brown or black [4]. Under a dissecting microscope, there is an abrupt change between the normal, straight hair or feather barb and the curled and darkened outer portion of the hair or barb. Higher temperatures cause the hair or feather to char, turn to ash, and break off. It is not unusual in high-heat burns to have a focal or diffuse absence of plumage or pelage, with only follicles remaining of the external covering.

2.2 Fire

The fires to which domestic animals are exposed are most often present in an enclosed space, such as a house or a room within a house. From a legal perspective, it is important for the veterinary forensic expert to establish whether the animal was alive during the fire or dead prior to ignition of the surroundings. In some house fire incidents, it can be challenging to determine a cause of death if the animal is partially or fully consumed by the flames. However, even in cases in which the entire body surface area has been charred, internal organs often remain only mildly altered. Radiographic, gross, and histologic examination of burned remains still provides valuable information on the condition of the animal at the time of death and the cause of mortality.

Muscles that are exposed to the broad heat of a fire react by contracting. In humans, this contraction of major muscle bundles results in a "pugilistic pose" wherein the limbs assume a crouching and defensive posture: the hands close, the knees bend, and the elbows flex. Animals that are burned may have an arched back and flexed limbs, reflective of contraction of the most powerful muscle bundles.

In a fire situation, the most dangerous elements are inhaled gasses and particulates. Fire-related deaths are more often attributed to inhalation injury than to physical burning of the skin. The products of combustion are dictated by the objects that are on fire. The smoke that is produced is inconsistent from fire incident to fire incident and may include particulates, aerosolized fluids and solids, superheated air, and gasses in varying quantities and types. In addition to these harmful substances, combustion uses up the oxygen in a confined space, resulting in a low-oxygen environment. Irritants that may be produced by the combustion of objects include ammonia, sulfur dioxide, hydrogen chloride, and phosgene. These may have direct effects on the airways, resulting in edema and inflammation. Asphyxiants displace oxygen both in the environment and physiologically, making this class of agent highly dangerous in an enclosed space situation. The most common fire-derived asphyxiants are carbon monoxide (CO) and cyanide (CN).

Smoke may originate not only from the obvious flames of a fire but also from items that are smoldering [5]. Smoldering occurs when an object is exposed to heat sufficient to cause thermal decomposition, but the relative oxygen concentration in the immediate surroundings is insufficient to support flame. This high-heat decomposition, or pyrolysis, still results in the release of particulates, gasses, and superheated air that can be detrimental to humans or other animals in the area.

Standard evaluation of fire survivors, especially those showing signs of tachypnea, tachycardia, and CNS depression, should include blood gas analysis and CO-oximetry in addition to a thorough history and physical evaluation. Chest radiographs may initially be unremarkable, but edema, inflammation, and cast formation may result in an alveolar or interstitial pattern 2–36 h after the event. Additional delayed effects of smoke inhalation include cerebral edema due to prolonged hypoxia, and stenosis and fibrosis of airways. Similar to burn victims, infection may follow a fire event resulting in bacterial pneumonia.

2.2.1 Pulmonary Irritants

Soot and other fire-related particulates are produced at the upper surface of the fire. In wildfires, these particulates are carried up and away on the wind. In an enclosed space, however, smoke fills a room from top to bottom and may be present below the surface of the flames. Soot on the mucosal surfaces of the trachea, esophagus, or stomach is a sign of vitality and respiration during a fire [6]. The absence of soot in these areas, however, does not definitively indicate that the animal was dead at the time of the fire. Elevated levels of CO and cyanide produced by a fire may induce toxicity, unconsciousness, and death before the animal is exposed to particulate matter in the air. Conversely, when soot is detected in the airways or upper GI tract, toxic or lethal levels of carboxyhemoglobin (COHb) and CN are almost always detected [7].

Grossly, soot and fire-related particulates appear as a black coating on the mucosal surface of the trachea. Swallowing during the fire results in black, smudgy material in the esophagus and stomach. In acute deaths, the material is extracellular and associated with the surface mucus layer. Particles that are smaller than 3 μm in size may reach the alveoli [5].

In a fire situation, animals may be exposed to superheated air. The temperature of this inhaled air declines quickly distal to the larynx. Thus, animals that survive exposure to a burning structure rarely have direct thermal injury caudal to the vocal cords. Damage due to inhalation of steam, however, may occur in the more distal portions of the trachea [1]. Postmortem exploration of whether an animal was alive during the thermal event should include histologic sampling of the trachea from at least three locations. Areas immediately adjacent to the larynx may exhibit loss of epithelial cilia, mucus production, and deposition of soot particles at the surface. These changes decrease and disappear in distal portions of the trachea. Edema of the lower airways may occur up to 24 h after inhaling superheated air. Animals that survive for a period of time after inhalation of hot gasses may develop acute respiratory distress syndrome, and/or pseudomembranous or purulent tracheobronchitis.

In some cases, delayed responses to the inhalation of superheated or smoke-laden air may occur. A common pathologic response to smoke inhalation in humans is the development of tracheobronchial polyps [8]. Histologically, these polyps are composed of granulation tissue and fibrosis with little inflammation. The presence of polyps may induce a chronic, dry cough and persist for up to 6 months. In animals, asthma or chronic obstructive pulmonary disease may develop weeks or months later. Additionally, inhaled carcinogens produced by the combustion of plastics may eventually cause neoplasia.

2.2.2 Carbon Monoxide

Carbon monoxide is naturally occurring and may be present in the body at base levels around 1%. Animals that live in the environment of a smoker may have slightly elevated levels. Carbon monoxide binds to hemoglobin with approximately 200 times greater affinity than oxygen. Approximately 85% of systemic CO is bound to hemoglobin, forming carboxyhemoglobin (COHb). Circulating COHb is taken up by the tissues in the same manner as oxyhemoglobin but is incapable of providing resources for aerobic respiration.

Normal atmospheric CO concentration in an average home is generally 10 ppm or less. Increased volume fraction of atmospheric carbon monoxide may be a result of combustion of carbon-based materials in an enclosed space. Stoves that use wood, propane, or other petroleum products consume oxygen and produce CO_2. If the environment in which the stove is located is not vented properly, oxygen within the space becomes less available, and consumption of CO_2 will produce CO. OSHA limits human exposure to CO to 50 ppm, averaged over an 8-h period. The peak exposure limit for some operations is 200 ppm.

Animals breathing in an environment with an increased volume fraction of CO develop elevated levels of COHb. The COHb competes with oxygenated hemoglobin for uptake into cells where it interferes with aerobic respiration and production of ATP. The cells become hypoxic and organs throughout the body are affected [9]. Additionally, CO induces the release of NO and guanylate cyclase [1] which acts on the vasculature, causing vasodilation. The combination of vasodilation and low blood oxygen saturation results in ischemia-reperfusion injury. This damage is most commonly seen in cardiomyocytes and neurons, especially those in the basal ganglia. In addition to neuronal cell death, acute myocardial infarction and rhabdomyolysis may be seen in animals that survive the initial event.

Antemortem diagnosis of CO poisoning can be done by measuring the amount of circulating COHb. Blood gas analyzers with CO-oximetry can accurately measure the amount of COHb, as well as oxyhemoglobin and methemoglobin saturation [1, 5]. Routine blood gas analysis without CO-oximetry calculates the amount of these compounds and does not directly measure their levels. Thus, in cases of toxicity, some measurements using this method may be artificially high. The relative amount of blood COHb decreases when the animal is removed from the smoke environment. Thus, measurements of blood gasses upon admission to the clinic may not reflect the peak levels that the animal experienced. Blood gas analysis is inaccurate for animals found dead at the scene. The most accurate measurement modality for postmortem blood samples is the gas chromatography-thermal conductivity detector method (GC-TCD) described by Lewis et al. [10].

Clinical signs of CO toxicity may be seen when COHb rises above 10% [1]. Animals may become dyspneic, cyanotic, and lethargic. Due to decreased oxygen saturation of the blood, animals may be tachycardic. Acute fatality may occur when blood levels of COHb are 50–80%. There is no direct correlation between COHb levels and the presence or intensity of clinical, gross, or histologic signs, though levels above 10% are considered to be indicative of toxicity. Other historical factors, such as evidence of fire, closed windows, and/or combustion materials, can help point toward CO toxicity.

The blood and mucus membranes of animals that have died of carbon monoxide poisoning are unnaturally bright red. Aside from dilation and congestion of vessels, histologic lesions of acute

CO poisoning are not evident. In comparison to pure hypoxic events, toxicity from CO poisoning may have a delayed course. Animals that survive an initial insult may exhibit morbidity and mortality hours, days, or months after an event. Animals that initially show improvement with supportive care may reverse clinical course and develop seizures or other CNS disturbance. The pathophysiology of delayed CO poisoning is not entirely clear, but changes of selective neuronal necrosis are most commonly seen in the pallidum, substantia nigra, cerebellum, and hippocampus. Capillaries in these areas may exhibit plump, reactive endothelial cell nuclei with occasional lymphocytes in the Virchow-Robin spaces [11]. Necrosis of the deep cerebral white matter may also occur in delayed CO toxicity. Computed tomography can also be helpful in delineating symmetrical neuronal loss in the globus pallidus and other basal ganglia [12].

2.2.3 Cyanide

Cyanide also inhibits oxidative phosphorylation by binding to ferric ion cytochrome a_3, part of cytochrome oxidase in the mitochondria. Like CO, cyanide toxicity causes a decrease in ATP production and disrupts cellular aerobic respiration [1].

In a fire situation, hydrogen cyanide (HCN) is produced through the combustion of nitrogenous materials, such as wool, silk, mattresses, and upholstery [7]. The effects of inhaled HCN are immediate and may include dyspnea, seizures, bradycardia, and loss of consciousness. Clinical signs may be seen when concentrations of HCN reach 200 ppm in the air.

Gross necropsy findings are inconsistent and may include a bitter almond smell and cherry red discoloration of the skin and mucus membranes. Due to the rapid onset of death due to cyanide inhalation, histologic effects are rare. There are no delayed effects of cyanide inhalation as are reported in CO toxicity.

Animals that survive a cyanide inhalation event may have metabolic acidosis but normal blood gas and CO-oximetry results. Normal levels of COHb in the blood of animals exposed to smoke or fire and exhibiting clinical signs of hypoxia should alert the veterinarian to the possibility of cyanide inhalation. Concentrations of cyanide in deceased animals can be measured in the heart blood via modified microdiffusion and photometry. Some toxicology labs have specific packaging and sampling requirements for cyanide samples.

Because the production of HCN during a fire depends on the material being burned, there is no strong correlation between measured COHb and HCN in fire- or smoke-inhalation victims [7]. HCN is more commonly detected in closed-space fire events than in other types of fire situations.

2.3 Erythema Ab Igne

Chronic exposure to a heat source that is cooler than the burn threshold (<45 °C) may result is an erythematous and hyperpigmented condition called erythema ab igne [13]. Heat sources may include heating pads, heat lamps, space heaters, or hot water bottles. Chronic heat source exposure in animals may result in localized alopecia and a reticulated or interlacing pattern of hyperpigmentation and erythema. Microscopically, there may be keratinocyte atypia, thinning of the epidermis, single-cell keratinocyte necrosis, and adnexal atrophy [14].

2.4 Scalds

Scalds occur when the skin comes in contact with hot liquids. Scalding is associated with partial-thickness skin damage, and full-thickness burns and charring do not occur. The hair coat of mammals initially provides protection against the hot liquids. However, once the liquid reaches the skin, the hair acts as an insulator, holding the heat to the surface and potentially increasing the injury. Scalds may have an intentional or unintentional etiology [15]. In humans, intentional scalds most often occur when a child is held or suspended in a body of hot water, such as a tub or sink. In these cases, the scalds are of uniform skin depth and degree and have well-defined margins between the affected and unaffected skin. Accidental scalds happen when hot liquids are dropped or pulled onto the body. In these cases the scald margins and depth of damage are irregular, due to movement of the body at the painful stimulus and cooling of the liquid as it pours over the skin. In veterinary forensics, the pattern of intentional scalds and scalds due to neglect may mimic accidental human scalds as hot liquids may be poured over or splashed onto an animal. Other indications of neglect, such as matted hair and ill-fitting collars, may exist in these cases to assist the forensic veterinarian in their assessment of the case.

2.5   Radiation

Nonionizing radiation has low energy and does not generally have an adverse impact on DNA or other cellular components. Common sources of nonionizing radiation include television sets, cell phones, and radios. Ionizing radiation is capable of eliciting molecular change in the cell, which may be harmful. Humans and other animals are exposed to ionizing radiation every day in the form of sunlight, natural decay of uranium and thorium in the soil, and natural radioactive minerals in food.

The sun produces ultraviolet radiation of wavelengths between 100 and 400 nm that is further subdivided into UV-A (315–400 nm), UV-B (280–315 nm), and UV-C rays (100–280 nm; [16]). The Earth's ozone layer filters out the shorter UV-C rays and most of the UV-B rays before they reach the surface [17]. The 5–10% of UV-B rays that do pass through the ozone layer to affect animals penetrate the skin superficially, with very little reaching the dermis. As the primary instigator of sunburn, these rays may be directly absorbed by DNA, resulting in molecular rearrangements, and also precipitate inflammation by inducing cytokines and vasoactive mediators. This inflammatory cascade results in the visible sunburn or superficial burn. Gross changes and the pain associated with them peak between 24 and 48 h postirradiation. Extended exposure to UV-B rays may result in keratinocyte apoptosis. The epidermal

response to chronic exposure involves hyperkeratosis, upregulation of epidermal melanin production, and increased thickness of the epidermal layer as protection against further UV damage.

UV-A rays can penetrate deeply into the dermis and incite reactive oxygen species (ROS), which can then directly damage DNA. ROS may oxidize guanine, resulting in its transformation into 8-hydroxy-2′-deoxyguanosine, which pairs with adenine. This changes a G/C pair into an A/T pair. Cellular DNA repair mechanisms correct these defects in the vast majority of instances, but missed maintenance of certain mutations may result in carcinogenesis.

In contrast to nonionizing radiation, far ultraviolet light, X-rays, gamma rays, and all particle radiation from radioactive decay are regarded as ionizing radiation. Ionizing radiation most notably causes hydrolysis of water, resulting in the formation of reactive oxygen species which can directly harm DNA and other macromolecules [18]. The most common effect of ionizing radiation is carcinogenesis resulting either from direct neoplastic transformation of a cell or inactivation of tumor suppressor molecules, such as p53 and retinoblastoma. The most commonly reported neoplasm related to non-sunlight, ionizing radiation exposure is leukemia, though thyroid tumors [19], hemangiosarcoma, osteosarcoma, and pulmonary adenocarcinoma have also been documented [20].

Reactive oxygen and nitrogen species may continue to be generated in an irradiated cell, even after the ionizing event has ceased. Additionally, the excessive generation of these species can be passed to the cellular progeny through cell division and to adjacent cells through intercellular mechanisms of communication.

High doses of ionizing radiation—such as is given in radiotherapy—and chronic exposure to low-level radiation have been associated with myocardial fibrosis and pericardial adhesions in both humans and animals [21]. Narrowing of vessels in the heart and brain may lead to congestive heart failure and thrombotic or embolic central nervous system infarction. There may also be an effect on epithelial cells at the transitional zone of the lens, resulting in posterior subcapsular cataracts and cortical cataracts. Nuclear cataracts are not associated with ionizing radiation.

Mitochondrial DNA and proteins are also affected by ionizing radiation. Resulting defects in mitochondrial function can result in aberrations of protein manufacture and transport and accelerated cellular aging.

2.6   Sources of Thermal Injury in Wildlife

Outside of a domestic situation, the dangers of electrothermal injury do not necessarily decrease. Wild animals are subject to wildfires, commercial electricity and heat sources, and lightning. The effects of industrial gas flares and the solar industry are discussed below. Electrocution is addressed later in this chapter.

2.6.1   Gas Flares

Landfill management and the production of energy from fossil fuels often involve the disposal of excess volatile gasses. These gasses are often transmitted up a tall, chimney-like stack and directly released or burned in the upper portions of the stack. Gas flare stacks are at least 30′ tall and burning may be intermittent or constant. Birds and insects may be attracted to the gas flares because of the light emitted from them. Birds may also be pursuing the attracted insects as prey items.

Birds that fly in close proximity to the gas flares may experience temperatures sufficient to singe the feathers. The pattern of singeing is different from that of burns or electrocution in that the feathers are diffusely affected. When birds fly over a gas flare, all the feathers over the ventral aspect of the body and inner aspects of the wings are exposed to heat. The outer edges of the feather barbs are affected first and will curl and darken synchronously. Charring of the skin and burning of the feather shafts are generally not seen because birds do not fly into the flame itself for a prolonged period of time. Damage to the feathers may be sufficient to impair flight, and birds may crash to the ground, sustaining additional blunt force injuries.

2.6.2   Solar Energy Equipment

There are three different types of commercial solar power-generating facilities: photovoltaic, solar power tower, and parabolic trough. Thermally, the most dangerous modality to birds is the solar power tower. These facilities utilize thousands of large mirrors to reflect the sun's rays, measured in solar flux units, onto a centrally located tower. Within the tower is a fluid that is heated by the concentrated rays and, through vaporization and cooling cycles, runs a generator. The concentration of the sun's rays around the top of the tower produces a very high solar flux or solar intensity. This potential energy turns into heat when it comes into contact with an object.

The concentrated solar energy around the tower also emits light, which attracts flying insects, including monarch butterflies. The insects, in turn, attract insectivorous birds, which attract avian aerial predators. As the insects and birds fly into the solar flux field, their bodies are heated by the concentrated rays. Low-intensity exposure results in diffuse feather singeing similar to that in gas flare exposure. In contrast to the frank heat of a gas flare, however, solar energy is absorbed differentially based on the color of the surface being affected. Sun energy is absorbed more by darker feathers or integument than by light feathers or integument. Thus, in low-level solar intensity exposure, dark bands on the feathers may be singed or otherwise affected more than lighter bands. Additionally, only the surface of feather that is exposed to the solar flux will become superheated. Areas of the vane that are shaded by other feathers appear to be less affected or unaffected by the solar flux (Fig. 2.2).

Exposure to high levels of solar flux may cause severe singeing of the feathers or immediate combustion of the whole body. Birds may be completely incinerated mid-flight leaving little to nothing for the pathologist to examine.

Fig. 2.2 Feather from a common raven (*Corvus corax*). This raven flew into and was exposed to solar flux around a solar power tower. In physical position on the wing of the bird, only a strip of the feather adjacent to the shaft was exposed to the solar flux. Because other portions of the feather were shaded by the adjacent flight feathers, only the exposed strip became singed

2.7 Microwave Burns

Microwave ovens (or "microwaves") produce microwave radiation within the electromagnetic spectrum. Units for residential use produce microwaves of around 2.45 gigahertz and wavelengths of approximately 12 cm in length. They heat food via a method known as dielectric heating. Water and other molecules present in food have asymmetrical charges, meaning that one side of the molecule is more positive than the other side. Microwaves act to move these molecules so that the charges are aligned in the same direction. The shifting polarity of the waves then causes the molecules to rotate 180° back and forth. The movement and collisions required to achieve alignment and rotation results in the production of energy in the form of heat.

The effects of microwave radiation are limited in depth due to the resistance of the object being microwaved. The production of thermal energy is lost as the microwaves travel deeper into the tissue. Also, molecules that are more electrically symmetrical (e.g., fats) or tightly packed (e.g., bone) are less able to be moved and aligned by the microwaves, making heating less efficient. The electrical asymmetry of water makes this substance an efficient target for microwave radiation.

In a microwave oven, microwaves are produced in a magnetron that is positioned focally at a top corner of the unit. The microwaves are initially generated unidirectionally but then bounce off the walls of the chamber with continued generation. Eventually, the waves scatter and bounce throughout the chamber, hitting food from many directions.

Humans are generally indirectly injured by microwaves, through scalds or burns from food that has been heated in a microwave oven. Animals, however, may be small enough to fit in the chamber of a microwave and be exposed directly to this radiation. Due to the interfaces between the skin, panniculus adiposus, and muscle, damage from microwaves is limited to the superficial portions of the body. The area of the body affected depends on the size of the animal, the duration of exposure, and the power level setting. Larger animals may prevent or limit the bouncing of microwaves off the walls of the chamber, absorbing the radiation before it contacts the opposite wall of the chamber [22]. This may result in focal or multifocal burns, rather than diffuse damage to the skin.

Microwave radiation causes coagulative necrosis of the skin and a leathery gross appearance. As with direct thermal burns, the depth of damage dictates the sensitivity of the lesions. Penetration of the waves is often deep enough to produce anesthesia in the affected tissue. Unlike thermal burns, however, the transition from normal to damaged tissue in a microwave burn is often abrupt with little tapering of gross and microscopic changes. Due to vascular thrombosis and, perhaps, immunosuppression, inflammation around the burn is delayed and mild.

Reepithelialization is often slow, and sequelae to the event, including septicemia and multiorgan failure, may mirror those of thermal burns.

2.8   Post-Burn Sequelae

Sequelae to major burns may include multiple organ failure, septicemia, insulin resistance, hyperglycemia, and fat and muscle wasting. In adult humans, these conditions are more likely to occur when over 40% of the TBSA has been burned. Serious disorders may occur when over 60% of the TBSA of children has been burned [23].

Immunosuppression in the post-burn period is largely orchestrated by interactions between macrophages and dendritic cells [24]. In the peracute post-burn period, dendritic cells may mediate the humoral immune response to the insult. Later activity results in the stimulation of macrophages throughout the system. Macrophages produce both inducible nitric oxide synthase (iNOS) and prostaglandins. Both PGE_2 and nitric oxide (NO) suppress T cell proliferation, the effects of which may be seen several days after the thermal injury. Additionally, macrophages that, as a result of thermal injury, have been stimulated into producing NO and PGE_2 are resistant to the anti-inflammatory effects of IL-10. Macrophages stimulated by nonthermal injury are normally sensitive to the effects of IL-10. This cytokine activity results in a period of immunosuppression post-burn.

The activity of dendritic cells and NO is also implicated in the breakdown of the barrier function in the gut lining after thermal injury. NO causes instability of the cell membranes of enterocytes and endothelial cells. This disruption allows enteric bacteria access to the circulation. Suppression of the immune system then allows proliferation of bacteria within the circulatory system.

Inflammatory mediators are mobilized immediately after a burn injury. mRNAs are differentially expressed in burn-damaged dermis to coordinate these mediators, with some being upregulated and some downregulated to promote healing. Inflammatory mediators involved in repair of burns include Notch-1 and Notch-2, VEGF-A, TGF-beta, and COL1A2 [25].

Severe burns result in pathophysiologic alterations that negatively impact the structure and function of mitochondria [26]. Mitochondria-rich muscle tissue acts as a reservoir for amino acids and proteins that are required during the healing phase. The combination of increased demand on muscle tissue and the decreased capacity of the energy-generating units results in muscle wasting in the post-burn period, often lasting for over 9 months in humans.

Cardiac functioning and rhythm is altered after severe burn events [27]. Beginning immediately after the burn injury and lasting for up to 72 h, cardiac function is severely depressed in what is referred to as the "ebb phase." Following this initial period, the "flow phase" is characterized by increased energy expenditure and heart rate which may last for more than a year. This process is thought to be mediated by beta-adrenergic receptors.

In studies of human burn victims, females had poorer outcome than males [28]. This increased risk of mortality was not associated with burn size and is contrary to the better outcome exhibited by human female victims of other types of trauma. Similar studies have not been explored in animals.

2.9   Electrothermal Injury

Electrothermal injury may occur when an animal completes a circuit with an object of sufficiently high current and voltage. The movement of electrical charges is dictated by the interactions between current, resistance, and potential difference (Fig. 2.3). The flow of electricity (current) between two points is measured in amperes (A). The difference in electrical potential between those two points is measured in volts (V). Material between the two points has an inherent resistance, measured in ohms, that affects the flow of electricity. Ohm's law states that the electrical current is directly proportional to the difference in electrical potential between two points and inversely proportional to the resistance between the points. Substances with low resistance, and thus amenable to current flow, include water and steel. Rubber and wood offer greater resistance and tolerate less flow of electricity. In

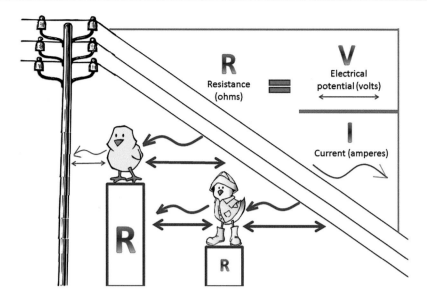

Fig. 2.3 The relationship between electrical potential, current, and resistance with regards to electrocution injury. Electricity flows between two points—in this case a ground wire and a power pole. The birds depicted have an inherent resistance that affects both the current of elec-tricity and the electrical potential between those two points. The greater resistance provided by the dry bird on the left limits the flow of electricity through the body, whereas the wet bird in the right allows greater flow and, thus, greater injury

real-world situations, animals that are wet or in contact with moisture or metal provide relatively little resistance to the flow of electricity. Dry skin or contact with dry, nonmetallic substrate is more protective against the full flow of current.

Electrical currents may be either alternating (AC, cyclically flowing back and forth) or direct (DC, unidirectional flow). Residential electricity is AC, whereas electricity in batteries and light-ning is direct. Regardless of whether the electric-ity alternates or flows in one direction, the path the current takes through the body follows the route of least resistance and is usually the short-est distance between the contact points.

Injuries resulting from contact with an elec-trothermal source include physiologic distur-bance of the cardiac rhythm, physical damage to soft tissues (burns), and/or indirect, mechanical injury as a result of a fall or muscle contraction.

2.9.1 Electrocution

Events involving contact with a source of elec-tricity are classified as either high voltage (>1000 V) or low voltage (<1000 V). Domestic animals may suffer electrical injury due to con-tact with exposed live wires, Tasers, and jumper cables or contact with water that is then exposed to an electrical current. Wildlife, especially birds, may be exposed to the higher voltage electricity in power lines. Additionally, proximity to very high-voltage sources may induce an electric arc without physical contact with an electrical source. The arc may contact an animal, resulting in electrocution, or pass near an animal. Air sur-rounding an electrical arc may reach tempera-tures up to 20,000 °C and cause singeing of hair or burned skin.

Exposure to high-voltage electrical conduc-tors often results in severe electrical burns because of the heat energy caused by contact with the electricity source. The epidermal effects of low-voltage exposure may be subtle or absent, depending on the duration of exposure. Brief exposure to a low electrical potential difference may cause no visible soft tissue damage. Longer exposure—as when an animal is trapped against the electrical source—may result in mild to severe burns.

Muscles contract in response to the physiologic electrical currents passing through the nerves. Exposure to rapid, exogenous current induces tetanic or sustained contraction until the source of electricity is removed. All muscles within the path of the current are affected, but the effect of contraction of larger muscles will be stronger in relation to smaller muscle bundles. Muscular contraction may be strong and fast enough to cause fractures or joint dislocations. In heavily muscled animals exposed to high-voltage shocks even of very short duration, violent contraction may result in compartment syndrome. This may also occur with prolonged exposure to low-voltage current.

The nervous system provides the least resistance to the flow of exogenous electricity. Thus, the brain, spinal cord, and peripheral nerves are acutely susceptible to electrothermal injury. Neurons may undergo conformational change that leads to increased cellular permeability, or electroporation, which eventually results in cell death [29]. Electrocution may cause a direct effect on the eyesight through damage to the optic nerve or occipital lobe of the brain. The current also affects the intima and adventitia of blood vessels through heat damage. This results in increased vascular permeability and thrombosis. Microscopic changes that may be evident in survivors within hours of electrocution include edema and local ischemic change. Eosinophilic neuron cell bodies with pyknotic nuclei, indicating neuronal necrosis, may follow.

Circulatory damage due to electrocution may also manifest in other areas of the body. Vascular stasis, rhabdomyolysis, and ischemia may lead to transient or severe disseminated intravascular coagulation. These effects may be acute or delayed.

Following the immediate effects of the electrocution event, secondary effects of temporary paralysis or autonomic disturbances may begin within a few days. Late effects of electrocution start to manifest 5 days after the event and include brain stem dysfunction and movement disorders. These delayed effects may be due to free radicals released from damaged neurons, causing progressive demyelination [30].

In humans, the motor neuronal system is more affected by electrocution injury than the sensory system. This may be due to the relative physiologic emphasis placed on the motor system in humans. Animals often have one or more highly developed senses, depending on their evolutionary ecology. Thus, evaluation of a suspected or confirmed electrocution victim should include assessment of the potential effect of electrical current and heat on the sensory neurons.

Skin burns may occur at the site of contact in electrocutions with AC power or at entry and exit points in DC or AC electrocution. Because electrical energy is translated into heat energy at points of contact with an animal, burns due to electrocution can be described the same way as burns due to direct thermal heat injury. The effects of electrocution may be subtle, resulting in little to no discernible burns to the skin. Minor or focal damage to the hair or feathers of an electrocution victim can be highlighted by viewing the affected skin through a red filter while illuminating the area with an alternate light source (ALS) tuned to wavelengths between 530 and 560 nm [31]. Keratin that has been electrothermally damaged has photoluminescent properties that make it glow bright orange-red when viewed through a red filter under these wavelengths of visible light. Glabrous skin that has been damaged by heat or electricity may appear grossly to be merely abraded, ashy, or scratched (Fig. 2.4). These lesions, however, can be differentiated by

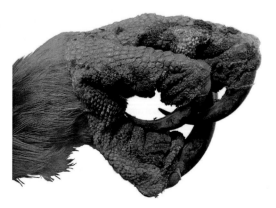

Fig. 2.4 Left foot of a golden eagle (*Aquila chrysaetos*). Ashy discoloration of the skin on the medial aspect of the third digit is a result of electrothermal injury

Fig. 2.5 Inner aspect of the left humerus of a bald eagle (*Haliaeetus leucocephalus*) that had singed feathers over both wings. The biceps muscle (B) and scapular head of the triceps (SHT) muscle are discolored brown due to the electrical current that passed through the soft tissues of the wings

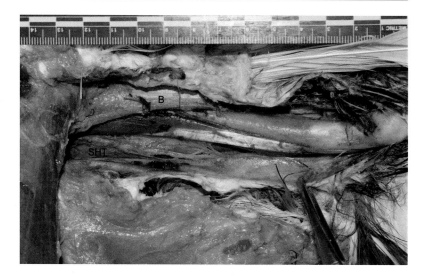

Fig. 2.6 Right leg and tail of a common raven. The foot has been amputated and cauterized by an electrical current emanating from a power line

the use of an ALS as traumatically damaged skin does not photoluminesce.

Electrocution from contact with power within a home infrequently results in visible burns of the skin. Gross and histologic changes may be seen in prolonged contact with in-home electrical contacts. More commonly, effects of this low-voltage electrocution result in cellular disturbances that may be witnessed behaviorally, grossly, and histologically if an animal survives the initial insult. Assessment of the scene and a careful history are often needed to diagnose electrocution of an animal with little to no visibly discernible singeing or burning.

Metal particles from electrical wires may be transferred to the skin with which it has direct contact [32]. Arcing of electricity may also result in metal deposition. The metal is not generally detectable grossly or radiographically and must be explored via histochemical analysis or scanning electron microscopy of skin at the point of contact. Iron, copper, or aluminum can be detected on electrocuted skin via these methods.

Wild birds may be exposed to lower-voltage distribution power lines or higher-voltage transmission lines [4]. High-voltage electrocution is more likely to result in singeing of the plumage and burns to the skin. Rapid vaporization of water at the point of electrical contact can result in separation of the skin from the underlying muscle or bone. In these cases, the affected subcutis and musculature appear coagulated, dry, and discolored brown (Fig. 2.5). Muscle may take on the appearance of cooked meat with tan discoloration and separation of myofibers. With very high-voltage events, thermal amputation and cauterization of digits or limbs may occur (Fig. 2.6). In low-voltage electrocution of wild birds, subtle singeing of feathers and skin may occur on the inner aspects of the wings distal to the humeroulnar joints and on the feet and legs distal to the stifles.

The special sense organs, the respiratory system, and the GI tract may also suffer direct damage due to an electrocution event [1]. Because of the high water content in the eye, an electrical current may cause the retina to detach or may cause direct damage to the cornea. Vascular damage within the eye itself may result in intraocular hemorrhage or thrombosis. Cataracts may develop weeks to years after an animal receives an electrical injury to the head or neck. Rupture of the eardrums is a common sequel to electrocution in humans but is not well documented in mammals. Hearing loss due to nerve and soft tissue damage in the ears may manifest immediately after the electrocution event or may have delayed development.

Electrical arcing may result in the production of ozone, which can act as an irritant to mucus membranes and the lungs [1]. Inhalation of ozone may result in pulmonary edema and hemorrhage. High-voltage electrical injury may cause rapid vaporization of fluids due to heat energy production. The expansion of gasses may result in tears in the intestinal wall or intra-abdominal hemorrhage.

Blunt force trauma may be secondary to electrocution injury. Electrical arcs from power lines may produce a blast force that propels an animal into objects or to the ground. Also, birds that are electrocuted on power poles may fall to the ground. Mild bruising may be evident. Hemopericardium is a common sequel to power pole electrocution and may result from direct electrical damage to the vasculature or deceleration injury upon hitting the ground. In deceleration injury, the heart base vessels are torn, resulting in hemorrhage into the pericardial sac.

Animals that are partially or fully submerged in water that becomes electrically excited may be electrocuted. In these instances, burning of the skin does not occur, but a line of demarcation between the electrified water and the air may be noted on the skin. Similar to scalds and depending on the duration of exposure to the electrified water, damage to the skin may be superficial or deep.

Histologically, there may be separation of the skin layers [3]. Intraepidermal separation of the skin is much more common in electrocution injury than in skin that has been exposed to a flame or hot objects. The presence of concurrent intraepidermal and subepidermal separation is also more common in electrocuted skin than in heat-damaged skin. Similar to heat-related burns, there may also be elongation of basal cell nuclei and smudging or coagulation necrosis of the dermal collagen.

2.9.2 Lightning Strike

Animals remaining outdoors during a thunderstorm may be hit by a lightning flash. Flashes that travel between the atmosphere and the ground are termed "lightning strikes" [33]. The duration of a strike is incredibly brief, lasting only around 300 ms. However, a flash of lightning may transmit energy up to 10^{10} J at an electromagnetic frequency of up to 10 MHz. This amount of energy is capable of boiling water instantaneously. The trunks of trees that are struck by lightning may crack or explode due to the rapid boiling of the internal sap and expansion of steam within a rigid framework. Humans and other animals, being soft bodied and more malleable, can better absorb the effects of gas expansion. However, tears in the soft tissues may result if the expanding gas overwhelms the elastic capacity of the affected tissue.

Direct lightning strike occurs when a shaft of electrically charged air passes through an animal and contacts the ground. Animals may also be struck by a sideflash, current that emanates from a nearby object that was directly struck by the flash. In contrast, a contact strike happens when an animal is in direct contact with something, such as a metal wall or fencepost that is directly hit by lightning. Additionally, lightning may travel to the ground through a conductor (e.g., tree, building) and travel through the ground to an animal standing close by (ground strike).

Lightning may travel over the surface of the body instead of using the body as a direct conduit in its path to the ground [1]. This event is termed a "flashover" and does not generally result in soft tissue burns or cardiac arrhythmias. Transformation of water on the surface of the body into steam may result in torn clothing. Internal and external pressure differences may also result in rupture of the tympanic membranes or contusion of internal organs.

Clinically, lightning strike may result in immediate cardiac asystole and respiratory arrest. These conditions may result from depolarization of the myocardium and transient paralysis of the medullary respiratory center.

Physical evidence of the lightning strike may be subtle on both the animal and the surrounding ground. Rarely, arborizing or fernlike patterns may be seen on the ground due to the movement or charring of grass or substrate by the rapidly traveling bolt of current. These patterns are referred to as keraunographic markings when seen on the earth. Similar markings may be seen on glabrous human skin following lightning strike and are referred to as Lichtenberg figures [34]. Histologic alterations have not correlated well with this visible manifestation and they are not true burns. These patterns on the skin may disappear within 12–24 h of the initial injury. Similar findings have not been reported in animals, likely because fur or feathers obscure the change.

Cases of individual or group electrocution due to lightning strike have been documented in livestock and, rarely, in wildlife [31, 35, 36]. Herds of cattle, swine, or caribou may be exposed to inclement weather. Moisture on the pelage due to precipitation decreases the resistance of the skin to the electrical current. Additionally, the tendency of animals to congregate under trees during a storm also increases the chances of ground strike, as current may initially strike the tree and travel through the wet ground and up the legs of the surrounding animals.

Occasionally, large flocks of birds, such as snow geese, may fly through an electrostatic field in the atmosphere, triggering a lightning flash, similar to the effect of an aircraft [31]. The flash may originate at an extremity of the flock (e.g., the lead bird) and pass through all the birds within the group. Because of the immediate, debilitating muscular and cardiopulmonary effects of the lightning flash, the entire flock may fall to the ground. Gross changes of electrothermal injury in these events may be subtle and include slight discoloration and curling of feathers on the lateral aspects of the neck and leading edges of the patagia (Fig. 2.7). The eardrums may be ruptured. More common are signs of blunt force impact with the ground and deceleration injury, such as subcutaneous bruising, liver laceration, and vascular tears.

External evidence of lightning strike in mammals may include linear or patchy areas of singed hair. These areas may be highlighted by wetting the hair or using an alternate light source to look for photoluminescent, singed hairs as previously described in Section 2.9.1 (Fig. 2.8). Charring or burning of the skin due to lightning strike is uncommon. Bloat may be accelerated in lightning victims, appearing even in freshly killed animals. The bloat may be robust and explosive—care should be taken on initial incision of the carcass to avoid rapid release of gasses trapped in body cavities and luminous organs.

Lightning strike may cause muscular contraction similar to that seen in anthropogenic electrocution. Food animals are bred to have robust muscle mass and may be more susceptible to fractures or dislocations as a result of lightning strike. In one case report [36], lightning affected a small herd of pigs; one died at the scene and three presented with hind limb paralysis. In all three survivors, strong and rapid contraction of the hind limb musculature resulted in fractures of the spine at the lumbosacral junction and transection of the spinal cord. Sagittal transection of the spine in this case revealed the lesions, as external signs of blunt force trauma or burns were not present.

Histologic changes in lightning strike victims are present only when there is gross evidence of tissue damage and are similar to those in anthropogenic electrocution events. Animals that survive the initial strike and die hours or days later may have microscopically evident inflammation or necrosis of the skin, skeletal muscle, or heart.

Fig. 2.7 Inner aspect of the right wing of a snow goose (*Chen caerulescens*). This was one of many geese that were found dead in a muddy field after a thunder storm and determined to have been struck by lightning. (**a**) At room light, a patch of apteria is lined by feathers that are discolored brown. (**b**) When illuminated by 560 nm wavelength light and viewed through a red filter, the feathers surrounding the area of alopecia photoluminesce bright orange

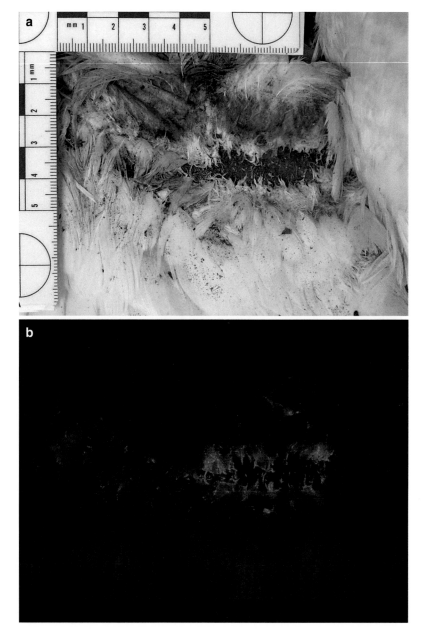

2.10   Chemical Burns

The skin and external covering (hair in mammals) provide protection against exogenous chemicals with which an animal may come into contact. The hair coat may act as a barrier to exogenous chemicals, preventing some amount of the compound from reaching the skin. However, once the chemical penetrates the pel-age and contacts the skin, the hair coat may also prolong the contact between the chemical and the skin as flushing of the affected area to remove the offending agent may be less efficient.

The most harmful chemical classes are strong acids and bases. Pets may be exposed to battery or hydrochloric acid in abuse situations. These acids cause coagulation necrosis, and the depth of skin damage is dictated by the pH of the com-

Fig. 2.8 Hair on the flank of a gray wolf (*Canis lupus*). This wolf was found dead after a thunderstorm and was determined to have been struck by lightning. (**a**) The patch of hair is curled but of normal coloration. (**b**) The same patch of hair is examined using X-ray florescence spectroscopy. The singed hair is brightly florescent

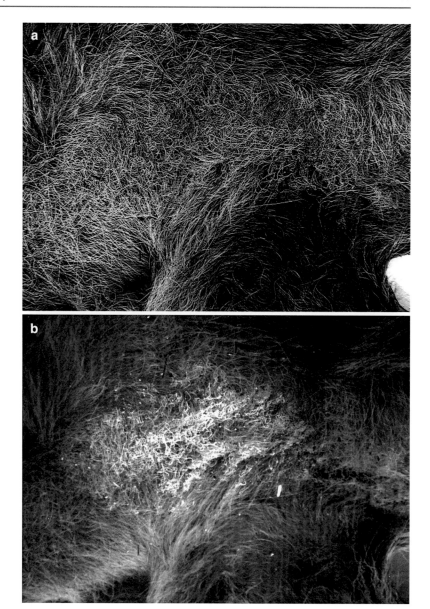

pound and the duration of direct exposure. For example, contact with sulfuric acid—with a pH of 0.3–2.1—for as little as 1 min may cause full-thickness necrosis of the skin [1]. The burn created may be blanched or brown and leathery. Due to nerve damage, the center of the lesion may be non-painful.

Acids may also volatilize, affecting the respiratory tract and mucus membranes in gas suspension. Some acidic compounds may produce a systemic effect after absorption through the skin.

For example, chromic acid in contact with as little as 1% of the body surface area may cause renal and hepatic damage, coagulopathy, and CNS disturbances [37]. Specific changes include acute renal tubular and hepatocyte necrosis due to the effect of the absorbed compound's effect on epithelial structures. In severe cases, there may be intravascular hemolysis, which contributes to renal and hepatic failure.

Because of the ability of alkaline chemicals to solubilize lipids, burns from basic chemicals tend to penetrate deeper into the skin. The result is a liquefactive necrosis—in contrast to the coagulative necrosis of acid burns—and the gross appearance is soft and gelatinous. The visible effects of alkali burns may take several hours to days to fully develop. Alkaline chemicals that animals may come into contact with include bleach, lye, and calcium oxide (lime). Lye is directly corrosive and is found in many household cleaning agents. Deep penetration of the skin by lye may allow the passage of hydroxyl ions and result in systemic effects. Calcium oxide is a commonly used gardening compound and combines with water to form calcium hydroxide, which has a pH of 11.

Differentiation between chemical burns and natural dermatopathology (e.g., atopy, lupus) rests largely in the distribution of the lesions. Many systemic hypersensitivity or autoimmune disorders manifest as symmetrical hair loss or inflammation around the eyes and nose, often sparing the mucus membranes in these areas. A chemical burn to the face would affect the skin, corneas, and mucus membranes to an equal degree. Also, the act of pouring or splashing a chemical on an animal will usually produce a pattern of injury that is asymmetrical and of varying severity throughout the wound area.

Legal Note The findings and conclusions in this chapter are those of the author and do not necessarily represent the views of the US Fish and Wildlife Service.

References

1. Tintinalli JE, Stapczynski JS, Ma OJ, Yealy DM, Meckler GD, Cline D, editors. Tintinalli's emergency medicine: a comprehensive study guide. 8th ed. USA: McGraw-Hill Education; 2016.
2. Jackson D. The diagnosis of the depth of burning. Br J Surg. 1953;40:588.
3. Üzün İ, Akyıldız E, İnanıcı M. Histopathological differentiation of skin lesions caused by electrocution, flame burns and abrasion. Forensic Sci Int. 2008;178:157–61. https://doi.org/10.1016/j.forsciint.2008.03.012.
4. Kagan R. Electrocution of raptors on power lines: a review of necropsy methods and findings. Vet Pathol. 2016;53:1030–6. https://doi.org/10.1177/0300985816646431.
5. Fitzgerald K, Flood A. Smoke inhalation. Clin Tech Small Anim Pract. 2006;21:205–14. https://doi.org/10.1053/j.ctsap.2006.10.009.
6. Stern A, Lewis R, Thompson K. Toxic smoke inhalation in fire victim dogs. Vet Pathol. 2014;51:1165–7. https://doi.org/10.1177/0300985813519134.
7. Stoll S, Roider G, Keil W. Concentrations of cyanide in blood samples of corpses after smoke inhalation of varying origin. Int J Legal Med. 2016. https://doi.org/10.1007/s00414-016-1426-0.
8. Shin B, Kim M, Yoo H, Kim S, Lee J, Jeon K. Tracheobronchial polyps following thermal inhalation injury. Tuberc Respir Dis. 2014;76:237–9. https://doi.org/10.4046/trd.2014.76.5.237.
9. Choi IS. Carbon monoxide poisoning: systemic manifestations and complications. J Korean Med Sci. 2001;16:253–61.
10. Lewis R, Johnson R, Canfield D. An accurate method for the determination of carboxyhemoglobin in postmortem blood using GC-TCD. J Anal Toxicol. 2004;28:59–62. https://doi.org/10.1093/jat/28.1.59.
11. Kent M, Creevy K, deLahunta A. Clinical and neuropathological findings of acute carbon monoxide toxicity in Chihuahuas following smoke inhalation. J Am Anim Hosp Assoc. 2010;46:259–64. https://doi.org/10.5326/0460259.
12. Dettmeyer RB. Forensic histopathology: fundamentals and perspectives. Berlin: Springer-Verlag; 2011.
13. Miller K, Hunt R, Chu J, Meehan S, Stein J. Erythema Ab igne. Dermatol Online J. 2011;17:28.
14. Walder EJ, Hargis AM. Chronic moderate heat dermatitis (erythema ab igne) in five dogs, three cats and one silvered langur. Vet Dermatol. 2002;13(5):283–92.
15. Maguire S, Moynihan S, Mann M, Potokar T, Kemp AM. A systematic review of the features that indicate intentional scalds in children. Burns. 2008;34:1072–81. https://doi.org/10.1016/j.burns.2008.02.011.
16. D'Orazio J, Jarrett S, Amaro-Ortiz A, Scott T. UV radiation and the skin. Int J Mol Sci. 2013;14:12222–48. https://doi.org/10.3390/ijms140612222.
17. Lopes D, McMahon S. Ultraviolet radiation on the skin: a painful experience? CNS Neurosci Ther. 2016;22:118–26. https://doi.org/10.1111/cns.12444.
18. Azzam EI, Jay-Gerin J-P, Pain D. Ionizing radiation-induced metabolic oxidative stress and prolonged cell injury. Cancer Lett. 2012;327:48–60.
19. Suzuki K, Mitsutake N, Saenko V, Yamashita S. Radiation signatures in childhood thyroid cancers after the Chernobyl accident: possible roles of radiation in carcinogenesis. Cancer Sci. 2015;106:127–33.
20. International Agency for Research on Cancer (2000) Evaluation of carcinogenic risks to humans. Ionizing radiation. Part 1: X- and Gamma (g)-radiation, and neutrons. Lyon, France.
21. Little M. A review of non-cancer effects, especially circulatory and ocular diseases. Radiat Environ Biophys. 2013;52:435–49.

22. Reedy LM, Clubb FJ Jr. Microwave burn in a toy poodle: a case report. J Am Anim Hosp Assoc. 1991;27:497–500.

23. Jeschke MG, Pinto R, Kraft R, Nathens AB, Finnerty CC, Gamelli RL, Gibran NS, Klein MB, Arnoldo BD, Tompkins RG, Herndon DN. Morbidity and survival probability in burn patients in modern burn care. Crit Care Med. 2015;43(4):808–15.

24. Schwacha M, Chaudry I. The cellular basis of post-burn immunosuppression: macrophages and mediators. Int J Mol Med. 2002;10:239–43. https://doi.org/10.3892/ijmm.10.3.23.

25. Zhou J, Zhang X, Liang P, Ren L, Zeng J, Zhang M, Zhang P, Huang X. Protective role of microRNA-29a in denatured dermis and skin fibroblast cells after thermal injury. Biol Open. 2016;5:bio.014910. https://doi.org/10.1242/bio.014910.

26. Porter C, Herndon D, Sidossis L, Børsheim E. The impact of severe burns on skeletal muscle mitochondrial function. Burns. 2013;39:1039–47. https://doi.org/10.1016/j.burns.2013.03.018.

27. Guillory A, Clayton R, Herndon D, Finnerty C. Cardiovascular dysfunction following burn injury: what we have learned from rat and mouse models. Int J Mol Sci. 2016;17:53. https://doi.org/10.3390/ijms17010053.

28. Summers J, Ziembicki J, Corcos A, Peitzman A, Billiar T, Sperry J. Characterization of sex dimorphism following severe thermal injury. J Burn Care Res. 2014;35:484. https://doi.org/10.1097/BCR.0000000000000018.

29. Johl H, Olshansky A, Beydoun S, Rison R. Cervicothoracic spinal cord and pontomedullary injury secondary to high-voltage electrocution: a case report. J Med Case Rep. 2012;6. https://doi.org/10.1186/1752-1947-6-296.

30. Reisner AD. Possible mechanisms for delayed neurological damage in lightning and electrical injury. Brain Inj. 2013;27:565–9.

31. Viner T, Kagan R, Johnson J. Using an alternate light source to detect electrically singed feathers and hair in a forensic setting. Forensic Sci Int. 2014;234:e25–9.https://doi.org/10.1016/j.forsciint.2013.10.033.

32. Jacobsen H. Electrically induced deposition of metal on the human skin. Forensic Sci Int. 1997;90:85–92.

33. Rakov VA, Uman MA. Lightning: physics and effects. Cambridge: University Press; 2003.

34. Wetli CV. Keraunopathology: an analysis of 45 fatalities. Am J Forensic Med Pathol. 1996;17:89–98.

35. Shaw GE, Neiland KA. Electrocution of a caribou herd caused by lightning in central Alaska. J Wildl Dis. 1973;9:311–3.

36. Van Alstine W, Widmer W. Lightning injury in an outdoor swine herd. J Vet Diagn Invest. 2003;15:289–91. https://doi.org/10.1177/104063870301500313.

37. Sharma B, Singhal P, Chugh K. Intravascular haemolysis and acute renal failure following potassium dichromate poisoning. Postgrad Med J. 1978;54:414–5. https://doi.org/10.1136/pgmj.54.632.414.

Neglect

N. Bradley-Siemens, A.I. Brower, and R. Reisman

3.1 Introduction

More than 30% of reported animal abuse in the United States involves some form of animal neglect [1] (Fig. 3.1). Neglect may be unintentional or deliberate (gross, willful, cruel, or malicious) and takes a variety of forms such as starvation, lack of basic physical care (e.g., grooming), unsanitary living conditions, abandonment, and failure to provide veterinary care. More complicated cases related to small- and large-scale hoarding often include a combination of the forms listed. Neglect may lead to death due to disease, starvation, and dehydration, and it may present with a multitude of other health problems related to living in unsanitary, crowded, and otherwise unacceptable conditions. The veterinary forensic pathologist must be familiar with necropsy findings in these circumstances and be able to connect them with relevant crime scene information, including housing, environment, and lack of veterinary care. This is accomplished through review of material provided by law enforcement or humane investigators (reports, photos, and videos) or direct assessment of a scene before or after seizure, within the context of necropsy findings [1].

3.2 Defining Neglect

3.2.1 Failure to Provide Adequate Food, Water, Shelter and Veterinary Care

The Humane Society of the United States defines animal neglect as a condition in which an animal's caregiver or owner does not provide food, water, shelter, or veterinary care sufficient for the animal's survival. Medical problems associated with neglect can, at first glance, seem less severe than a single act of violent abuse. However, most cases of neglect include prolonged suffering. The cumulative discomfort, distress, and pain that a neglected animal experiences when not provided health care, proper nutrition, or shelter can be extreme and may result in permanent injury or death [2]. Simple neglect, the failure to provide basic needs to an animal, may not always be considered a criminal act. Some cases can be addressed by intervention from animal welfare agencies by providing resources and education on adequate animal care. Willful, cruel, or malicious neglect is committed with the intention of harming an animal and is more commonly prosecuted.

N. Bradley-Siemens, D.V.M., M.N.M. (✉)
A.I. Brower, D.V.M., D.A.C.V.P.
Department of Pathology and Population Medicine, Midwestern University College of Veterinary Medicine, Diagnostic Pathology Center, 5725 West Utopia Rd, Glendale, AZ 85308, USA
e-mail: nbradl@midwestern.edu

R. Reisman, D.V.M.
ASPCA, New York, NY, USA

© Springer International Publishing AG 2018
J.W. Brooks (ed.), *Veterinary Forensic Pathology, Volume 2*,
https://doi.org/10.1007/978-3-319-67175-8_3

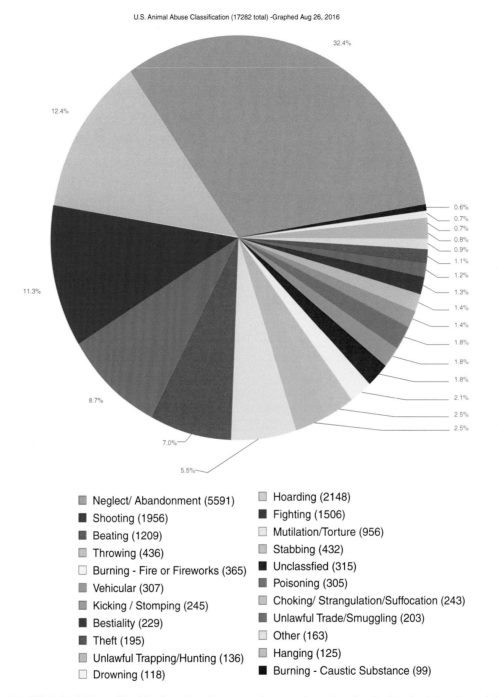

Fig. 3.1 US Animal Abuse Classifications. http://www.pet-abuse.com/pages/cruelty_database/statistics.php and the AARDAS project

While all 50 US states have misdemeanor and felony-level animal cruelty laws to varying degrees, court interpretation of these laws influences legal outcomes. For example, the New York State Misdemeanor Animal Cruelty Law, the first animal cruelty law established in the United States, does not require veterinary care as written, but it includes the word "sustenance" in the phrase *animals must be provided with food, water, and sustenance*. The term sustenance has been interpreted during the application of the law to mean care of the animal's health needs, including veterinary care. This example helps to illustrate the way in which animal cruelty becomes a legal designation. While the veterinary pathologist can play a key role in building the case for animal cruelty, the final determination is not made by the medical professional but by the legal body examining it.

In the United States, animal cruelty laws differ in every state, and laws and their applications vary greatly across different countries. The five freedoms for animal welfare were established in the United Kingdom in 1965 and have served as a guide in assessing the welfare and care of animals globally. They include freedom from hunger or thirst; freedom from discomfort; freedom from pain, injury, or disease; freedom to express normal behavior; and freedom from fear or distress. In the same year that the five freedoms were established, the United States signed into law the Animal Welfare Act (AWA). The AWA is the only federal US law regulating the treatment of animals, and it provides the key legal reference in cases of animal neglect. In the United States, when criminal charges or sentencing is pursued in an animal neglect case, legal decisions are based on a "reasonable person" standard, in consideration of the five freedoms, and under the guidance of the Animal Welfare Act [3].

Forensic veterinary medicine, or legal medicine, is veterinary medicine practiced in a legal context. Veterinary clinicians and pathologists who practice forensic veterinary medicine should be familiar with the animal cruelty laws in their regions and the language used. For instance, starvation, a cause of death familiar to veterinary pathologists, is not a word used in animal cruelty law. Rather, animal cruelty laws state that animals must be provided with adequate food. While

designating a cause of death is the responsibility of the veterinary pathologist, ultimately, it is the responsibility of law enforcement to determine the specific circumstances that led to an animal's compromised health, and it is up to the courts to determine if these circumstances constitute neglect.

The types of medical problems that are prosecuted as cases of individual animal criminal neglect include long-term inadequate nutrition; extreme lack of general physical care, such as strangulating hair mats in long-haired dogs; unsanitary living conditions that result in secondary disease such as severe dermatitis or pododermatitis; inappropriate restraint such as embedded collars; exposure to environmental extremes including both heat and cold; and "failure to treat" any medical condition for which a reasonable person would recognize that an animal needs medical care. In all of these situations, it is necessary to demonstrate that neglect resulted in tissue injury and deviation from a state of comfort (discomfort, distress, or pain). It is not uncommon for criminal animal neglect to be associated with human neglect involving a child, elder, or other dependent in a household. Variable numbers of animals may be affected, and the scale of animal neglect can range from an individual animal to large-scale hoarding and overwhelmed shelters, sanctuaries, and puppy mills [4, 5].

3.3   Findings Compatible with Neglect

3.3.1   Lack of Adequate Nutrition

Basic nutrition of domestic species is a standard part of veterinary education, and consideration of nutritional requirements can help veterinary pathologists interpret postmortem findings in cases of starvation and dehydration. Understanding the basic nutritional requirements in the species examined also helps define the pathogenesis of lesions and increases the likelihood that important components of medical histories and investigation data will be correctly interpreted. The Association of Shelter Veterinarians has produced Guidelines for Standards of Care in Animal Shelters that provides nutritional basics when housing and caring for animals [3]. Included are the provisions that fresh, clean, readily accessible water be available at all times (unless there is a medical reason to withhold it); food should be fresh, palatable, and free from contamination; food needs to be of sufficient nutritional value to meet normal daily requirements to attain normal development and maintain normal body weight; and food should be consistent with the nutritional requirements and health status of the individual. The amount and frequency of feeding vary depending on life stage, species, size, activity level, health status of the animal, and the diet chosen. When multiple animals are in an enclosure, monitoring is necessary to ensure no one animal is excluded from food or water sources, and food in animal enclosures should be examined regularly to ensure that it is free from debris and not spoiled [3].

Calorie requirements for dogs and cats are provided in Table 3.1. At a minimum, healthy dogs and cats over 6 months of age must be fed once per day. Ideally, dogs should be feed twice daily. Cats should have multiple small meals or a minimum of twice per day feeding. Healthy puppies and kittens must be fed small amounts of food frequently or have food constantly available (free choice) all day to support higher metabolic rates and prevent life-threatening fluctuations in blood glucose levels (hypoglycemia). Any animal that is debilitated, underweight, pregnant, or lactating should receive more frequent feedings to support increased metabolic needs [3].

Cats are true carnivores and have higher protein requirements than dogs. They do not possess the ability to manufacture or synthesize some essential nutrients, including taurine, arginine, and vitamin A. All these nutrients are present in prey they would naturally consume, and commercial diets fed to cats must include these nutrients as well.

Inadequate nutrition results in a compromise of every body system and tissue. There are well-established relationships between nutrition and maintenance of immune status and between reduced immunity and increased susceptibility to infection and infestation. Cell-mediated immunity may become impaired within 3–5 days of anorexia [6]. Parasite infestation or bacterial infection can catalyze further decline in animals who already have marginal nutritional status. Further, infections and parasitic infestations may cause reduced food intake, increased energy consumption, catabolism of muscle protein, and depletion of glycogen and fat stores. Inadequate nutritional status, if persistent and not corrected, may progress to protein-calorie malnutrition. In a state of malnutrition, cell-mediated immunity remains impaired, and infections may recur or persist [7].

A dog that is visibly emaciated has lost a substantial amount of both body fat and muscle tissue, resulting in a body weight that is at least 20–25% less than an ideal weight (Fig. 3.2 and 3.3). This loss of body tissue is evidenced by:

1. Visual and palpable prominence of skeletal structures, including the ribs, vertebral spinous processes, pelvic bones, and margins and spine of the scapula
2. Loss of round shape of temporal muscles on the sides of the head
3. Severe abdominal tuck and extreme hourglass shape when looking at the dog from above (Fig. 3.4) (Purina Body Condition Scale, [8, 9]).

Table 3.1 Daily maintenance energy requirements for dogs and cats

Animal	MER[a] (kcal/day)
Healthy adult dogs	
Intact	$1.8 \times$ RER[b]
Neutered	$1.6 \times$ RER
Obese prone	$1.4 \times$ RER
Healthy puppies	
<4 months old	$3 \times$ RER
>4 months old	$2 \times$ RER
Healthy adult cats	
Intact	$1.4 \times$ RER
Neutered	$1.2 \times$ RER
Obese prone	$1.0 \times$ RER
Healthy Kittens	$2.5 \times$ RER[c]

Sanderson, Sherry Lynn. *Nutritional Requirements and Related Diseases of Small Animals.* Merck Veterinary Manual. Permission for Use Approved by Merck & co Inc. Publishing: http://www.Merckvetmanual.Com/
[a]MER = maintenance energy requirement
[b]RER = resting energy requirement
[c]Kittens can alternatively be fed free choice

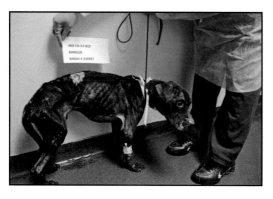 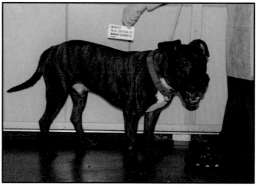

Figs. 3.2 and 3.3 Before and after images of a dog illustrating weight gain from a neglected condition to normal. The dog's entry weight was 27.3 # (Fig. 3.2), and the final weight was 55 # (Fig. 3.3), a 100% increase in overall body weight. This dog also had severe multifocal, decubital ulcers, not an uncommon finding in an emaciated dog

Label	The ASPCA Animal Hospital
	424 E 92nd Street, New York, N.Y. 10128 (212) 876-7700

Purina Body Condition Scoring for Underweight Animals

Body condition is determined by both looking at the animal and feeling the animal

☐ 1 **Emaciated**
- No palpable fat (post mortem; no significant subcutaneous or body cavity fat stores)
- Obvious loss of muscle mass including; temporal muscles, supraspinatus, infraspinatus, epaxial, gluteal and leg muscles
- Prominence (visually and by palpation) of skeletal structures (i.e. ribs, vertebral spines, pelvic bones, spine of scapula and femur) due to loss of body fat and muscle
- Severe abdominal tuck and extreme hourglass shape

☐ 2 **Very Underweight**
- No palpable fat (post mortem; no significant subcutaneous or body cavity fat stores)
- Definite loss of muscle mass
- Ribs, lumbar vertebrae and pelvic bones easily visible and/or palpable due to loss of body fat and muscle
- Prominent abdominal tuck. Hourglass shape to torso

☐ 3 **Thin**
- No palpable fat (post mortem; no significant subcutaneous or body cavity fat stores)
- Minimal loss of muscle mass
- Ribs easily palpated (may be visible) Tops of lumbar vertebrae visible. Pelvic bones becoming prominent
- Obvious waist and abdominal tuck

☐ 4 **Underweight/Lean**
- Waist visible from above. Abdominal tuck evident
- Ribs easily palpable with minimal subcutaneous fat
- No muscle loss
- May be normal for lean breeds such as sighthounds

☐ 5 **Ideal**
- Abdomen tucked slightly when viewed from the side
- Waist visible from above, just behind the ribs
- Ribs palpable without excess subcutaneous fat

Fig. 3.4 Purina Body Condition Scoring for Underweight Animals (ASPCA). Permission for use approved by Nestle Purina Pet Care Center

Pica, the ingestion or craving of nonfood objects, is a common behavior exhibited by starving animals. Items commonly ingested are rocks, plastic, wood, and dirt, but nearly any material may be found in the gastrointestinal tract. These foreign items can cause internal damage to the gastric mucosa or intestinal lining resulting in ulcerations, hemorrhage, or perforation of gastrointestinal walls. Pica may also be a symptom of extreme boredom seen with strict confinement or restriction of movement. Ingested foreign objects may be visible in feces at the scene, and melena can be observed if upper intestinal bleeding results from these nonfood items [10]. Foreign items are commonly recovered from the stomach and intestine at the time of postmortem examination of emaciated animals (Figs. 3.5, 3.6, 3.7, 3.8 and 3.9).

Cannibalism is a behavior that may be initiated or exacerbated by high-stress environments such as overcrowding and unsanitary housing conditions. It may be observed in mothers of puppies and kittens and in environments in which there is insufficient food, water, or shelter or in which there are continuous perceived threats (noise, smells, and large numbers of animals). Hoarding environments often have a combination of these factors. The type of cannibalism exhibited by companion animals may only involve the feet and lower extremities of the consumed ani-

mal. This is not a normal predatory feeding pattern and may indicate reluctance of an animal to feed upon its own species. Other situations may involve eating the whole body with the exception of the head and tail. Bones of intact or disarticulated remains may be found at the scene or in the gastrointestinal content of deceased animals. Animals may take a portion of the body to another location, leaving bones scattered in a hoarding scene at which animals are starving. If partially consumed animal remains are discovered in an enclosed structure without access to other animals from the external environment, it can be reasonably concluded that the other animals within the confined structure are consuming the

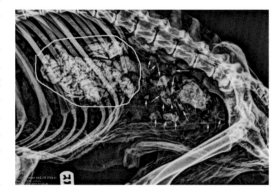

Fig. 3.5 Radiograph of a mummified dog (MD). The radiopaque shadows are pieces of glass within the gastrointestinal tract

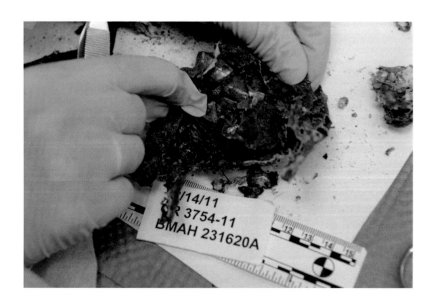

Fig. 3.6 Dry stomach tissue removed from MD's body contains many pieces of broken glass

Fig. 3.7 All of the glass that was removed from MD's intestinal tract. Pieces of a gasket were also found, suggesting that the dog ate a broken mason jar. A presumptive test for blood tested positive from a swab from the dog's lips. This is consistent with the dog cutting its lips as it ate the broken glass

Fig. 3.8 Pica. The image shows dirt and rocks eaten by a deceased Rottweiler dog

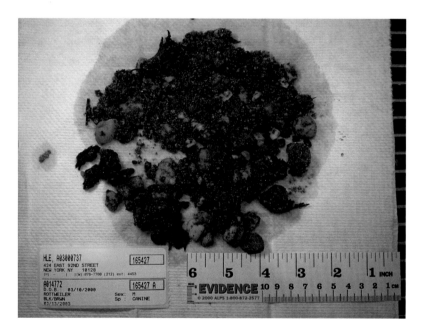

deceased animals; otherwise postmortem consumption by traditional scavenger species should be suspected [10]. Careful examination of remains may be required to differentiate normal postmortem decomposition from cannibalism or predation. Evidence of tooth marks, puncture wounds, and consumed remains in gastric content can be very helpful in making these distinctions, but in their absence, a definitive conclusion may not be possible.

3.3.2 Starvation and Dehydration

Starvation, also referred to as protein-calorie malnutrition, results from a diminished or absent intake of protein and calories. The rate of starvation is influenced by tissue demand, and the result is gradual depletion of lean body mass (muscle) and adipose tissue (Figs. 3.10, 3.11 and 3.12). While uncomplicated starvation causes a progressive decrease in metabolic rate in an effort to conserve energy, stress,

Fig. 3.9 Pica. The image shows razor blades, sharp pieces of plastic, and packages of ketchup found in a dog's stomach postmortem

Fig. 3.10 Canine; starvation and dehydration. Ribs and bony prominences over the shoulders, rear legs, and hips are evident, as are overgrown nails

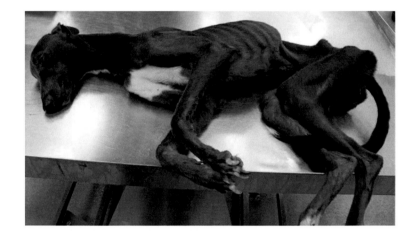

Fig. 3.11 Canine; starvation and dehydration. In addition to an emaciated body condition, fecal and urine soiling across the rear leg is evident, suggesting a period of lateral recumbency

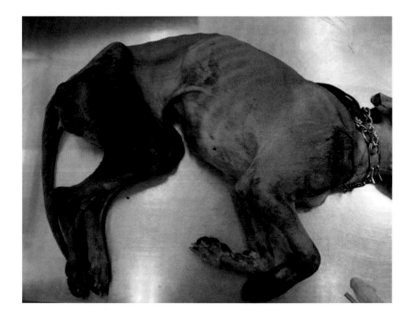

Fig. 3.12 Canine; starvation and dehydration. Eyes sunken deep in their orbits, temporal muscle wasting, and reduction in size of the neck

and trauma, other diseases may increase the metabolic rate and hasten tissue depletion. The rate of starvation and potential consequences should also be considered in the context of an animal's age and reproductive status. Young and growing animals and pregnant animals have increased nutritional demands as compared to adults [6]. Starvation results in weight loss and diminished growth capacity of bone structures in young animals. Pregnant animals enduring starvation may give birth to unhealthy neonates and dead feti [6].

Gross evidence of starvation may include changes in hair coat, which may appear thin, dry, and dull or may be brittle (stiff). Hairs may epilate easily. In addition, abnormal accumulation of skin scale may be noted (Figs. 3.13 and 3.14). Wound healing is also

Fig. 3.13 This dog had decubital ulcers on his head, extremities, back, pelvis, and proximal tail

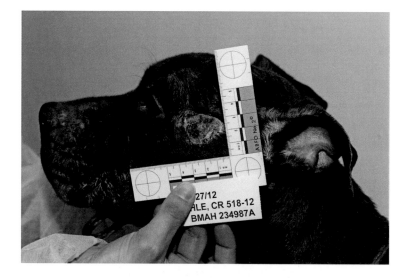

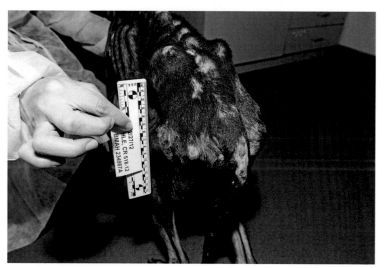

Fig. 3.14 He also had dry skin and a lusterless hair coat

hindered by malnutrition, creating the potential to develop secondary bacterial and yeast infections [6, 11].

Dehydration can occur concurrently in starving animals. Dehydration develops from deprivation of water or the animal's inability to drink. Severe dehydration may cause life-threatening electrolyte imbalances, and water deficits of 15–20% of an animal's body weight can lead to death [6].

3.3.3 Neglect Related to Inappropriate Shelter and Environment

An animal's environment may hold the most important information in a neglect case. There may be multiple problems observed at a scene where neglect has occurred. The most common findings include overcrowding, short tie-outs, and lack of shelter with overexposure to the elements. There may be insufficient amounts of water or undrinkable water (Fig. 3.15), inappropriate food for the age and species of animal, or food unfit for consumption. Environments may be malodorous, with feces and urine covering surfaces (Fig. 3.16). Additionally environments

may be disheveled and dirty or cluttered with hazardous debris and objects (Figs. 3.17 and 3.18). Examination of an environment should include noting signs of animal illness such as vomit or diarrhea and evidence of flea or tick infestation. An estimate should be constructed for the duration of the existing conditions. This can be evaluated based on the presence of dried or moldy feces, debris covering pens or cage doors, moldy food, and algae present in the water sources. In the event the animal has been tied outside, there may be a path or indentation in the ground and a lack of grass where the animal has been tethered. There may be plant material overgrowing existing kennels or cages. In the case of a deceased animal, entomological evidence should be considered to assist with time of death estimates [6, 11, 12].

3.3.4 Hypothermia and Hyperthermia

Hypothermia results from exposure to low environmental temperatures and occurs when the body's heat loss exceeds production. This is usually the result of inadequate shelter or lack of acclimation. There may not be any definable

Fig. 3.15 Image showing the sink as the main source of water; it was set to drip at slow rate. The image also shows large accumulations of cat hair surrounding the faucet from attempts to drink

Fig. 3.16 Hoarder scene; over one inch of feces is caked to the floor in the hallway of this condominium

Fig. 3.17 Debris in the home of a hoarder preventing room access

lesions on an animal with uncomplicated hypothermia [6], but physical evidence may include areas of edema, hemorrhage, ischemia, and dry tissue necrosis, referred to as frostbite. In domestic animals, ears, digits, the scrotum, and tail tips are most often affected. Areas of frostbite may have a blue, swollen appearance early on, eventually tissues will appear dry and shrunken, and ultimately the tissue may slough. Petechial hemorrhages related to frostbite are reported in lungs but are nonspecific [6].

Hyperthermia leading to heat stroke is caused by exposure to a hot environment where the animal's physiologic mechanisms used to cool the body become overwhelmed. The animal becomes incapable of preventing its body temperature from rising to a harmful or even fatal level. The typical presentation of a heat stroke patient

Fig. 3.18 Cats in the same condominium were discovered among debris and other objects

includes vomiting, diarrhea, severely elevated temperature (temperatures exceeding 103.5 F in dogs), and collapse. Organ damage or failure may occur and most commonly involves the liver, kidney, brain, and circulatory system [7]. In animal abuse cases, hyperthermia usually occurs in the summer months and results from leaving an animal in a hot vehicle, in a structure, or in an outside environment without protection from high temperatures and direct sunlight. Temperature is influenced by relative humidity. When the humidity rises, the heat index will be higher than the actual recorded temperature; thus, it is important to record data on both temperature and humidity at the scene [10].

Veterinarians may be asked to examine or necropsy a variety of animals affected by heat stroke, including horses, cows, pigs, and cats, but dogs are more commonly encountered in forensic investigations than other species [7]. In dogs, the majority of heat is removed through radiation and conducted from the surface of the body into the surrounding air. Remaining heat is dissipated by evaporation from the tongue and upper respiratory tract while the dog is panting. The loss of heat through evaporation is adversely affected by increased humidity; thus, environments with elevated temperatures and high relative humidity are

potentially more dangerous because they make it more difficult for dogs to adequately keep their body temperature within a normal physiologic range [7].

There are factors that can predispose an animal to heat stroke. These include water deprivation, obesity, exercise intolerance, lack of acclimation to a hot environment, medications, and some central nervous system diseases. Brachycephalic dog breeds and those with upper respiratory diseases are also more vulnerable, and any animal with a prior history of heat stroke should be considered at increased risk of repeated events. Dehydration can worsen the effects of heat stroke by causes conflicting demands within the body. When the body is heat stressed, peripheral blood vessels must dilate to dissipate heat. However, when an animal is dehydrated, the body will vasoconstrict peripheral vasculature to maintain blood volume. These antagonistic processes can result in cerebral hypothermia [6].

Before a diagnosis of heat stroke is made, other causes of death should be ruled out through complete postmortem examination. The diagnosis of death caused by heat stroke is often then a diagnosis of exclusion based largely on the crime scene and other environmental information. Pathologists should be aware that heat stroke can speed the onset of rigor mortis, but it can also cause permanent rigidity of the body that can be mistaken for rigor mortis. Rigor mortis is a temporary rigidity occurring postmortem that is related to loss of ATP and calcium ion changes. In addition to rigor mortis, the muscular rigidity caused by heat stroke may also result from the coagulation, dehydration, and ultimately shortening of muscle proteins due to heat [6, 7].

All organs may be discolored deeply red or brown from vascular congestion, and this may involve the mucous membranes [7]. Heat stroke may result in generalized autolysis of the tissue, especially with the body cavities. Autolysis can make additional diagnostic or histological testing difficult. Gross examination may demonstrate disseminated intravascular coagulation (DIC) with petechiation across the skin, on the surface of organs, and within body cavities. There may also be cerebral edema and areas of intraparenchymal hemorrhage. Intestinal contents may be bloody, and stomach ulcerations may be present. The heart may display evidence of muscular ischemia, hemorrhage, and necrosis [6].

3.3.5 Inappropriate Restraint

A common presentation of this form of neglect includes a dog tethered, alone or with other dogs, in a yard or enclosure, often but not necessarily having been abandoned. Embedded collars are a common finding in these situations. In some jurisdictions, embedded collars may be a felony offense depending on the severity and duration of injury. A collar usually becomes embedded over time, as the animal grows. This process can result in infection and disfigurement of the neck. As a collar constricts the increasing size of the neck, pressure necrosis of the skin and underlying tissue may result. The constriction of the collar on blood vessels may result in edema and swelling of the head and neck regions. Animals with embedded collars often suffer from starvation and malnutrition (Figs. 3.19, 3.20 and 3.21). In an extreme case, the author has observed vessel laceration from infiltration of a collar that resulted in exsanguination.

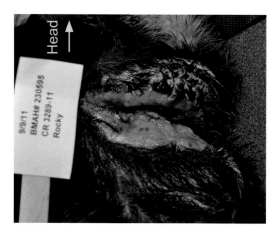

Fig. 3.19 An embedded collar wound with excessive scar tissue formation. This wound was estimated to be a minimum of 3 months old, based on the concept that it takes 5–7 days for a granulation bed to form and scar tissue accumulates at approximately 1.0 cm per month

Collars must be collected for evidence. When necessary, removal should be done by cutting the collar while avoiding the fastened or tied area. These areas may preserve trace evidence such as fingerprints that could be used to identify an abuser. The circumference of the neck should be measured in the area of the neck that is not swollen and compared with the length of the collar to which it was fastened or secured. Maggots may also be present in the infected wounds of an embedded collar via myiasis. These insects can help establish the duration of injury. Wounds resulting from an embedded collar typically begin to form granulation tissue in 5–7 days. Granulation tissue grows at a rate of approximately 1.0 mm per day and slows as the lesion ages to 1 roughly 1.0 cm per month (NY State College of Veterinary Medicine Dept. of Pathology).

3.3.6 Lack of Veterinary Treatment

Insufficient or absent veterinary care is a common occurrence in animal hoarding (Figs. 3.22, 3.23 and 3.24) and fighting situations and in instances of economic hardship. Animals may present in advanced states of disease, with treatable parasite infestations, untreated wounds,

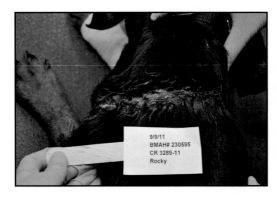
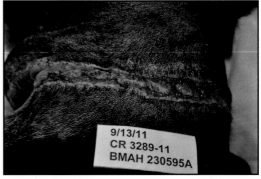

Figs. 3.20 and 3.21 The left side of the dog's neck before and after it was shaved. The unique patterned skin wound is consistent with an embedded chain

Fig. 3.22 Severe matting of the neck and head to front limbs right side

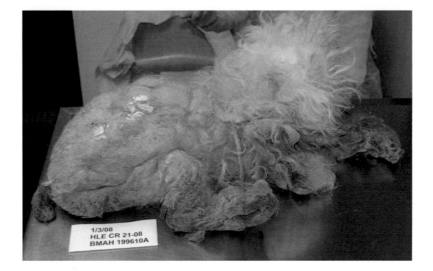

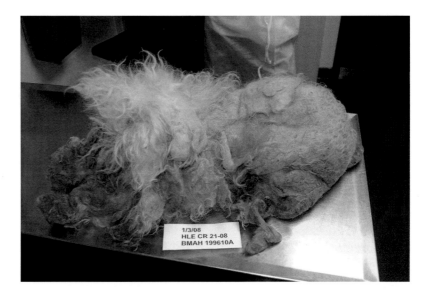

Fig. 3.23 Severe matting of the neck and head to front limbs left side

Fig. 3.24 After shaving and removal of mats

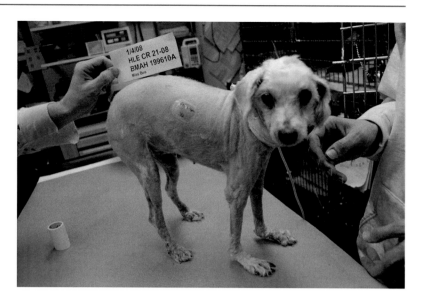

infections, or traumatic injuries. While it is not uncommon for animals to become injured accidentally, failure to treat such an injury may be considered neglect when injuries are not addressed and pain, distress, or even death results from failure to seek medical attention. Information related to when and how the injury occurred, the immediate action taken, and later actions taken if any can be crucial in determining this form of neglect. The pathologist should be given access to or provided with any interviews, reports, and photography that may point out inconsistencies in time sequences, clinical signs, and treatments administered [7]. This is especially true in bone fracture cases. Acute bone fractures will have evidence of fresh hemorrhage around the fracture site and within surrounding soft tissues. There may be clot formation within the fractured fragments of the bone and fibrous strands connecting the bone segments involved. There will be an absence of bone repair. If a yellow, serum-like fluid around a fracture site or within surrounding soft tissues is present, it may suggest a hematoma of a longer post-traumatic period. Any callus formation at the fracture site grossly or radiographically can assist with assessing duration of healing since the traumatic event. Infection may become an underlying issue and may assist in assessment and duration of any treatment [7].

3.4 Neglect Cases Examined

3.4.1 Evaluation of the Scene or Environment

Involvement in neglect cases from an investigatory and testimonial standpoint is greatly enhanced when the pathologist or forensic veterinarian can be present at the scene during the investigation and subsequent seizure of animals and animal remains. If this is not possible, review of crime scene photographs, video, or any medical records generated as a result of the investigation may be crucial to forming or substantiating conclusions generated in a necropsy. A scene evaluation, summarized in Table 3.2, should cover the following areas: ventilation, sanitation, types of confinement and surfaces, access to and quality of food and water, food storage, husbandry, and veterinary care. Figures 3.25, 3.26, 3.27 and 3.28, taken from animal neglect crime scenes, illustrate some common findings.

Ideally the following information should be sought firsthand or gathered from the investigation team prior to conducting a postmortem examination. General observations and environmental findings should be documented in detail and include the number of live and deceased animals found at the scene; the physical signs of dis-

Table 3.2 Crime scene evaluation

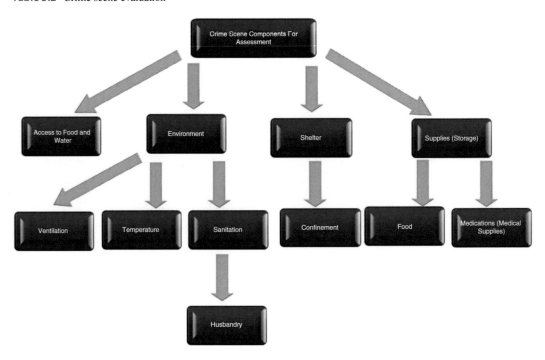

Fig. 3.25 Forced entry into the house of a hoarder by police

ease in animals; the type of environment and description of materials found in it; the type of care, if any, that was being provided; and the types of behaviors animals in the environment were exhibiting. A veterinarian should evaluate any medication found at the scene, noting what was used to treat, how it was stored, and expiration dates. Additional information may be obtained from veterinarians listed on prescription labels. The availability and how food is stored should be documented. There may actually be food present that is not being given to animals.

Fig. 3.26 Entryway into home of the second floor condominium

The overall cleanliness of the environment (Fig. 3.29), including the presence of urine and feces or rotting food, can contribute to parasite infestations, gastrointestinal diseases, and respiratory, skin, and eye irritation. Instruments to measure levels of ammonia and hydrogen sulfide present from urine and fecal contamination can provide important data. Ammonia can be detected by humans at 10 parts per million (ppm) or less. The Occupational Safety and Health Administration (OSHA) advises any level exceeding 50 ppm is an extreme danger to health and life (Fig. 3.30). Ammonia gas is water soluble and will react with the moist membranes of the eyes and respiratory tract. Ocular changes may include epiphora, conjunctivitis, and corneal ulceration. Respiratory effects may include clear or purulent nasal discharge, bronchial constriction, tachypnea, and hyperplasia of the alveolar and bronchiolar epithelial tissues (Figs. 3.31 and 3.32) [10].

3.4.2 Postmortem Examination

Forensic veterinary pathologists are tasked with linking historical and environmental evidence of neglect with physical postmortem findings.

General Considerations for Necropsy in Suspect Cases of Neglect (Table 3.3)

1. Rule out natural disease
   (a) Metabolic or other pathologic causes of fatal wasting
2. Inadequate or inappropriate nutritional support
   (a) Gross or histologic changes that may be associated with the following:
      i. Inadequate food quantity
      ii. Poor food quality
      iii. Unbalanced diet
3. Secondary changes due to nutritional deficiency
   (a) Infections or delayed healing relatable to impaired immune function
4. Dehydration and/or starvation
5. Secondary changes due to extreme environmental conditions

3.4.2.1 Discriminating between Natural Disease and Malnutrition

Necropsy examinations in very emaciated animals may discover natural disease or physiological causes that could account for advanced weight loss. The forensic veterinarian or veterinary

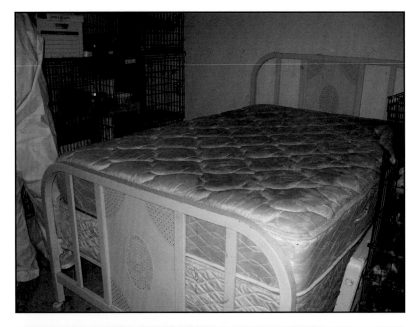

Figs. 3.27 and 3.28 Both sides of a mattress the cat owner slept on soaked in urine and feces. The owner simply turned over for use

pathologist needs to assess the level of involvement these factors played in the decline of the animal's body condition and document whether adequate veterinary treatment was sought for prolonged weight loss [7]. There is a variety of underlying conditions that may lead to an emaciated condition, including chronic infections, heart disease, and cancer. Clinical histories may be crucial in determining if the animal was receiving treatment for an underlying condition vs. if the condition was being neglected.

A gross external examination of the body should include documentation of what would have been apparent to the owner or caregiver, and

Fig. 3.29 Feces overflowing litter boxes and no food or water present in any kennels or cages present at this home

Fig. 3.30 Personal protective equipment (PPE) worn by personnel due to high levels of ammonia

it should include a clear indication of the body condition of the animal. In cases of neglect, poor body condition is generally due to a combination of fat and muscle atrophy, with atrophy of muscle beginning 24 h after the onset of starvation. Atrophy of the back and thigh muscles may be the first to be involved, but the process will eventually extend to all of the muscle groups in the body. It should be noted that depletion of glycogen deposits in muscle tissue of emaciated animals can interfere with the normal process of rigor mortis, potentially influencing estimates of the postmortem interval [7].

To relay body condition in a postmortem report, many pathologists rely on a body condition scoring system such as the Purina Body

Figs. 3.31 and 3.32 Severe ocular (Fig. 3.31), aural (Fig. 3.32), and dental disease (not shown) throughout the group of neglected cats

Condition Scale [8, 9], which has a 9-point classification scheme from emaciation to overweight condition. The use of these systems reduces ambiguity and simplifies arguments in criminal prosecution, but the use of scoring systems is somewhat controversial among pathologists. The controversy comes from fact that standardized systems are based on physical characteristics of living, upright animals. There is no standard system to evaluate the body condition of animals postmortem. The appearance of features such as bony prominences and muscle groups can vary postmortem and in lateral recumbency, and depending on the postmortem interval, changes in color and the condition of the carcass can ren-

der the criteria used in these systems irrelevant. Therefore, it is more reliable to clearly describe the amount of subcutaneous and visceral adipose found, and to give an impression of overall muscle mass, than to indicate a numerical body condition score in a postmortem report. In addition, a standard set of photographic images should be taken to accurately depict external features; typically this was done with four views: left side, right side, dorsum, and ventrum. Photographic documentation should then continue with postmortem dissection.

External examination of the body should be in keeping with traditional necropsy techniques. The following findings are not specific for but are

Table 3.3 Necropsy flowchart for cases of neglect

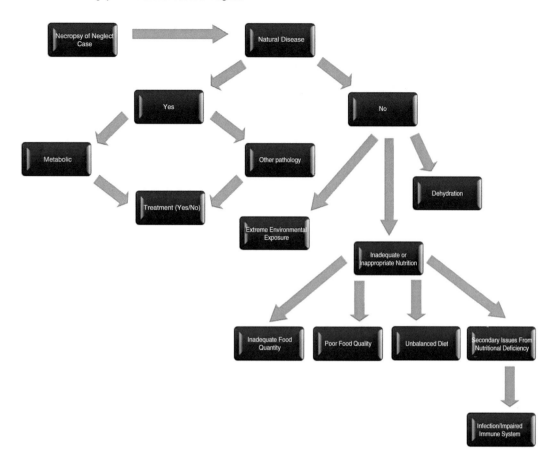

commonly encountered in cases of neglect. Oral examination may reveal significant dental disease, which may be associated with inappropriate diet or malnutrition and may fit with failure to seek veterinary care. The presence of parasites, such as ear mites and ticks, and evidence of mange or dermatophytosis and secondary pyoderma or other skin conditions are also common. Dogs often have overgrown toenails that may be embedded or split. Scars, wounds, or abscesses from fighting due to overcrowding or inadequate or minimal food sources may be present and should be measured, described, and photographed. Hair loss, as previously described, may be associated with poor nutrition but may also be the consequence of stress-related self- or allogrooming. Severe matting of perineal and hind limb hair often incorporates feces and/or urine, which may result in skin scalding and infection

(Figs. 3.33, 3.34 and 3.35). Depending on location, excessive matting can inhibit movement, impair sight, or interfere with urination and defecation [11, 12].

3.4.2.2 Necropsy Findings Associated with Long-Term Inadequate Nutrition and Dehydration

External findings consistent with starvation and dehydration are common in cases of neglect and include sunken eyes within their orbits and resulting protrusion of the third eyelid; dry, tacky oral mucous membranes; extensive muscle wasting and lack of palpable subcutaneous adipose; and tight adherence of the skin to underlying tissues.

On internal examination, fat deposits within the omentum and mesentery are usually the first to be depleted and may be grossly reduced. As fat continues to be utilized from under the skin, near

Fig. 3.33 Severe matting left hind limb and tail effecting ambulation

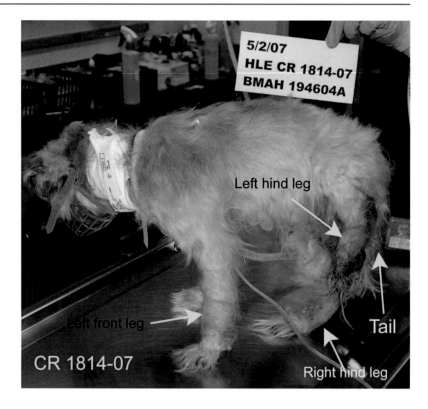

the heart (Fig. 3.36), around the kidneys, and from bone marrow, it will become grossly apparent in these tissues, often creating a gelatinous or "serous" appearance. This gross change is due to replacement fat droplets with proteinaceous fluid, which in severe cases may reduce overall colloidal pressure [7]. Atrophy due to starvation may also be seen in the liver, skin, thyroid glands, and testes.

The presence or absence of gastric and intestinal content should always be noted and the content described. In cases of starvation, hemorrhage in the form of ecchymoses or petechia in gastric mucosa occurs when the stomach is empty for prolonged periods. Gastric and duodenal erosions and ulcers may also be present, and melena may be identified anywhere from the stomach to the colon (Figs. 3.37 and 3.38). Because of the potential for criminal prosecution, it is important to look at gastric erosions and ulcers grossly and microscopically and rule out underlying causes for these lesions. The argument could be made in court that an animal had a medical cause for gastric erosion or ulceration that then caused

inappetence and weight loss. Gross and histopathologic examination of gastric mucosa can help to age the mucosal injury and allow comparison with the expected time for weight loss found in a patient. In cases of starvation, ingesta of poor or nonnutritive quality may also be found. Animals may resort to ingestion of feces, rocks, sand, and other materials in their environment when they run out of food to eat [11].

In starvation some differences may be seen in the gastrointestinal tracts of ruminants versus companion animals. In a healthy ruminant, the rumen can account for about 25% of live weight. In an underweight animal, the rumen weight may exceed 25% of live weight due to the loss of body condition and consumption of poor-quality feed. The presence of food in the rumen is used as evidence that an animal was being fed; however, this may not be true. Many severely malnourished animals have large quantities of fibrous material present in the rumen. This emphasizes the importance of collecting and analyzing rumen contents in evaluating the nutritional value of ruminant feed. Ruminant intestinal content is the result of

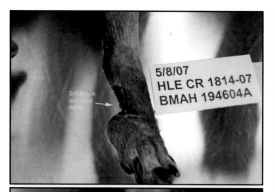

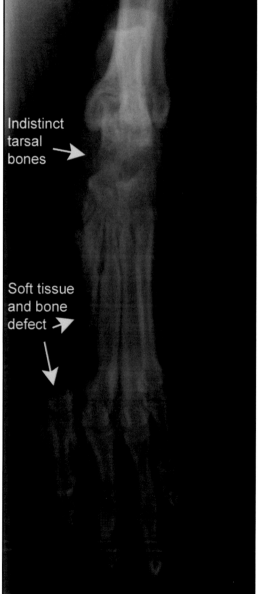

Indistinct
tarsal
bones →

Soft tissue
and bone
defect ↗
↓

Figs. 3.34 and 3.35 Left hind limb from Fig. 3.33, after hair removal, observes soft tissue and bone damage from matting resulting in annular constriction

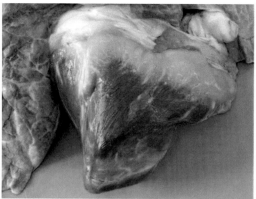

Fig. 3.36 Bovine heart, serous atrophy of fat

the slow and continuous digestion of fibrous material in the rumen and may be variably present in cases of starvation [7].

Companion animals (monogastrics) such as dogs and cats do not store food in their stomachs for very long periods. Food will usually pass to the intestinal tract within hours in dogs and cats, and after several days of starvation, the gastrointestinal tract may be entirely empty. Gastric ulceration may result from diminished blood flow to the lining of the stomach, especially in dogs, and can result in perforation of the gastric wall. Additionally, these animals will ingest indigestible materials due to the extreme hunger they are experiencing. The stomach can become severely distended with this type of material. Large intestinal fecal matter may be dry or sticky in the presence of this foreign material. Dogs and cats that have succumbed to starvation generally have less malodorous gastrointestinal tract contents than those of healthy animals [7].

Organs in the body will atrophy as emaciation progresses. This will be most evident in the liver, spleen, pancreas, thymus, and salivary glands. Histologically, the hepatic cells may show atrophy. The lymph nodes of juvenile animals can be enlarged and edematous. Bone marrow fat is one of the last fat reserves used in the body, and loss of this reserve is typically associated with profound malnutrition and starvation. The gross appearance of the marrow in these states is typically red and watery with grossly and histologically decreased fat content. Bone marrow fat can be quantified using solvent extraction techniques

Fig. 3.37 Gastric ulcers in an emaciated dog

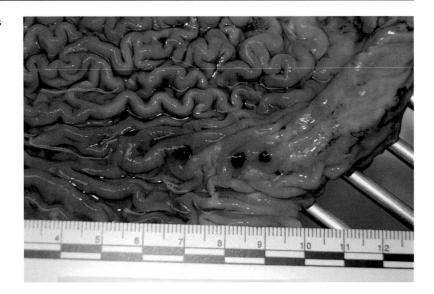

Fig. 3.38 A stomach with melena due to gastric erosions/ulcers filled with debris. The pain from the gastric epithelial injury did not prevent this dog from eating

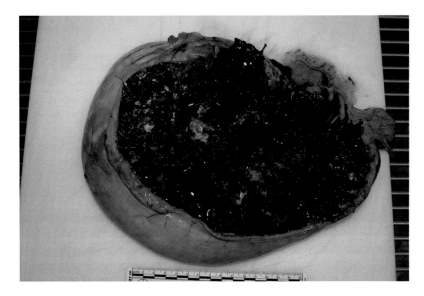

and compared against established normal ranges to support postmortem findings in cases of starvation. Radiographs will assist with bone growth analysis in long bones illustrating any growth arrest lines [7].

3.4.3 Hoarding: A Special Case of Neglect

Hoarding is an excellent example of the potentially complex nature of animal neglect. These cases routinely involve several of the forms of neglect covered in this chapter, scene investigation, live animal and postmortem examinations, and interagency collaboration. In addition, animal hoarders commit animal neglect by actions that are routed in complex and often misunderstood human mental conditions [4].

Hoarding and saving behaviors can be symptoms in a number of complex neuropsychiatric disorders. Compulsive hoarding is listed in the *Diagnostic and Statistical Manual of Mental Disorders (DSM-5)* under obsessive-compulsive disorder (OCD), but in 2013, it was recognized by the American Psychiatric Association as a distinct form of mental illness, and it is generally viewed as a related OCD spectrum disorder by mental health experts [13]. Animal hoarding is the compulsive urge to amass and control animals without regard to negative consequences to the animals or the individual. Stereotypes include the elderly neighborhood "crazy cat lady," but the syndrome is much broader and more complicated than most realize. Mental health conditions and personality disorders among animal hoarders shape the form of neglect that animals experience and create important barriers to meaningful intervention. Further, animal hoarding has almost 100% recidivism, usually because aspects of mental health in the hoarder are not addressed [2]. While over 70% of animal hoarders are women [2], animal hoarding spans most socioeconomic and demographic boundaries and can involve any species of animal [2, 6]. The average age of women who hoard is 52.6 years and is 48.7 years for men [6].

There are three types of animal hoarding classifications. There is the overwhelmed caregiver, who is aware that there is a problem with the animal care he or she is providing. Hoarding in these cases is often tied to a change in the person's health, financial state, or personal life and relationships. There is the rescue hoarder, who denies any problems exist with the animal care that is being provided. His or her obsession to save animals negates an inability to care for them. The exploiter is the most extreme and least common type of animal hoarder. This type of hoarder is unwilling to recognize any problems or the legitimate concerns of others for the animals in their care. He or she has no empathy for animals or people and disregards any harm caused [2, 5].

Animal hoarding is an extremely complex form of neglect but is defined by the presence of three key features: (1) clutter and disorganization, (2) excessive acquisition of animals, and (3) difficulty discarding or relinquishing animals (Figs. 3.39, 3.40, 3.41 and 3.42). Most hoarding situations begin as selfless acts of concern to save animals. Eventually, compulsive caregiving behavior is increased in an attempt to gratify unfulfilled human needs, while the requirements of the animals are disregarded or ignored [2]. Hoarding may take place in an individual's home or other facility (Figs. 3.43, 3.44, 3.45 and 3.46), either of which may be illegitimately identified as a rescue or animal sanctuary. Some may have legal nonprofit status with a 501.c.3. In comparison to legitimate animal welfare organizations, animal hoarders will not take appropriate action when faced with declining conditions. In these instances, they may not choose to stop taking in animals, increase staffing, or increase overall resources to resolve animal problems related to health, housing, sanitation, and nutrition.

Due to the high incidence of recidivism among animal hoarders, these individuals are usually

Figs. 3.39 and 3.40 Ice chest found in closet under debris (Fig. 3.39), full of individually wrapped cat remains (Fig. 3.40); empty dry ice packaging was also present

Fig. 3.41 Deceased cat, from ice chest severely decomposed in wrapping material

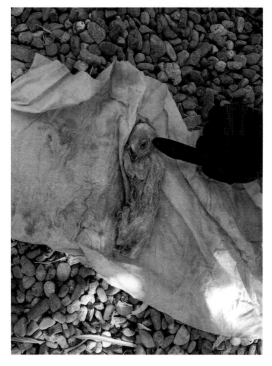

Fig. 3.42 Severely decomposed kitten removed from wrapping material

hoarders. If intervention or prosecution has been sought, law enforcement will have information about this person as well. These agencies can provide prior veterinary medical records or necropsy reports and crime scene photographs. These can help with establishing timelines for injuries or diseases and chronicity of the overall problem.

According to a 2006 presentation by R.L. Lockwood on Hoarding: Psychology and Punishment, typical animal hoarding behaviors include:

- Reluctance to admit visitors to home.
- Will not divulge how many animals are present in the dwelling.
- Continued acquisition of new animals even with declining health of resident animals.
- Desire to provide care for animals who are paralyzed or have contagious diseases.
- The number of staff/volunteers assisting the caregiver, if any, is not sufficient for the number of animals present.

known to the animal welfare community in a given area. In many instances, the local animal control or humane society humane investigator has a long-standing case log with individual

Hoarding warning signs that veterinarians may experience include a client who brings in multiple animals that may have only been seen once. The animals are not seen for preventative

Fig. 3.43 Former print shop. Entire floor filled with milk jugs and empty cat food bags and cans. The large quantity of urine and feces produced by approximately 100 cats caused the floor to rot. Cats were literally falling through the floor to the office space below

Fig. 3.44 One of over 100 cats living in dilapidated print shop

care but are presented with extreme illness or injury. The animal hoarder will often have multiple veterinarians within the community. There may be a foul odor from the animal, animal's car-

rier, or the owner-caregiver [6]. In cases of hoarding where scene investigation is required, law enforcement will typically work in conjunction with humane officers to establish cause, serve

Fig. 3.45 Barrels of dead cats in the print shop

warrants, and investigate properties. A fire department hazmat team may be called to assess an environment for human safety prior to the investigation. It is ideal that a forensic veterinarian or pathologist also be present at the scene when the search warrant is served. In lieu of this, all photos, videos, or scene sketches and notes should be scrupulously reviewed by the forensic veterinarian or veterinary pathologist. Many hoarding cases will have multiple agencies assisting with a scene investigation.

Postmortem examinations often reveal gross and histologic evidence of infectious diseases that are commonly covered in standard vaccination protocols. Viruses that are hardy in the environment and readily transmitted through contact, fecal-oral routes and/or carried on fomites do particularly well in hoarding environments. In the case of feline hoarding, pathologists should look for lesions consistent with feline panleukopenia virus, FIP, FIV, and FeLV and upper respiratory pathogens such as herpesvirus. Pyogenic infections, such as those caused by beta-hemolytic streptococcus and *Staphylococcus* sp., are also associated with close, unsanitary living conditions [14].

Fig. 3.46 Close-up of barrel filled with discarded deceased cats

References

1. Animal Legal Defense Fund. Animal neglect facts. http://aldf.org/resources/laws-cases/animal-neglect-facts/ Obtained: August 2, 2016.
2. Patronek GJ, Loar L, Nathenson JN. Animal hoarding: structuring interdisciplinary responses to help people and communities at risk. Hoarding of Animals Research Consortium; 2006.
3. Association of Shelter Veterinarians. Guidelines for standards of care in animal shelters; 2010.
4. Frost, R.O., Patroneck, G., Arluke, A., Steketee, G. The hoarding of animals: an update psychiatric times; 2015. http://www.psychiatrictimes.com/addiction/hoarding-animals-update. Obtained:August 2, 2016.
5. Frost RO, Patronek G, Rosenfield E. A comparison of object and animal hoarding. Depress Anxiety. 2011;28(10):885–91.
6. Merck MD. Veterinary forensics: animal cruelty investigations. 2nd ed. Ames, IA: Wiley; 2013.
7. Munro R, Munro HMC. Animal abuse and unlawful killing: forensic veterinary pathology. Edinburgh: Elsevier Limited; 2008.
8. Laflamme DP. Development and validation of a body condition score system for dogs: a clinical tool. Canine Pract. 1997a;22:10–5.
9. Laflamme DP. Development and validation of a body condition score system for cats: a clinical tool. Feline Pract. 1997b;25:13–8.
10. Merck MD. Veterinary forensics: animal cruelty investigations. Ames, IA: Blackwell Publishing; 2007.
11. Gerdin JA, McDonough SP, Reisman R, Scarlett J. Circumstances, descriptive characteristics, and pathologic findings in dogs suspected of starving. Vet Pathol. 2016;53(5):1087–94.
12. Gerdin JA, McDonough SP. Forensic pathology of companion animal abuse and neglect. Vet Pathol. 2013;50(6):994–1006.
13. Saxena S. Editorial. Am J Psychiatr. 2007;164:3.
14. Morrow BL, McNatt R, Joyce L, McBride S, Morgan D, Tressler C, Mellits C. Highly pathogenic beta-hemolytic streptococcal infections in cats from an institutionalized hoarding facility and a multi-species comparison. J Feline Med Surg. 2016;18(4):318–27.

Environmental Injuries

4

Doris M. Miller

4.1 Normal Physiology of Thermoregulation under Normal Conditions in Animals

In animals the thermoregulatory center is the anterior hypothalamus which regulates the core body temperature depending on the environmental temperature. [1]. The body core consists of the essential organs such as the brain, heart, lungs, liver, and kidneys. Behavioral changes have been observed with variations in hypothalamic temperature in dogs [2]. Hypothalamic heating caused the dogs to sprawl, while during hypothalamic cooling they would curl up [2]. In a cold environment, blood flow is directed away from the skin and peripheries into the core. In a warm environment, blood flow is increased to the skin.

4.2 Hypothermia

4.2.1 Definition

Hypothermia is a lowering of the animal's core body temperature below what is physiologically acceptable for that species [1, 3, 4]. Hypothermia is a general body cooling while frostbite is a focal or localized area of hypothermia.

4.2.2 Risk Factors

Critically ill, cachectic, debilitated, and injured animals have impaired thermoregulatory responses and also may not be able to retain or seek heat [5, 6].

Hypothermia is also reported in certain poisonings such as alcohol and acetaminophen poisoning [7]. Postanesthetic hypothermia (<36.4 °C) occurs in up to 32% of canine surgical patients due to redistribution of heat from the core to peripheral tissues [1, 8].

Neonates have underdeveloped thermoregulatory mechanisms [9–11]. Neonates have limited response to epinephrine and norepinephrine and thus are unable to adequately vasoconstrict at the periphery or have protective vasodilation. While they can sense cold temperatures and move toward heat, they cannot piloerect their fur. Their increased body surface area predisposes them to increased heat loss. Hypothermic neonates (<94 °F or 34.4 °C) will have poor to weak suckling response, hypomotile intestines, and tachycardia [9, 11].

4.2.3 Pathophysiology

While there is a variation in physiological responses at specific temperatures among species and animals, in general for dogs and cats, a rectal temperature of

D.M. Miller, D.V.M., Ph.D., D.A.C.V.P.
Anatomic Pathology—ADVL, University of Georgia,
College of Veterinary Medicine, Athens, Georgia
e-mail: miller@uga.edu

© Springer International Publishing AG 2018
J.W. Brooks (ed.), *Veterinary Forensic Pathology, Volume 2*,
https://doi.org/10.1007/978-3-319-67175-8_4

less than 28–31.1 °C (82–88 °F) results in the inability to regain normal body temperature [3, 6]. Hypothermia in adult animals results in an endocrine response (catecholamines release) to increase metabolism to improve thermogenesis, shivering, and behavioral responses to escape cold [6, 11–13]. Shivering is caused by the resultant hypothalamic stimulation of reflexes in the spinal cord that cause muscle contractions which lead to an increase in body temperature [3, 11, 12, 14]. There is piloerection resulting in the trapping of warm air near the body, while vasoconstriction maintains warm blood in the vital internal organs.

Hypothermia causes increased circulating catecholamines with an increased respiratory rate, decreased total body oxygen consumption, heart rate, cardiac output, and electrolyte abnormalities initially [5, 6, 13]. Depending on the severity of the hypothermia, there is hypoglycemia and potassium alteration, the latter due to intracellular shifting rather than a true loss [6]. Continued or prolonged hypothermia leads to failure of the thermoregulation system and progressive multiorgan failure [6, 11, 15, 16]. Renal failure and acute tubular necrosis secondary to depressed renal blood flow, reduced glomerular filtration rate, decreased blood pressure, and diuresis occur [5, 17]. There is eventual respiratory depression, lactic acidosis, and pulmonary atelectasis associated with or due to the compromised pulmonary gas exchange and decreased tissue perfusion. This leads to hypoxia, pulmonary edema, and acute respiratory distress syndrome or pneumonia. In dogs, hypothermia has been reported to cause a delay in clot formation, prolonged QT interval, and bradycardia. In the brain this can cause symptoms ranging from depression to coma [6]. As the core body temperature continues to drop, the gastrointestinal blood flow decreases. Vasoconstriction in hypothermia results in a decreased blood flow to tissues leading to tissue hypoxia and to diminished resistance to infection associated with impaired oxidative killing by neutrophils, decreased phagocytosis, impaired chemotaxis, and depression of cytokines and antibodies.

Frostbite is caused by the effect of freezing on a part of the body of a live animal [3–5, 18]. The extremities are the most susceptible, and gross appearance of the tissue can vary from pale and cold to dark bluish. Necrosis followed by sloughing may develop and take as long as 4–15 days [4]. The degree or severity of frostbite is best evaluated after initial treatment in the live animal, but the outcome may not always be predicted accurately due to the delayed vascular lesions [19, 20]. Hypothermia causes a shunting (vasoconstriction) of oxygen and blood away from the peripheral tissues (ear tips, toes, feet, mammary gland, tail) which can result in cell death, microvascular thrombosis, intracellular and extracellular ice crystal formation, membrane damage, and cell lysis in the live animal (Fig. 4.1) [3–5, 18]. This injury is due to the direct damage to the keratinocytes and endothelial cells from the hypothermia causing the formation of ice crystals (intracellular and extracellular) and inadequate blood supply to the area. Experimental studies have shown that the earliest changes are hyperemia of superficial and deep dermal vessels, vacuolization of keratinocytes, individualization of cells, and pyknosis seen within hours of injury. Leukocyte emigration, microabscesses, and vasculitis were present within 24 h. However, medial vascular degeneration and thrombosis often were not evident until 1–2 weeks following frostbite injury [19, 20].

4.2.4 Macroscopic Lesions

Macroscopic lesions associated with hypothermia are nonspecific and often depend on the duration of the hypothermia prior to death. As the core body temperature continues to drop, the gastrointestinal blood flow decreases. This can lead to erosions of the stomach and intestines. Hemorrhagic pancreatitis has been reported due to decreased perfusion. Continued hypothermia causes decreased cardiac output, decreased myocardial oxygen metabolism, and hypovolemia with resulting atrial and ventricular fibrillation [4–6].

Hypothermia-induced coagulation abnormalities (reversible platelet sequestration, decreased platelet aggregation, and prolonged bleeding times)

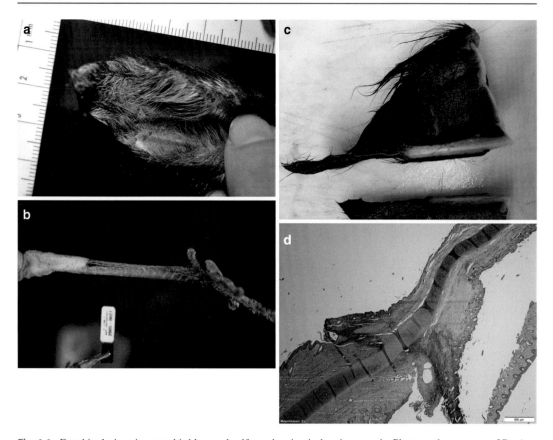

Fig. 4.1 Frostbite lesions in a cat, bird leg, and calf ear showing ischemic necrosis. Photographs courtesy of Dr. Ann Cavender (**a**), Dr. Tabitha Viner (**b**) and Dr. Doris Miller (**c** and **d**)

are often missed in the clinical setting due to coagulation tests conducted at normal (98.6 °F) temperatures [6]. These disorders rapidly reverse once normothermia is reestablished especially if the duration of hypothermia is less than 6 h [15, 16].

4.2.5 Microscopic Lesions

When hypothermia was induced in dogs, there were histopathological changes in the liver, kidneys, and adrenal glands [21]. These changes were reported to be depletion of hepatic glycogen and increased lipid in the liver, adrenals, and renal tubules, degenerative changes in the central lobules of the liver, and miliary necrosis in the myocardium [15, 16, 21]. These are nonspecific and could not be related directly to the cause of death during hypothermia by the researchers [16, 21]. Fisher et al. did not find any significant changes in the heart, lungs, adrenals, kidneys, and pancreas of 40 dogs in experimental hypothermia of 2–24 h duration. [22] There was, however, focal pancreatitis in approximately 10% of the dogs [22].

4.3 Hyperthermia

4.3.1 Definition and Types

Hyperthermia which is an elevation of the core body temperature above normal can occur in response to fever, environmental conditions (elevated temperature and/or humidity), exercise, pathologic conditions (tumors, eclampsia, seizures, malignant hyperthermia), and drugs such as caffeine (result of excessive muscular activity), amphetamines, and cocaine [1, 4, 7]. Heatstroke is a form of hyperthermia associated with a systemic inflammatory response that can lead to multiorgan dysfunction. Heatstroke has been said to be the oldest known disease [23]. Hyperthermia due to heatstroke is considered a medical emergency (temperature > 106 °F or 41 °C) that occurs when the body cannot maintain its normal temperature through its regular thermoregulatory system [3, 24]. Cases of heatstroke have been reported in animals being left in parked cars, tied in the sun with no shade available, and not acclimated prior to exercise (exertional heatstroke) [1, 4, 24–27].

4.3.2 Risk Factors

Risk factors identified for the development of heatstroke are obesity (fat provides insulation and is a poor thermal conductor), breed (brachiocephalic, golden retrievers, Labrador retrievers), body weight, high environmental temperature and humidity, lack of acclimation, lack of access to potable water, confinement in a poorly ventilated space, hair coat thickness and color, cardiovascular or neurologic disease, advanced age, dehydration, some medications, and previous heatstroke or heat injury [24, 25, 28–31].

Fat is an effective insulator that can slow the transfer of body heat which is protective in hypothermia but can be problematic with hyperthermia [6]. In dehydrated cats, it has been shown that there is a reduction in the evaporative response (respiratory rate) to elevations in core body temperature suggesting that dehydration results in an increase in threshold hypothalamic temperature for evaporation with a change in the thermoregulatory system [32]. Dehydrated camels, donkeys, steers, sheep, goats, dogs, and antelope have elevated body temperatures with decreased rates of water loss through sweating or panting when compared with their hydrated counterparts [28, 32, 33].

4.3.3 Pathophysiology

The physiologic response to heat stress has two components—the acute-phase response and the heat shock response [24, 25, 34]. The acute-phase response involves the endothelial cells, leukocytes, epithelial cells, and cytokine release in an attempt to protect tissues [34].

The heat shock response is a rapid molecular cytoprotective mechanism that involves production of heat shock proteins which have also been detected in tissue injury, inflammation, and bacterial infections [34].

During hyperthermia, blood shifts from the mesenteric circulation to the muscles and skin to facilitate heat dissipation and tissue oxygen demands [24, 35, 36]. Within the intestines, there is resulting hypoxia, intestinal ischemia, and hyperpermeability, often resulting in bloody diarrhea [24, 35]. The resulting inflammatory cytokine release, reactive oxygen, and nitrogen generation by the injured tissue cause increased intestinal permeability with release of endotoxins into the bloodstream [24]. This is a mechanism similar to that described with sepsis, and the gross and microscopic lesions are similar [24, 35].

The most commonly observed serum biochemistry abnormalities in hyperthermia are increased creatinine kinase, alanine aminotransferase, aspartate aminotransferase, alkaline phosphatase, and neutrophilia with a left shift, hypoglycemia with thrombocytopenia, and nucleated red blood cells [24–26, 37]. Hyperthermia causes endothelial injury which activates the coagulation and complement cascades causing DIC and a systemic inflammatory response syndrome [24, 29, 34]. The hepatic injury due to hypoperfusion and microembolism can potentiate the hemostatic abnormalities [26, 29, 38]. There is an increased prothrombin time and activated partial thromboplastin time [38]. As a consequence of direct renal thermal tissue damage and severe hemoconcentration, azotemia and tubular necrosis are a frequent finding at necropsy. The pulmonary lesions of edema, alveolar hemorrhages, and infarcts are due to the injury to the pulmonary endothelium [24]. Most tissues of the body except the brain, spinal cord, and nerves can withstand temperatures up to 112 °F (44 °C) for up to 1 h before irreversible damage occurs [3]. It has been suggested, however, that the cause of death in canine heatstroke is due to the hemodynamic deterioration, DIC, and pulmonary changes rather than the CNS lesions [24, 35, 39]. This is due to the altered cardiovascular function combined with coagulation abnormalities and increased metabolic demand leading to multiorgan failure which quickly leads to death [25, 31].

4.3.4 Clinical Signs and Relationship to Mortality

The most common clinical signs associated with heatstroke are tachypnea, collapse, bleeding (petechial, hematochezia), shock, diarrhea, seizures, and either hyper-, normo-, or hypothermia on presentation [24–26, 29]. The body temperature can vary depending on the treatment and length of time since treatment was initiated. Cooling of the body continues after termination of treatment and should be stopped before the body reaches a normal range. This is due to the return of peripheral blood to the body core and the movement of the warmer core to the periphery [6, 24, 40].

Negative indicators for survival after hyperthermia can include seizures, coma, coagulopathy (prothrombin time > 18 s, partial thromboplastin time > 30s), hypothermia, and more than 18 nucleated red blood cells per 100 white cells [25, 26, 29]. Excessive panting often leads to respiratory alkalosis. Development of acute renal failure and metabolic acidosis develop [25].

4.3.5 Macroscopic Lesions

Descriptions of postmortem lesions in natural and experimentally induced cases of hyperthermia have been reported [26, 29, 35, 37, 38]. Natural cases of heatstroke had multiorgan lesions compatible with hyperthermia-induced disseminated intravascular coagulation and a systemic inflammatory response syndrome [26, 29, 34, 35, 37, 38]. All organs have a vascular congestion, an increased onset of rigor mortis, and an increased rate of postmortem changes due to the increased body temperature in hyperthermia (Fig. 4.2) [41].

4.3.6 Microscopic Lesions

Microscopic lesions in natural cases included pulmonary edema, infarction, or hyperemia; mild to severe multifocal to coalescing subendocardial, myocardial, and epicardial hemorrhages; severe, diffuse visceral, and parietal peritoneal hemorrhages; hemorrhages in the serosal, muscular, and submucosal layers of the gastrointestinal tract; splenomegaly due to congestion; renal congestion, mild to severe renal tubular degeneration and necrosis; and mild to severe brain edema and hyperemia [34, 36, 42–44]. There also was mild to moderate fibrinoid thrombosis of the microvasculature adjacent to the hemorrhagic areas in all affected tissues [35, 38]. Some of the dogs had mild to severe necrosis of the mucosa of the intestines [35, 40]. In another study in which only six dogs were necropsied, the lesions were acute renal tubular necrosis, renal infarcts, diffuse serosal hemorrhages, skeletal muscle hemorrhages, gastrointestinal hemorrhage, icterus, pancreatitis (one animal), and cerebral hemorrhages [29]. Metarubricytosis has been frequently reported in cases of heatstroke [24, 35, 45]. The mechanism of this release of nRBC (nucleated red blood cells) has not been established positively. There may be a thermal injury to the bone marrow, or it may be mediated by the cytokines produced during the systemic inflammatory response [29, 35, 45].

4.4 Challenges of Confirming Hypothermia and Hyperthermia in Animals

As other conditions can give similar lesions as those found in hypothermia and hyperthermia (such as sepsis), the final diagnosis may be a challenge in animals found dead with very little history. There is no single diagnostic test or pathognomonic lesion that can confirm injury due to hyperthermia or hypothermia. The pathologist should be provided with detailed history and information about the circumstances and environment in which the animal was found.

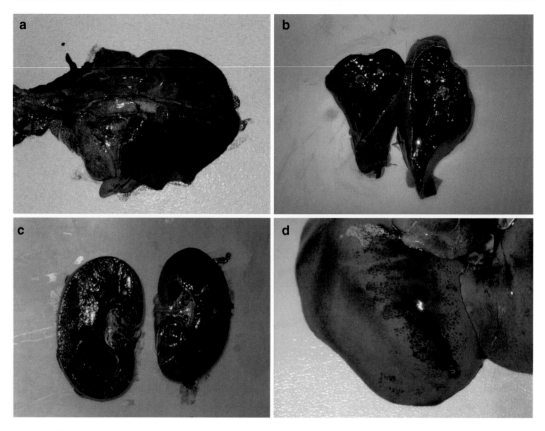

Fig. 4.2 Necropsy lesions of canine dying from hyperthermia. Note lung hemorrhages, congested kidneys and hepatic hemorrhages. Photographs courtesy of Dr. Corrie Brown (**a–c**) and Dr. Daniel Rissi (**d**)

Photographs of the scene may be beneficial. Conditions under which the body was stored or maintained prior to the presentation for the necropsy is essential. Ice crystals and their effects on cellular morphology occur in carcasses frozen after death. Frostbite can present with local tissue changes similar to those observed in primary vasculitis, chemical burns, and systemic illness. However, examination of other organs and sections of the skin in addition to the history and location of the lesion on the animal's body (ears, tail, scrotum) can help to determine the etiology as frostbite. In summary, necropsy findings are often nonspecific, and correct sampling at the scene, thorough postmortem examination, and interdisciplinary cooperation of all professionals involved are essential for a definitive diagnosis in cases involving suspected hypothermia and hyperthermia.

References

1. Miller JB. Hyperthermia and hypothermia. In: Ettinger SJ, Feldman EC, editors. Textbook of veterinary internal medicine: diseases of the dog and cat. PA: Elsevier; 2000. p. 6–10.
2. Hellstrom B, Hammel HT. Some characteristics of temperature regulation in the unanesthetized dog. Am J Phys. 1967;213(2):547–56.
3. Ghayourmanesh S, Bull AW. Hyperthermia and hypothermia. Magill's Medical Guide (Online Edition). 2015;1:1–9.
4. Merck MD, Miller DM, Reisman RW. In: Merck MD, editor. Veterinary forensics animal cruelty investigations. 2nd ed. IA: Wiley; 2013. p. 207–32.
5. Mathews KA. Accidental hypothermia & frostbite. Proc N Am Vet Conf. 2004;18:179–82.
6. Oncken AK, Kirby R, Rudloff E. Hypothermia in critically ill dogs and cats. Comp Cont Edu Pract Vet. 2001;23(6):506–20.
7. Sinclair L, Merck M, Lockwood R. Poisoning. In: Sinclair L, Merck M, Lockwood R, editors. Forensic

investigation of animal cruelty. USA: Humane Society Press. p. 139–53.

8. Rigotti CF, Jolliffe CT, Leece EA. Effect of prewarming on the body temperature of small dogs undergoing inhalation anesthesia. J Am Vet Med Assoc. 2015;247(7):765–70.

9. Khan FA, Dutt R, Deori S, Das GK. Fading puppy complex—an overview. Intas Polivet. 2009;10(11):335–7.

10. Palmiere C, Teresinski G, Hejna P. Postmortem diagnosis of hypothermia. Int J Legal Med. 2014;128(4):607–14. https://doi.org/10.1007/s00414-014-0977-1.

11. Thomovsky E. Hypothermia in neonates: prevention and treatment. Proc N Am Vet Conf. 2015;29:1095.

12. Hammel HT, Wyndham CH, Hardy JD. Heat production and heat loss in the dog at 8–36 °C environmental temperature. Am J Phys. 1958;194(1):99–108.

13. Meyer DM, Horton JW. Effect of moderate hypothermia in the treatment of canine hemorrhagic shock. Ann Surg. 1988;207(4):462–9.

14. Auld CD, Light IM, Norman JN. Accidental hypothermia and rewarming in dogs. Clin Sci. 1979;56:601–6.

15. Caranna LJ, Neustein HB, Swan H. Pathologic changes in experimental hypothermia. Arch Surg. 1961;82(1):147–52.

16. Fisher B, Fedor EJ, Lee SH. Rewarming following hypothermia of two to twelve hours. Ann Surg. 1958;148(1):32–43.

17. Moyer JH, Morris G, DeBakey ME. Hypothermia: I. Effect on renal hemodynamics and on excretion of water and electrolytes in dog and man. Ann Surg. 1957;145(1):26–40.

18. Fell EH, Hanselman R. Prevention of shock and death by immediate application of a pressure dressing to the severely frozen limbs of dogs. Ann Surg. 1943;117(5):686–91.

19. Schoning P, Hamlet MP. Experimental frost-bite in Hanford miniature swine. I Epithelial changes. Br J Exp Path. 1989;70:41–9.

20. Schoning P, Hamlet MP. Experimental frost-bite in Hanford miniature swine. II Vascular changes. Br J Exp Path. 1989;70:51–7.

21. Knocker P. Effects of experimental hypothermia on vital organs. Lancet. 1955;269:836–40.

22. Fisher ER, Fedor EJ, Fisher B. Pathologic and histochemical observations in experimental hypothermia. Arch Surg. 1957;75(6):817–27.

23. Hartman FW, Major RC. Pathological changes resulting from accurately controlled artificial fever. Am J Clin Pathol. 1935;5(5):392–410.

24. Bruchim Y. Canine heatstroke. Israel J Vet Med. 2012;67(2):92–5.

25. Andress M, Goodnight M. Heatstroke in a military working dog. US Army Med Dep J. 2013:34–7.

26. Drobatz KJ, Macintire DK. Heat-induced illness in dogs: 42 cases (1976–1993). JAVMA. 1996;209(11):1894–9.

27. McLaren C, Null J, Quinn J. Heat stress from enclosed vehicles: moderate ambient temperatures cause significant temperature rise in enclosed vehicles. Pediatrics. 2005;116(1):109–12.

28. Baker MA. Thermoregulatory responses to exercise in dehydrated dogs. J Appl Physiol. 1984;56(3):635–40.

29. Bruchim Y, Klement E, Saragusty J, Finkeilstein E, Kass P, Aroch I. Heat stroke in dogs: a retrospective study of 54 cases (1999–2004) and analysis of risk factors for death. J Vet Intern Med. 2006;20:38–46.

30. Gerdin JA, McDonough SP, Reisman R, Scarlett J. Circumstances, descriptive characteristics, and pathologic findings in dogs suspected of starving. Vet Pathol. 2015:1–8.

31. Johnson SI, McMichael M, White G. Heatstroke in small animal medicine: a clinical practice review. J Vet Emerg Crit Care. 2006;16(2):112–9.

32. Doris PA, Baker MA. Effect of dehydration on thermoregulation in cats exposed to high ambient temperatures. J Appl Physiol. 1981;51(1):46–54.

33. Baker MA, Nijland MJM. Selective brain cooling in goats:effects of exercise and dehydration. J Phys. 1993;471:679–92.

34. Romanucci M, Salda LD. Pathophysiology and pathological findings of heatstroke in dogs. Vet Med Res Rep. 2013;4:1–9.

35. Bruchim Y, Loeb E, Saragusty J, Aroch I. Pathological findings in dogs with fatal heatstroke. J Comp Pathol. 2009;140:97–104.

36. Segev G, Aroch I, Savoray M, Kass PH, Bruchim Y. A novel severity scoring system for dogs with heatstroke. J Vet Emerg Crit Care. 2015;25(2):240–7.

37. Krum SH, Osborne CA. Heatstroke in a dog: a polysystemic disorder. JAVMA. 1977;170(5):531–2.

38. Bhavani MS, Kavitha S, Bhat AA, Nambi AP. Coagulation parameters in dogs with heat stroke—a short study. J Anim Res. 2015;5(2):381–3.

39. Oglesbee MJ, Alldinger S, Vasconcelos D, Diehl KA, Shinko PD, Baumgartner W, Tallman R, Podell M. Intrinsic thermal resistance of the canine brain. Neuroscience. 2002;113(1):55–64.

40. Bosak JK. Heat stroke in a great Pyrenees dog. Can Vet J. 2004;45:513–5.

41. Munroe R, Munro HMC.: Animal abuse and unlawful killing Forensic veterinary pathology. PA: Saunders Elsevier; 2008. p. 70.

42. Bjotvedt G, Hendricks GM, Sundquist KL. Exertional heat stroke in two racing greyhounds. Calif Vet. 1983;11:9–13.

43. Larson RL, Carithers RW. A review of heat stroke and its complications in the canine. Iowa State Univ Vet. 1983;45(1):4–10.

44. Segev G, Daminet S, Meyer E, De Loor J, Cohen A, Aroch I, Bruchim Y. Characterization of kidney damage using several renal biomarkers in dogs with naturally occurring heatstroke. Vet J. 2015;206:231–5.

45. Aroch I, Segev G, Loeb E, Bruchim Y. Peripheral nucleated red blood cells as a prognostic indicator in heatstroke in dogs. J Vet Intern Med. 2009;23:544–51.

Poisoning

5

Lisa A. Murphy and Rebecca Kagan

5.1 When to Suspect a Poisoning

Poisonings make up a small percentage of veterinary cases. Based on the limited available data for reported animal poisonings, the majority (>99%) appear to be accidental rather than intentional [1]. Dogs account for approximately 75% of reported malicious poisonings and about 15% involve cats [2]. The remaining 10% include equine, food animal, exotic, and wildlife cases.

Sudden or unexpected death of one or more previously healthy animals may warrant a suspicion of poisoning, especially if no other obvious causes of death such as trauma or disease can be found. Susceptibility to most toxic substances is not limited to a single animal type, so finding more than one affected species could also indicate a poisoning. Furthermore, finding one or more ill or dead animals in proximity to a carcass, common food or water source, or other suspect bait materials may indicate a potential source of intoxication. While some toxicants can be inhaled or absorbed through skin or mucous membranes, ingestion will be the most common route of exposure.

5.2 Importance of History Taking

Determination that an animal has died or developed illness due to poisoning requires pulling together what can variably be either sparse or vast quantities of information, including but not limited to case histories, observed signs and symptoms, medical records, clinical test results, postmortem findings, and toxicologic analyses. Key elements of a possible poisoning case may be missing, incomplete, or difficult to verify, and samples suitable for testing may be inadequately preserved or otherwise not suitable or available for analysis. Clinical signs in poisoning cases are often nonspecific and may not have been observed at all if the animal is simply found dead. Even when a thorough necropsy can be performed, poisoning cases may also lack specific gross or histologic lesions. For these reasons, taking a thorough history will be critical to identifying a potential poisoning case and ideally discovering the likely source of the toxicant. Elements of a good history in a suspected poisoning case should include questions about the exposure, the environment, and the animal [1].

L.A. Murphy, V.M.D., D.A.B.T. (✉)
University of Pennsylvania School of Veterinary
Medicine, Philadelphia, PA, USA
e-mail: murphylp@vet.upenn.edu

R. Kagan, D.V.M., D.A.C.V.P.
U.S. Fish & Wildlife Service National Forensics
Laboratory, Ashland, OR, USA
e-mail: rebecca_kagan@fws.gov

© Springer International Publishing AG 2018
J.W. Brooks (ed.), *Veterinary Forensic Pathology, Volume 2*,
https://doi.org/10.1007/978-3-319-67175-8_5

5.2.1 Exposure History

Establishing a good exposure history can be critical in determining which poisons to test for. Questions to ask include whether the owner, caretaker, or other observer witnessed the animal ingesting or otherwise coming into contact with something unusual. If so, what can they tell you about the object or substance's size, shape, state (solid or liquid), color, and location? How soon afterward were problems first noted? If people or other animals were observed in the same vicinity, did any of them seem to be affected as well?

5.2.2 Environmental History

The goal of the environmental history is to identify the potential source(s) of a toxicant [3]. This should ideally be done by visiting the site to gather as much firsthand information as possible and to facilitate the collection of a wide variety of fresh sample types for analysis. In many cases the environmental history may instead rely on interviews and information provided by others who were at the scene instead, such as owners, caretakers, investigators, or even members of the general public who were present. Photographs and diagrams in addition to written and oral eyewitness accounts may be helpful for more fully reconstructing the scene where the suspected poisoning may have occurred.

The extent and nature of an animal's environment may vary widely, with numerous opportunities for a toxic exposure. Pet animals can be confined to a residence or a fenced yard or roam a larger immediate area within an urban, suburban, or rural neighborhood. Dogs may regularly walk the same route with their owners or routinely visit the same park. Horses and livestock are generally kept in a fenced yard or pasture; however, the size of this area may vary greatly and include or abut many potential sources of toxicants, such as wooded areas, streams or bodies of water, housing developments, and public roadways. Free-roaming wildlife may frequent a variety of these environment types over the course of a single day or season. Previously reported sightings of the affected animal or group may suggest additional locations that should be examined.

Potentially toxic substances may be found in plain sight or more often mixed into a variety of edible items such as canned pet foods, grain, pelleted feeds, raw or cooked meat, and processed human foods such as hot dogs. Other evidence of intentional baiting can include carcasses and completely or partially empty plates, cans, and containers that otherwise seem out of place. The environment should also be examined for the presence of naturally occurring toxicants such as poisonous plants, toxic mushrooms, and water sources contaminated by harmful algal blooms. Housing areas, locations where food is prepared or stored, and water sources should all be inspected in cases involving domestic animals or captive wildlife.

5.2.3 Animal History

The minimum animal history should document its signalment and any pertinent health history as available [1]. Signalment includes species, approximate age, reproductive status if known, and breed if applicable. When multiple animals are involved, additional data should include the total number of animals in each species group or age class, along with how many affected animals died or recovered.

Medical information or husbandry records should be reviewed when available. Special attention should be given to previous vaccinations, prior health problems, current medications, animal movements, and other management details and perhaps most importantly when the animal either first became ill or last seemed normal. For any treatments administered, it should be noted whether or not any response or clinical improvement was observed. When there are indications that blood, serum, urine, gastrointestinal contents, or other patient samples were collected, especially prior to the administration of any treatments, it should be determined if those samples have been retained and appropriately preserved for possible toxicologic analysis.

5.3 Sample Collection and Storage

Toxicology testing can be expensive and very specific, so samples for testing are often collected and held pending necropsy, histology, and ancillary test results. Samples should be collected in individual containers such as specimen cups, jars, or sealable plastic bags and carefully labelled with the case identifier, date, tissue type or source, and other descriptive information, including the name of the person collecting the sample [3]. When in doubt, samples for toxicology testing should be frozen in separate labelled containers. While formalin-fixed tissues for histology may be critical to ruling out other possible causes of death, they are rarely useful for toxicology testing. Recommendations about sample types and quantities to collect for veterinary toxicology testing have been previously published by multiple authors [1, 3–5]. Even though individual analyses in the toxicology laboratory may involve gram or microliter sample quantities, larger amounts increase the number of tests that can be run and ensure that testing can be repeated to confirm the results of screening tests. It may also be necessary to verify results obtained by one analyst or laboratory by having the testing performed by a second individual or facility at the request of a defense attorney. Tables 5.1, 5.2 and 5.3 provide a useful summary of the types of samples that are valuable

Table 5.1 Environmental samples to collect for toxicology testing

Sample type	Amount	Special instructions
Feeds or baits	500 g	Use glass jars or paper or plastic bags
Plants	Entire plant or representative branch plus photographs for trees and large shrubs	Press and dry or freeze
Mushrooms	Whole mushroom	Keep cool and dry in a loosely sealed paper bag
Water	1 L	Clean glass jar
Bedding material	500 g	Keep cool and dry in paper or plastic bags

Table 5.2 Antemortem samples to collect for toxicology testing

Sample type	Amount	Special instructions
Whole blood	5–10 mL	Preserve with EDTA or heparin and refrigerate
Serum	5–10 mL	Spin and remove from clot then freeze Use special tube for zinc
Urine	50–100 mL	Plastic screw-top container
Milk	30 mL	Refrigerate
Ingesta and feces	At least 100 g	Freeze
Injection or application sites and biopsy specimens	Variable	Freeze
Hair	10 g	Tie mane or tail hair to note origin

Table 5.3 Postmortem samples to collect for toxicology testing

Sample type	Amount	Special instructions
Ingesta	At least 100 g	Freeze
Liver	100 g	Freeze
Kidney	100 g	Freeze
Brain	½ of brain	Sagittal section, leaving the midline in formalin for histopathology
Fat	100 g	Freeze
Ocular fluid	1 eye	Freeze whole eye or extracted fluid
Injection site	100 g	Freeze

The findings and opinions contained herein are those of the author and do not necessarily reflect the views of the US Fish and Wildlife Service

to collect when investigating a possible animal poisoning. Sampling can be separated into the categories of environmental (Table 5.1), antemortem (Table 5.2), and postmortem samples (Table 5.3).

5.3.1 Environmental Samples

Environmental samples that should be collected include any available food sources (whether or not they are consistent with the animal's normal diet), water, soil, plants, mushrooms, bedding or nesting material, and other items that animals may have had access to (Table 5.1). Containers or structures should be carefully inspected for the presence of any potentially toxic contents. Food or feed samples should not be pooled into the same container unless they are from the same common source. Dilution or masking of a potential toxicant may result in a failure to readily detect it in a pooled sample, particularly if it is present at low concentrations or sporadically distributed throughout the sampled material.

Plant and mushroom specimens require special handling to avoid excessive deterioration before a definitive species identification can be made. Ideally entire specimens should be provided to an expert botanist or mycologist rather than partial samples or fragments collected from the environment or an animal's gastrointestinal contents. Hay should be carefully inspected for suspicious weeds, seeds, or foreign material. For large trees and shrubs, high-quality photographs can be helpful. Plants should be wrapped in newspaper or pressed and dried. Mushrooms should be placed in a loosely closed paper bag and kept cool. Dry hay can be sealed into plastic bags.

Water samples should be collected from the place where the water initially enters the location in question; any pipes, tanks, or storage containers used to move it around the property; and the sites where animals may actually drink, such as bowls, troughs, or puddles [4]. All of these different water sources could be subject to contamination resulting in animal illness.

5.3.2 Antemortem Samples

A complete set of antemortem animal fluid samples should include whole blood, serum, and urine (Table 5.2). Gastrointestinal contents are extremely valuable, particularly in cases of acute illness or death, and in live patients are typically available in the form of either vomitus or stomach contents obtained with a stomach tube during a gastric lavage decontamination procedure. Milk should be obtained from lactating animals as some compounds can be excreted into milk, pos-

ing a risk for both offspring and humans who may consume it. As with environmental samples, pooling of bodily fluids and stomach contents from multiple animals is not recommended.

5.3.3 Postmortem Samples

During the course of the necropsy, the pathologist performs a gross examination in addition to collecting representative tissue samples to be placed into formalin for histopathology, sampled for microbiology as appropriate, and refrigerated or frozen into separate containers for toxicology testing. A typical checklist of tissues to collect includes liver, kidney, brain, fat, and ocular fluid (Table 5.3). Collection of tissues from areas suggestive of injection or topical application sites should include a wide area of skin and underlying tissues. Other unusual or suspicious sites or lesions on the exterior of the animal or within the body should also be documented and sampled. Photographs and written reports from the gross necropsy may help direct subsequent toxicology testing, based on the presence or absence of visible lesions. If not collected before the animal's death, using a syringe to obtain urine from the urinary bladder and blood from the heart should be attempted.

5.3.4 Sample Storage

Samples for toxicologic analysis should ideally be stored in individually labelled containers. Glass or hard plastic containers (polypropylene or polystyrene) with screw caps are less likely to leach contaminants into samples than soft plastics or metals [6, 7]; however, they are subject to cracking when frozen [1]. Sealable soft plastic bags (e.g., Whirl-Pak® bags) may be most practical unless toxicologic analysis is delayed, or volatile or potentially plastic-degrading chemicals are being collected. Care should be taken to avoid cross-contamination of samples and their containers.

Blood and other fluid samples should not be stored and transported in syringes. In addition to the risk of sample loss or injury from the needle during transport, rubber in the syringe plunger can contaminate the sample with zinc. Zinc contamination can be avoided by using commercially available, rubber-free blood collection tubes and supplies.

Dry samples such as hair, grains, pelleted feeds, and hay can be sealed in a paper envelope or bag [1] and kept at room temperature. For the feed samples, breathable containers that do not retain moisture will avoid mold growth after collection that may make the later detection of mycotoxins difficult to interpret.

5.4 Common Toxicants in Domestic Pets and Wildlife

5.4.1 Anticholinesterase Insecticides

5.4.1.1 Sources
Anticholinesterase insecticides include organophosphates and carbamates, historically some of the most extensively used insecticides in agriculture, homes, and gardens and may be formulated as sprays, powders, or granules [8]. While the sale and use of some compounds in this class have become more restricted over time, at least in the United States, the wide distribution and highly potent nature of these insecticides continue to result in accidental and intentional animal poisonings. Examples of organophosphates and carbamates commonly implicated in animal poisoning cases by veterinary toxicology laboratories include aldicarb, methomyl, carbofuran, and terbufos. These insecticides can be absorbed through skin or inhaled; however, most exposures result from ingestion [9], including cases of secondary poisoning from consuming intoxicated prey species [10–12].

Because these poisons are highly toxic and some may have the potential to persist for at least some period of time, baited carcasses can kill many animals; both those that feed directly on the bait and those that feed on the dead scavengers. Scene findings suggestive of organophosphate or carbamate poisoning include the finding of multiple dead or clinically affected animals in one area, dead insects on the carcasses, the presence of a scavenged carcass, and body position indicating terminal convulsions. Formulations may be visible as dark granules or white or colored powder, but it also may be applied as a liquid.

5.4.1.2 Mode of Action and Affected Body Systems
Organophosphate and carbamate insecticides inhibit acetylcholinesterase (AChE). AChE is found in the brain and other nervous system tissues, red blood cells, and muscle and has a high and specific affinity for the neurotransmitter acetylcholine (ACh) [13]. When ACh is released by the nervous system, it stimulates a voluntary muscle, gland, pupil, blood vessel, or other smooth muscle. The function of AChE is to hydrolyze ACh, terminating its stimulatory effect. Organophosphate and carbamate insecticides inhibit AChE, resulting in prolonged overstimulation of the nervous system and skeletal muscles [8].

5.4.1.3 Expected Clinical Signs and Lesions
The onset of clinical signs associated with carbamates or organophosphates can occur within minutes or hours [13], meaning some animals will be simply found dead, and even symptomatic animals may die before veterinary care can be obtained. The initial signs typically consist of excessive salivation, accompanied by frequent urination and defecation [8], followed by muscle tremors and ataxia that may rapidly progress to seizures. Primary respiratory failure usually results from airway constriction; dysfunction of the diaphragm and intercostal muscles may be contributing factors [14]. Necropsy findings may include evidence of a recently ingested meal. Other, variable findings, may include pulmonary edema, systemic congestion, excessive gastrointestinal and respiratory fluids, and diarrhea.

5.4.1.4 Diagnosis
Cholinesterase activity can be measured in blood, brain, or retinal tissue to demonstrate exposure to an anticholinesterase. If brain is to be analyzed, a hemisection should be sampled, frozen, and tested

as quickly as possible [15]. It should be noted that cholinesterase levels can be falsely raised by decomposition and falsely lowered by prolonged freezing [16, 17]. It is important to utilize a laboratory that has established normal reference ranges for animal species of interest [13]. Compatible clinical signs, including acute death, and less than 25% of normal ChE activity support a diagnosis of organophosphate or carbamate toxicosis [18]. Analysis of vomitus, gastrointestinal contents, liver, and suspected source materials should all be performed to identify a specific insecticide.

Ideally, collection and testing of both stomach contents and brain is done. Detection of the toxin in the stomach contents in conjunction with low cholinesterase levels in the brain confirms cholinesterase-inhibiting poison as the cause of death. For species in which reference ranges are not established (which includes most wildlife), detection of poison in the stomach contents or on the skin is often enough to determine the cause of death.

For cases in which the victims are heavily scavenged, organophosphates and carbamates may still be on the mucosa of the oral cavity, esophagus, or stomach. If exposure was percutaneous, skin may be positive. Birds in particular are sensitive enough to absorb a fatal dose from just perching on a baited carcass. Dermal exposure should be suspected if gastric contents are negative but organophosphates or carbamates are present in other sources (other birds or the environment) and/or cholinesterase levels are low. Skin from the plantar surfaces of the feet should be tested as these are areas most likely to have made contact with a contaminated surface.

Due to the potential for toxicity from cutaneous or inhaled exposure, one should always take proper precautions when working with or transporting these types of cases. Always use PPE and work in a well-ventilated environment.

5.4.2 Rodenticides

5.4.2.1 Sources
Rodenticides designed to kill primarily rats and mice have been produced in a variety of colors and formulations, most typically in blocks or bars [19]. Pellets, powders, grain mixtures, and cracked corn [20] may also be vehicles for rodenticides. Following actions taken by the US Environmental Protection Agency (EPA) in 2008 to protect nontarget species including cats, dogs, and wildlife, consumer rodenticides produced after June 2011 no longer contain the second-generation anticoagulant rodenticides brodifacoum, difethialone, difenacoum, and bromadiolone. First-generation anticoagulants (warfarin, chlorophacinone, and diphacinone) are still permitted along with other nonanticoagulant rodenticides available for over-the-counter purchase such as bromethalin and strychnine [21].

5.4.2.2 Anticoagulant Rodenticides
Anticoagulant rodenticides have a long history of causing illness and death in nontarget cats, dogs, and wildlife [22–25]. These compounds continue to be regularly detected in animal poisoning cases, even after the EPA's 2008 changes to restrict their use by consumers.

Mode of Action and Affected Body Systems
Anticoagulant rodenticides inhibit vitamin K_1 epoxide reductase, depleting active vitamin K_1 and interrupting the liver's production of clotting factors II, VII, IX, and X [26, 27]. Animals are usually clinically normal for the first 24–72 h following exposure, while existing clotting factors still remain. Once clinical signs develop, hemorrhage can occur anywhere in the body.

Expected Clinical Signs and Lesions
The most common clinical signs of anticoagulant rodenticide poisoning are lethargy, coughing, dyspnea, and hemoptysis [27]. Hemorrhage can occur in almost any location including the brain, the gastrointestinal tract, and cavities such as the chest, abdomen, and joints. The most frequent postmortem findings are hemoperitoneum, hemothorax, and pulmonary hemorrhage [22]. In the absence of severe trauma or other obvious causes of hemorrhage, these findings should suggest possible anticoagulant rodenticide poisoning.

Diagnosis

Laboratory tests performed on blood to assess abnormal clotting include PT (prothrombin time), APTT (activated partial thromboplastin time), ACT (activated clotting time), and PIVKA (proteins induced by vitamin K antagonism). Animals may also develop anemia, thrombocytopenia, and hypoproteinemia [28]. Specific anticoagulant rodenticides can be detected in blood, liver, gastrointestinal contents, and potential source materials. Because there may be an extended period of time between ingestion of the toxin and death, analysis of liver rather than ingesta is standard. Toxin concentration does not necessarily correlate to the severity of clinical signs due to high potency and long half-life of these rodenticides.

Postmortem diagnosis requires both detection of the rodenticide and hemorrhage. Anticoagulant rodenticides can be present in wild birds (particularly owls) that have no clinical signs and/or have died due to an unrelated cause. Sublethal levels of anticoagulant rodenticides have not been linked to decreased fitness in raptors [23, 29].

5.4.2.3 Bromethalin

Mode of Action and Affected Body Systems

Bromethalin and its active primary metabolite desmethyl bromethalin uncouple oxidative phosphorylation. Decreased ATP levels and impaired sodium-potassium ion channel pumps cause fluid shifts into the brain and spinal cord [30], eventually leading to progressive, irreversible damage [31].

Expected Clinical Signs and Lesions

Experimental studies conducted in dogs produced two dose-dependent syndromes [32]. Sublethal doses in dogs resulted in the development of hind limb ataxia and paresis over 24–86 h, often progressing to hind limb paralysis. Higher doses caused severe muscle tremors and seizures. Other findings included cerebral edema and increased cerebrospinal fluid (CSF) pressure. Cats are even more sensitive to bromethalin, though their seizures develop later and are less severe than those observed in dogs [33].

Postmortem findings suggestive of bromethalin toxicosis include cerebral edema and white matter spongiosis with myelin vacuolization in the absence of inflammation [34–36].

Diagnosis

Bromethalin can be found in fat, liver, kidneys, and the brain [35]. Despite evidence showing an increasing trend in animal bromethalin exposures [37], testing for this rodenticide and its active metabolite, desmethyl bromethalin, is not widely available at diagnostic laboratories. A diagnosis of bromethalin toxicosis can be made based on exposure to bromethalin-containing rodenticides, compatible clinical and postmortem findings, and by ruling out other possible causes of death.

5.4.2.4 Strychnine

Mode of Action and Affected Body Systems

Following its rapid absorption, strychnine blocks the inhibitory action of the neurotransmitter glycine to motor neurons and interneurons [38, 39]. This results in mild to severe muscle spasms and convulsions, often characterized by extreme hyperextension of the body and limbs [21].

Expected Clinical Signs and Lesions

Severity of clinical signs varies with the exposure dose and signs typically develop within 10–120 min of ingestion [21]. Musculoskeletal signs develop gradually at first, often noticed as spasms and stiffness of the face, neck, and limbs. This is rapidly followed by generalized tonic-extensor type convulsions, with animals exhibiting an arched back and jaws clamped into a "sardonic grin." Increased sensitivity to sensory stimulation such as loud noises, light, and touch may also be present though are not completely specific to strychnine toxicosis. Hyperthermia may be present as a result of the muscle contractions and convulsions, and death most likely occurs due to hypoxia associated with respiratory paralysis.

Rhabdomyolysis and acute renal failure have been reported in strychnine-intoxicated humans [40]; however, similar findings have not been adequately described in animals. Rigor mortis occurs rapidly after death and may persist for days [20]. The postmortem examination may not reveal many lesions beyond pinpoint hemorrhages in the lungs due to asphyxia.

Diagnosis

In cases with compatible clinical signs, suspect bait material, stomach or crop contents, blood, urine, liver, and kidney should all be collected for strychnine analysis [20].

5.4.3 Avitrol

5.4.3.1 Sources

Most commonly known by its trade name, Avitrol®, 4-aminopyridine (4-AP) is a highly toxic, restricted use EPA-approved pesticide for the control of various bird species. It is also approved by the FDA for the treatment of human multiple sclerosis patients [41]. Avitrol is supplied as ready to use corn and grain products or pellets that can be mixed into grain-based feeds. The EPA registration of 4-AP powders was discontinued in 2007 [42].

5.4.3.2 Mode of Action and Affected Body Systems

4-AP selectively blocks potassium channels, prolonging action potentials. Enhanced interneuronal and neuromuscular synaptic transmission results in both cholinergic (diaphoresis, altered mentation, seizures) and dopamine-related (tremors, involuntary twitching, and muscle contractions) effects [43]. Rapidly metabolized and eliminated, relay toxicosis from the ingestion of dead birds is not expected [44].

5.4.3.3 Expected Clinical Signs and Lesions

As a target flock begins to feed on 4-AP-treated bait, the acute neurological signs that develop in the first few birds are meant to frighten and disperse the rest of the flock. In a review of nontarget exposures to 4-AP [42], the most commonly reported clinical signs in dogs were tremors, hypersalivation, seizures, tachycardia, and ataxia.

Necropsy findings in birds may include signs of trauma, due to the neurologic and flock responses to the toxin.

5.4.3.4 Diagnosis

Diagnosis is based on evidence of potential exposure to 4-AP-containing bait accompanied by acute neurological signs. Gastrointestinal contents can be tested for 4-AP; however, its rapid absorption may limit the quantity present for analysis. Detection in liver and kidney may also be possible.

5.4.4 Starlicide

5.4.4.1 Sources

3-Chloro-4-methyl benzenamine hydrochloride, also known as 3-chloro-4-methylaniline hydrochloride and DRC-1339, is another restricted use EPA-registered avicide, commonly known as Starlicide®. This product is supplied as ready to use feed products, pellets that can be mixed into grain-based feeds, and powders that can be applied to roosts and other surfaces. Extensive animal testing during the development of this product demonstrated that pest bird species such as blackbirds, corvids, rock doves, gulls, and starlings were among the most susceptible [44].

5.4.4.2 Mode of Action and Affected Body Systems

Following ingestion, Starlicide is rapidly hydrolyzed to what is believed to be the actual toxic compound, 3-chloro-*p*-toluidine (CPT), and within 2.5 h >98% of the oral dose can be detected in feces [44]. Nephrotoxicity appears to be the primary cause of death in birds and may be mediated by renal deacetylase in sensitive species [45]. In mammals and other birds, cardiac or respiratory arrest may occur.

5.4.4.3 Expected Clinical Signs and Lesions

CPT is believed to cause irreversible necrosis of the proximal convoluted renal tubule [44]. CPT may also have direct cytotoxic effects causing hemoconcentration, plasma protein loss, and ascites [46]. Clinical signs in experimentally poisoned starlings were first observed about 20–30 h after consumption; however, death can occur as quickly as within 3 h depending on the dose ingested [47]. Water consumption initially increases then decreases; birds become fluffed and listless, then finally become comatose, and die.

In starlings killed by Starlicide, characteristic deposits of white, fat-like material can be found within the body cavity and especially within the pericardial region [47]. Other findings may include hemorrhage and/or congestion within the kidneys, liver, and brain.

5.4.4.4 Diagnosis
Starlicide may be detectable in gastrointestinal contents and tissues, especially kidneys.

5.4.5 Pentobarbital

5.4.5.1 Sources
Improper disposal of animals euthanized with the short-acting barbiturate pentobarbital has resulted in relay toxicosis in many wild and domestic animal species [48–51]. Pentobarbital residues have been detected in compost piles greater than 1 year after the placement of euthanized horse carcasses [52].

5.4.5.2 Mode of Action and Affected Body Systems
Since pentobarbital is an anesthetic and anticonvulsant, significant and potentially life-threatening central nervous system depression can develop. The primary mechanism of action is through binding to γ-amino butyric acid (GABA) and enhancing its inhibitory effects [53].

5.4.5.3 Expected Clinical Signs and Lesions
Intoxicated animals display varying degrees of lethargy and ataxia and may eventually become comatose. Live or deceased animals may have physical injuries as a result of falls and other trauma due to their compromised state of alertness and coordination; however, other specific lesions may be absent at necropsy.

5.4.5.4 Diagnosis
Urine, stomach contents [54], suspect source material, and liver can all be submitted for gas chromatography–mass spectrometry (GC–MS) analysis that may detect both pentobarbital and phenytoin, another common ingredient in euthanasia solutions [53].

5.4.6 Ethylene Glycol (Antifreeze)

5.4.6.1 Sources
Ethylene glycol is the main ingredient in most antifreeze products, including those used in automobiles, and is also used as a solvent in the production of paints and plastics [55]. Less toxic antifreeze products such as propylene glycol are also available; however, due to its wide use and availability and well-known toxicity, ethylene glycol exposures are commonly reported in animals [37, 56].

5.4.6.2 Mode of Action and Affected Body Systems
Following ingestion and absorption from the gastrointestinal tract, ethylene glycol is primarily metabolized in the liver by alcohol dehydrogenase (ADH) [57, 58] to glycoaldehyde. Glycoaldehyde is oxidized to glycolic acid and then to glyoxylic acid [55]. Glyoxylic acid is primarily converted to oxalic acid. Calcium binds to oxalic acid, forming calcium oxalate crystals that can be detected in urine. Ethylene glycol itself shares similar toxicity characteristics with ethanol; however, the toxic metabolites adversely affect the kidneys and other body systems [59–61].

5.4.6.3 Expected Clinical Signs and Lesions
Ethylene glycol can be a gastric irritant, producing nausea, vomiting, and abdominal cramping [61] and also a central nervous system (CNS) depressant [62]. Accumulation of glycolic acid and other metabolites causes an often severe metabolic acidosis with systemic adverse effects [63]. Acute renal failure is the most severe consequence of ethylene glycol poisoning. While kidney function may recover with time and treatment,

many animals are euthanized once acute renal failure develops [56, 64] due to the guarded prognosis or financial constraints.

5.4.6.4 Diagnosis

The key features of hyperosmolality, metabolic acidosis, acute renal failure, and calcium oxalate crystalluria should raise the suspicion of ethylene glycol toxicosis [65]. Ethylene glycol can be directly measured in serum, urine, and kidney tissue, and may be determined using commercial test kits that can be used in a veterinary clinic permitting the accurate diagnosis of ethylene glycol toxicity in dogs. Acute tubular necrosis with calcium oxalate crystals will confirm ethylene glycol intoxication at necropsy, except in cases of rapid death due to metabolic acidosis.

5.4.7   Lead

5.4.7.1 Sources

Lead is ubiquitous in soil [66] and is also present in solder, lead-based paints [67], and leaded gasoline. Other lead sources that may result in exposures involving domestic animals and wildlife are automotive batteries, industrial waste, fishing sinkers, curtain weights, old putty and caulk, linoleum, antique golf balls, and lead arsenate pesticides [68–73]. Lead shot and bullets can be ingested directly from the environment or in carcasses [74–79]. Due to the frangible nature of lead-core hunting ammunition, improperly disposed gut piles continue to pose a significant danger to scavengers such as bald eagles, vultures, and California condors [80, 81]. Even in areas where lead shot is no longer used in hunting waterfowl, it is still used for upland game animals [82]. Humans with retained intra-articular bullets have developed clinical lead poisoning [83–86]; however, elevated hepatic lead levels have not been demonstrated in wildlife with chronically embedded lead projectiles [87].

5.4.7.2 Mode of Action and Affected Body Systems

Lead binds sulfhydryl groups, inhibiting hemoglobin synthesis by inactivating enzymes such as δ-aminolevulinic acid dehydratase (ALAD) and ferrochelatase and causing anemia [78]. Lead also interferes with many calcium-dependent processes, affecting multiple body systems and cell types [88], including central and peripheral neurotransmission [89].

5.4.7.3 Expected Clinical Signs and Lesions

Lead toxicosis has been described in many animal types; however, manifestation of clinical signs varies by species [90]. Dogs and cats commonly display nonspecific behavior changes, anorexia, lethargy, ataxia, vomiting, and diarrhea [91]. Psittacines variably develop anorexia, regurgitation, depression, diarrhea, anemia, and seizures [92]. Other birds such as waterfowl and raptors become weak and depressed with muscle atrophy and peripheral nerve dysfunction [93]. Raptors do not develop the renal effects seen in mammals [78].

5.4.7.4 Diagnosis

Many veterinarians will institute treatment for lead intoxication based on case history and clinical signs alone [94]. Diagnosis should be confirmed by measuring a lead level in blood, liver, or kidney; suspect gastrointestinal contents and metallic objects can also be tested for the presence of lead. In-house analyzers can be used to immediately determine blood lead levels [78]. Blood lead levels can additionally be used to monitor response to treatment in lead-intoxicated animal patients. Techniques developed to measure lead using dried blood spots on filter paper may be especially helpful when patient size limits blood draws to very small volumes [95].

Neither acute nor chronic lead intoxication is associated with specific lesions. In avian species, the finding of extremely thick and sludgy bile, sometimes in conjunction with reduced nutritional condition, should elevate suspicion for lead toxicity. Metal may or may not still be present in the gastrointestinal tract at the time of death and may be visible on radiographs if present. Laminar cerebral cortical necrosis may be evident on histopathology [90]; however, this finding should not be considered pathognomonic for lead toxicosis. Lesions found in birds may include myocardial necrosis, hepatocellular necrosis, brain edema, and renal tubular necrosis in waterfowl [93].

Legal Note The findings and conclusions in this chapter are those of the author and do not necessarily represent the views of the US Fish and Wildlife Service.

References

1. Gwaltney-Brant SM. Veterinary forensic toxicology. Vet Path. 2016;53(5):1067–77.
2. Gwaltney-Brant SM. Epidemiology of animal poisonings in the United States. In: Gupta RC, editor. Veterinary toxicology: basic and clinical principles. 2nd ed. London: Academic Press; 2012.
3. Galey FD. Diagnostic and forensic toxicology. Vet Clin North Am Equine Pract. 1995;11(3):443–54.
4. Galey FD. Diagnostic toxicology. In: Plumlee KN, editor. Clinical veterinary toxicology. St. Louis, MO: Mosby; 2004.
5. Poppenga RH. Diagnostic sampling and establishing a minimum database in exotic animal toxicology. Vet Clin North Am Exot Anim Pract. 2008;11(2):195–210.
6. Dinis-Oliveira RJ, Carvalho F, De Clercq D, et al. Collection of biological samples in forensic toxicology. Toxicol Mech Methods. 2010;20(7):363–414.
7. Millo T, Jaiswa AK, Behera C. Collection, preservation and forwarding of biological samples for toxicological analysis in medicolegal autopsy cases: a review. J Indian Acad Forensic Med. 2008;30(2):96–100.
8. Meerdink GL. Anticholinesterase insecticides. In: Plumlee KN, editor. Clinical veterinary toxicology. St. Louis, MO: Mosby; 2004.
9. Means C. Organophosphate and carbamate insecticides. In: Peterson ME, Talcott PA, editors. Small animal toxicology. 3rd ed. St. Louis, MO: Elsevier; 2013.
10. Hill EF, Mendenhall WM. Secondary poisoning of barn owls with Famphur, an organophosphate insecticide. J Wildl Manag. 1980;44(3):676–81.
11. Reece RL, Handson P. Observations on the accidental poisoning of birds by organophosphate insecticides and other toxic substances. Vet Rec. 1982;111(20):453–5.
12. Henny CJ, Kolbe EJ, Hill EF, et al. Case history of bald eagles and other raptors killed by organophosphorus insecticides topically applied to livestock. J Wildl Dis. 1987;23(2):292–5.
13. Fikes JD. Toxicology of selected pesticides, drugs, and chemicals. Organophosphorus and carbamate insecticides. Vet Clin North Am Small Anim Pract. 1990;20(2):353–67.
14. Kibler WB. Skeletal necrosis secondary to parathion. Toxicol Appl Pharmacol. 1973;25(1):117–22.
15. Mineau P, Tucker KR. Improving detection of pesticide poisoning in birds. J Wildl Rehabil. 2002;25(2):4.
16. Salaramoli J. Acetyl cholinesterase activity decreases by time after death in cow. Asian J Anim Vet Adv. 2008;3(6):453–6.
17. Villar D, Balvin D, Giraldo C, et al. Plasma and brain cholinesterase in methomyl-intoxicated free-ranging pigeons (Columba Livia f. Domestica). J Vet Diagn Invest. 2010;22(2):313–5.
18. Meerdink GL. Organophosphorus and carbamate insecticide poisoning. In: Kirk RW, editor. Current veterinary therapy X, small animal practice. Philadelphia: WB Saunders; 1989.
19. DeClementi C, Sobczak BR. Common rodenticide toxicoses in small animals. Vet Clin North Am Small Anim Pract. 2012;42(2):349–60.
20. Gupta RC. Non-anticoagulant rodenticides. In: Gupta RC, editor. Veterinary toxicology: basic and clinical principles. 2nd ed. London: Academic Press; 2012.
21. Talcott PA. Strychnine. In: Peterson ME, Talcott PA, editors. Small animal toxicology. 3rd ed. St. Louis, MO: Elsevier; 2013.
22. DuVall MD, Murphy MJ, Ray AC, et al. Case studies on second-generation anticoagulant rodenticide toxicities in nontarget species. J Vet Diagn Invest. 1989;1(1):66–8.
23. Albert CA, Wilson LK, Mineau P, et al. Anticoagulant rodenticides in three owl species from western Canada, 1988–2003. Arch Environ Contam Toxicol. 2010;58(2):451–9.
24. Rattner BA, Horak KE, Lazarus RS, et al. Assessment of toxicity and potential risk of the anticoagulant rodenticide diphacinone using eastern screech-owls (Megascops asio). Ecotoxicology. 2012;21(3):832–46.
25. Stansley W, Cummings M, Vudathala D, et al. Anticoagulant rodenticides in red-tailed hawks, Buteo jamaicensis, and great horned owls, Bubo virginianus, from New Jersey, USA, 2008–2010. Bull Environ Contam Toxicol. 2014;92(1):6–9.
26. Sheafor SE, Couto CG. Clinical approach to a dog with anticoagulant rodenticide poisoning. Vet Med. 1994;94:466–71.
27. Merola V. Anticoagulant rodenticides: deadly for pests, dangerous for pets. Vet Med. 2002;97:716–22.
28. Murphy MJ. Anticoagulant rodenticides. In: Gupta RC, editor. Veterinary toxicology: basic and clinical principles. New York: Elsevier; 2007.
29. Murray M. Anticoagulant rodenticide exposure and toxicosis in four species of birds of prey presented to a wildlife clinic in Massachusetts, 2006–2010. J Zoo Wildl Med. 2011;42(1):88–97.
30. Dorman D. Bromethalin. In: Plumlee KN, editor. Clinical veterinary toxicology. St. Louis, MO: Mosby; 2004.
31. Osweiler GD. Toxicology. Baltimore: Williams and Wilkins; 1996.
32. Dorman DC, Parker AJ, Buck WB. Bromethalin toxicosis in the dog. Part I: clinical effects. J Am Anim Hosp Assoc. 1990a;26:589–94.

33. Dorman DC, Parker AJ, Dye JA, et al. Bromethalin neurotoxicosis in the cat. Prog Vet Neurol. 1990c;1(2):189–96.
34. Dorman DC, Parker AJ, Buck WB. Bromethalin toxicosis in the dog. Part II: selected treatments for the toxic syndrome. J Am Anim Hosp Assoc. 1990b;26:595–8.
35. Dorman DC, Simon J, Harlin KA, et al. Diagnosis of bromethalin toxicosis in the dog. J Vet Diagn Investig. 1990d;2(2):123–8.
36. van Lier RB, Cherry LD. The toxicity and mechanism of action of bromethalin: a new single-feeding rodenticide. Fundam Appl Toxicol. 1988;11(4):664–72.
37. McLean MK, Hansen SR. An overview of trends in animal poisoning cases in the United States: 2002–2010. Vet Clin North Am Small Anim Pract. 2012;42(2):219–22.
38. Curtis DR, Hosli L, Johnston GAR. A pharmacological study of the depression of spinal neurons by glycine and related amino acids. Exp Brain Res. 1968;6(1):1–18.
39. Curtis DR, Duggan AW, Johnston FAR. The specificity of strychnine as a glycine antagonist in the mammalian spinal cord. Exp Brain Res. 1971;12(5):547–65.
40. Boyd RE, Spyker DA. Strychnine poisoning: recovery from profound lactic acidosis, hyperthermia, and rhabdomyolysis. Am J Med. 1983;74(3):507–12.
41. Rowan MJ. Central nervous system toxicity evaluation in vitro: neurophysiological approach. In: Blum K, Manzo L, editors. Neurotoxicology. New York: Marcel Dekker; 1985.
42. McLean MK, Khan S. A review of 29 incidents involving 4-aminopyridine in non-target species reported to the ASPCA animal poison control center. J Med Toxicol. 2013;9:418–21.
43. King AM, Menke NB, Katz KD, et al. 4-Aminopyridine toxicity: a case report and review of the literature. J Med Toxicol. 2012;8(3):314–21.
44. Eisemann JD, Pipas PA, Cummings JL (2003) Acute and chronic toxicity of compound DRC-1339 (3-chloro-4-methylaniline hydrochloride) to birds. USDA National Wildlife Research Center—staff publications paper 211.
45. Mull RL, Giri SN. The role of renal aromatic n-deacetylase in selective toxicity of avicide 3-chloro-p-toluidine in birds. Biochim Biophys Acta. 1972;27:222–8.
46. Borison HL, Snow SR, Longnecker DS, Smith RP. 3-chloro-p-toluidine: effects of lethal doses in rats and cats. Toxicol Appl Pharmcol. 1975;31:403–12.
47. DeCino TJ, Cunningham DJ, Schafer EW. Toxicity of DRC-1339 to starlings. J Wildl Manag. 1966;30(2):249–53.
48. Anderson JF, Filkins D, Stowe CM, Arendt TD. Accidental relay toxicosis caused by pentobarbital euthanasia solution. J Am Vet Med Assoc. 1979;175:583–4.
49. Fucci V, Monroe WE, Riedesel DH, Jackson LL. Oral pentobarbital intoxication in a bitch. J Am Vet Med Assoc. 1986;188:191–2.
50. Jurczynski K, Zittlau E. Pentobarbital poisoning in Sumatran tigers. J Zoo Wildl Med. 2007;38:583–4.
51. Verster A, Schroder HHE, Newbit JW. Accidental pentobarbital poisoning in a lioness. J South Afr Vet Assoc. 1990;61:37–8.
52. Payne J, Farris R, Parker G, Bonhotal J, Schwarz M. Quantification of sodium pentobarbital residues from equine mortality compost piles. J Anim Sci. 2015;93:1824–9.
53. Bischoff K, Jaeger R, Ebel JG. An unusual case of relay pentobarbital toxicosis in a dog. J Med Toxicol. 2011;7:236–9.
54. Kaiser AM, McFarland W, Siemion RS, Raisbeck MF. Secondary pentobarbital poisoning in two dogs: a cautionary tale. J Vet Diagn Investig. 2010;22:632–4.
55. Thrall MA, Connally HE, Grauer GF, et al. Ethylene glycol. In: Peterson ME, Talcott PA, editors. Small animal toxicology. 3rd ed. St. Louis, MO: Elsevier; 2013.
56. Khan SA, Schell MM, Trammel HL, et al. Ethylene glycol exposures managed by the ASPCA National Animal Poison Control Center from July 1995 to December 1997. Vet Hum Toxicol. 1999;41(6):403–6.
57. Blair AH, Vallee BL. Some catalytic properties of human liver alcohol dehydrogenase. Biochemistry. 1966;5(6):2026–34.
58. Coen G, Weiss B. Oxidation of ethylene glycol to glycoaldehyde by mammalian tissue. Enzymol Biol Clin. 1966;6(4):288–96.
59. Bovee KE. Ethylene glycol toxicity. Am J Clin Pathol. 1966;45(1):46–50.
60. Thrall MA, Grauer GF, Mero KN. Clinicopathologic findings in dogs and cats with ethylene glycol intoxication. J Am Vet Med Assoc. 1984;184(1):37–41.
61. Davis DP, Bramwell KJ, Hamilton RS, et al. Ethylene glycol poisoning: case report of a record-high level and a review. J Emerg Med. 1997;15(50):653–7.
62. Berger JR, Ayyar DR. Neurological complications of ethylene glycol intoxication: report of a case. Arch Neurol. 1981;38(11):724–6.
63. Jacobsen D, Ovrebo S, Ostborg J, et al. Glycolate causes the acidosis in ethylene glycol poisoning and is effectively removed by hemodialysis. Acta Med Scand. 1984;216(4):409–16.
64. Connally HE, Thrall MA, Forney SD, et al. Safety and efficacy of 4-methylpyrazole as a treatment for suspected or confirmed ethylene glycol intoxication in dogs: 107 cases (1983–1995). J Am Vet Med Assoc. 1996;209(11):1880–3.
65. Gaynor AR, Dhupa N. Acute ethylene glycol intoxication. Part II. Diagnosis, treatment, prognosis, and prevention. Compendium. 1999;21(12):1124–33.
66. Trampel DW, Imerman PM, Carson TL, et al. Lead contamination of chicken eggs and tissues from a small farm flock. J Vet Diagn Investig. 2003;15(5):418–22.
67. Wright FC, Younger RL, Riner JC, et al. Effects of daily oral subtoxic doses of a wet lead-based paint on cattle. Bull Environ Contam Toxicol. 1976;16(2):156–63.

68. Wuerthele HW. Golf balls as a source of lead poisoning. JAMA. 1928;91(25):1989.
69. Locke LN, Kerr SM, Zoromski D. Lead poisoning in common loons (*Gavia immer*). Avian Dis. 1982;26(2):392–6.
70. Berny PJ, Cote LM, Buck WB. Case reports of lead poisoning in dogs from the National Animal Poison Control Center and the Centre national d'Informations Toxicologiques Veterinaires: anecdotes or reality? Vet Hum Toxicol. 1992;34(1):26–31.
71. Lemos RAA, Driemeier D, Guimaraes EB, et al. Lead poisoning in cattle grazing pasture contaminated by industrial waste. Vet Human Toxicol. 2004;46(6):326–8.
72. Beyer WN, Gaston G, Brazzle R, et al. Deer exposed to exceptionally high concentrations of lead near the continental mine in Idaho, USA. Environ Toxicol Chem. 2007;26(5):1040–6.
73. Van der Merwe D, Carpenter JW, Nietfeld JC, et al. Adverse health effects in Canada geese (*Branta Canadensis*) associated with waste from zinc and lead mines in the tri-state Mining District (Kansas, Oklahoma, and Missouri, USA). J Wildl Dis. 2011;47(3):650–60.
74. DeMent SH, Chisolm JJ, Barber JC, et al. Lead exposure in an "urban" peregrine falcon and its avian prey. J Wildl Dis. 1986;22(2):238–44.
75. Samour JH, Naldo J. Diagnosis and therapeutic management of lead toxicosis in falcons in Saudi Arabia. J Avian Med Surg. 2002;16(1):16–20.
76. Clark AJ, Scheuhammer AM. Lead poisoning in upland-foraging birds of prey in Canada. Ecotoxicology. 2003;12(1–4):23–30.
77. Lance VA, Horn TR, Elsey RM, et al. Chronic incidental lead ingestion in a group of captive-reared alligators (*Alligator mississippiensis*): possible contribution to reproductive failure. Comp Biochem Physiol C Toxicol Pharmacol. 2006;142(1–2):30–5.
78. Redig PT, Arent LR. Raptor toxicology. Vet Clin Exot Anim. 2008;11(2):261–82.
79. Bannon DI, Parsons PJ, Centeno JA, et al. Lead and copper in pigeons (*Columbia livia*) exposed to a small arms-range soil. Arch Environ Contam Toxicol. 2010;60(2):351–60.
80. Finkelstein ME, Doak DF, George D, Burnett J, Brandt J, Church M, Grantham J, Smith DR. Lead poisoning and the deceptive recovery of the critically endangered California condor. Proc Nat Acad of Sci. 2012;109(28):11449–54.
81. Haig SM, D'Elia J, Eagles-Smith C, Fair JM, Gervais J, Herring G, Rivers JW, Schulz JH. The persistent problem of lead poisoning in birds from ammunition and fishing tackle. Condor. 2014;116(3):408–28.
82. Stansley W, Murphy L. Liver lead concentrations in raptors in New Jersey, USA, 2008–2010. Bull Environ Contam Toxicol. 2011;87(2):171–4.
83. Slavin RE, Swedo J, Cartwright J, et al. Lead arthritis and lead poisoning following bullet wounds: a clinicopathologic, ultrastructural, and microanalytic study of two cases. Hum Pathol. 1988;19(2):223–35.
84. Peh WC, Reinus WR. Lead arthropathy: a cause of delayed onset lead poisoning. Skelet Radiol. 1995;24(5):142–4.
85. Akhtar AJ, Funnye AS, Akanno J. Gunshot-induced plumbism in an adult male. J Nat Med Assoc. 2003;95(10):986–90.
86. Sokolowski MJ, Sisson G. Systemic lead poisoning due to an intra-articular bullet. Orthopedics. 2005;28(4):411–2.
87. LaDouceur EEB, Kagan R, Scanlan M, et al. Chronically embedded lead projectiles in wildlife: a case series investigating the potential for lead toxicosis. J Zoo Wildl Med. 2015;46(2):438–42.
88. Wismer T. Lead. In: Peterson ME, Talcott PA, editors. Small animal toxicology. 3rd ed. St. Louis, MO: Elsevier; 2013.
89. Bressler JP, Goldstein GW. Mechanism of lead neurotoxicity. Biochem Pharmacol. 1991;41(4):479–84.
90. Gwaltney-Brant S. Lead. In: Plumlee KN, editor. Clinical veterinary toxicology. St. Louis, MO: Mosby; 2004.
91. Kowalczyk DF. Lead poisoning. In: Kirk RW, editor. Current veterinary therapy IX. Philadelphia: W.B. Saunders; 1986.
92. LaBonde J. Toxicity in pet avian patients. Semin Avian Exotic Pet Med. 1995;4(1):23–31.
93. Locke LN, Thomas NJ. Lead poisoning of waterfowl and raptors. In: Fairbrother A, Locke LN, Hoff GL, editors. Noninfectious diseases of wildlife. 2nd ed. Ames: Iowa State University Press; 1996.
94. Mautino M. Lead and zinc intoxication in zoological medicine: a review. J Zoo Wildl Med. 1997;28:28–35.
95. Lehner AF, Rumbeiha W, Shlosberg A, et al. Diagnostic analysis of veterinary dried blood spots for toxic heavy metals exposure. J Anal Toxicol. 2013;37(7):406–22.

Anesthesia-Related Deaths

6

Josepha DeLay

6.1 Introduction

Perianesthetic mortality contributes to a small but important segment of the pathology caseload in veterinary diagnostic laboratories. The death of an animal while anesthetized or sedated is difficult for veterinarians and animal owners. In these situations, the goal of the necropsy is to identify and document preexistent disease conditions or complications of the surgical, anesthetic, or diagnostic procedure that may have caused or contributed to death. Anesthesia-related deaths are often particularly challenging for pathologists, as morphologic lesions indicative of the cause of death (COD) may be absent in a substantial proportion of cases [1, 2]. Lesions caused by resuscitation efforts may be present, complicating interpretation of the COD. Pathologists must also recognize the potential for litigation in these cases or for disciplinary action by the veterinary licensing body, and thorough written and photographic documentation of the necropsy must be undertaken to accommodate any future legal action.

6.2 Pathophysiology of Anesthesia-Related Deaths

General anesthesia is a complex physiologic state in which centrally acting drugs alter the state of consciousness. In doing so, numerous other physiologic processes are also affected including cardiovascular and respiratory functions. Anesthesia is a high-risk activity, although continuous improvements in drug safety and patient monitoring have decreased the risk over time of complication and death during anesthesia in humans and animals [3–7]. Clinical reports have identified rates of perianesthetic mortality in veterinary species ranging from 0.11% to 1.5% in dogs, 0.06–1.08% in cats, and 0.12–1.6% in horses [3, 5, 6, 8–12]. In contrast, the mortality rate due solely or in part to anesthesia in humans in developed countries is 0.002% and 0.009%, respectively [7]. Differences in the level of patient monitoring during anesthesia in human and veterinary medicine likely contribute to the overall lower mortality rate in humans [13]. In addition, the level of specialization among individuals involved in administration and monitoring of anesthetized patients is generally higher in human medicine compared to veterinary medicine [13].

The common pathways contributing to perianesthetic complication in all species involve

J. DeLay
Animal Health Laboratory, University of Guelph, Guelph, ON, Canada, N1G 2W1
e-mail: jdelay@uoguelph.ca

respiratory, cardiovascular (including hypovolemia), and/or central nervous (CNS) systems, all of which may culminate in cardiac arrest and death [14]. Most cases of perianesthetic death in dogs and cats involve lesions in the upper respiratory tract, lungs, or heart [1, 2]. Often multiple factors are involved sequentially, and determining the primary event precipitating the crisis situation is not possible. A detailed clinical history may provide insight regarding a specific incident that initiated the sequence of events leading to cardiac arrest, such as intravenous drug injection triggering anaphylaxis, or postanesthetic upper respiratory tract (URT) obstruction secondary to perilaryngeal and pharyngeal trauma induced by difficult endotracheal intubation. Necropsy confirmation of factors involved in perianesthetic mortality is limited to those conditions producing morphologic lesions that can be identified by gross or histologic examination. As a result, many conditions such as drug-induced central depression of cardiovascular or respiratory centers, cardiac dysrhythmia, or acid-base or electrolyte abnormalities cannot be confirmed after death. However, necropsy is valuable in identifying lesions indicative of disease that may have led to or resulted from these conditions, such as cardiomyopathy or adrenocortical insufficiency, and in excluding many other potential contributing factors in cases of anesthesia-associated death.

A variety of disease conditions may contribute to the common pathways of perianesthetic complication. For example, respiratory impediment may result from obstructive or infiltrative disease of the upper respiratory tract, lung, or pleura, or dysfunction of thoracic and intercostal muscles and diaphragm. Cardiac dysfunction could be caused by primary myocardial disease such as cardiomyopathy or myocarditis, or metabolic derangement or hypoxia impeding normal myocardial function. Any of these conditions may precipitate potentially fatal cardiac dysrhythmias. Previously unidentified congenital cardiac anomalies, such as subaortic stenosis, may also contribute to cardiac failure. Hypovolemia is an additional consideration as a cause of cardiovascular failure and cardiac arrest, and may be due to intraoperative or spontaneous hemorrhage, or relative hypovolemia due to redistribution of intravascular fluid volume and associated hypotension, as may occur in anaphylaxis. Interference with normal function of central nervous system (CNS) respiratory and cardiovascular centers may lead to respiratory and cardiac complications. Contributing factors to this central effect include preexistent inflammatory, infectious, ischemic, or neoplastic conditions involving CNS, metabolic disturbances, and effects of anesthetic drugs.

6.3 Necropsy Procedure and Reporting

The majority of cases of anesthesia-related death presented to diagnostic laboratories involve dogs and cats, reflecting the frequency of general anesthesia in these species [1]. Objective identification of necropsy lesions is vital to interpretation of the COD. Examination should follow the individual pathologist's routine procedure but with modification to include special attention to the upper airways, lung, and heart. Special techniques for evaluation of pneumothorax and venous air embolism may be included, as later described. The exam should also include evaluation for potential or known complications of the specific procedure for which the animal was anesthetized or sedated.

The exam should begin with a thorough review of the clinical history. Information provided to pathologists in cases of anesthesia-related death is often suboptimal [1], and every effort should be made to obtain a complete history that includes specific circumstances of the animal's condition prior to and during anesthesia [2]. Important information to include in the history includes the animal's signalment; physical condition prior to anesthesia, based on the American Society of Anesthesia (ASA) guidelines [4]; the presence of clinical disease at the time of anesthesia or sedation, including duration of the condition and current therapies; all clinical pathology and other ancillary test results; the procedure for which the animal was anesthetized or sedated; the method of anesthesia or sedation, including drugs administered; the timing (sedation/premedication, maintenance, recovery) of onset of anesthetic complication or death and the type of complication; if the animal was intubated at the time of death; the timing of the onset of complications with regard to injections, manipulations, or other procedures; and whether cardiopulmonary resuscitation (CPR) was attempted and what specific procedures were carried out [2]. Knowledge of these clinical details is important in directing the necropsy but is also critical for accurate interpretation of necropsy findings and in making conclusions regarding the COD. For example, in a brachycephalic dog that died with an endotracheal (ET) tube correctly in place during the maintenance phase of inhalant anesthesia, upper respiratory tract obstruction due to elongated soft palate or other anatomic features may be excluded as a contributing factor to death. If the timing of death and intubation status were not provided in the clinical history, the pathologist might erroneously conclude that elongated soft palate or other anomaly led to URT obstruction and death. These same anomalies may be of more importance if the dog died during recovery from anesthetic, after the ET tube was removed. The pathologist must have knowledge of the procedure for which the animal was anesthetized. The exam should include evaluation for potential complications specific to the procedure, such as careful evaluation of ovarian and cervical pedicles for evidence of hemorrhage in dogs and cats that die during recovery from ovariohysterectomy. Awareness of the presurgical ASA score for individual animals and of any preexistent disease conditions will provide a clinical context for interpretation of necropsy findings. The ASA score categorizes the animal's preanesthetic health status based on a set of predetermined criteria [4]. An increased ASA score has been associated with an increase in the risk of death during anesthesia in humans and animals [3, 6, 7, 9, 10], and knowledge of the presurgical status of individual animals and of any preexistent disease conditions will provide a clinical context for interpretation of necropsy findings.

Documentation of animal identity prior to beginning the exam should include external iden-tification photographs and recording of microchip number, tattoos, ear tags, and/or brands that may be present. The condition of preservation of the body and previous freezing or other storage conditions should be noted, as these may influence the interpretation of necropsy findings. Photographs should be used throughout the exam to record all external and internal lesions. A scale bar and case number label should be included in all photos. Full-body radiographs may be considered, concentrating on thorax and taken prior to the start of the necropsy, especially in cases in which pneumothorax or venous air embolism is suspected based on the clinical history. A complete external examination should include description and location of any skin incisions, the presence of intravenous catheters, shaved sites in skin, and the presence and location of any other appliances such as an ET tube or electrocardiogram (ECG) electrodes, for corroboration with clinical records. Any indication of external hemorrhage and its severity should be recorded and the volume measured or estimated, when possible. Evidence of subcutaneous emphysema will prompt investigation during the internal exam for tracheal laceration or rupture. External nares should be examined for discharge and for evidence of stenosis or other obstructive lesion. As in routine necropsies, body condition and hydration should be evaluated, as well as the color of oral mucous membranes and sclera.

The internal exam includes evaluation of all organ systems for evidence of acute or preexistent disease but should focus particularly on lesions involving the URT, lung, thorax, and heart. Careful consideration of the sequence of the exam is important, in order to preserve lesions that may be transient or easily destroyed such as body cavity hemorrhage or effusion, elongated soft palate or other URT obstruction, pneumothorax, ruptured pulmonary bullae, and air emboli. Evaluation of upper airways should include examination for submucosal edema supportive of anaphylaxis or acute trauma, and of the oropharynx, larynx, and trachea for potentially obstructive mucous plugs, vomitus, or foreign debris. Particularly in brachycephalic breeds, the position of the caudal edge of the soft palate with regard to the epiglottis should be assessed and measured, and the presence of laryngeal saccule eversion noted.

Prior to opening of the thoracic cavity, assessment for pneumothorax may be done by incising the diaphragm from the abdominal aspect and observing for an inrush of air into the thorax with collapse of the normal concavity of the diaphragm, indicative of normal negative intrathoracic pressure. An alternative method for assessment of pneumothorax involves careful dissection and excision of a mid-thoracic intercostal muscle to the level of parietal pleura. In the absence of pneumothorax, the lung should be visible directly subjacent to the parietal pleura [15]. The external aspect of the trachea and surrounding soft tissue may be examined in situ for evidence of laceration, or peritracheal or mediastinal emphysema. Evaluation of thoracic vena cava in situ for the presence of luminal air bubbles may support a diagnosis of venous air embolism, in cases for which the clinical history is suggestive of this condition. Interpretation of intravascular gas bubbles must be made with caution in bodies that are not well preserved, as gas accumulation in blood may reflect putrefaction [15]. The presence of an air embolus in the right cardiac ventricle may be assessed by filling the pericardial sac with water prior to removal of the pluck from the body, then incising the right ventricular wall, and observing for escape of gas bubbles [15, 16]. An alternative technique following pluck removal is to submerge the intact heart in water while incising the right ventricle, while again monitoring for gas bubbles [17].

In cases in which the pneumothorax is detected, the lungs should be evaluated for ruptured bullae following removal of the pluck from the body but prior to incision of the trachea and lung dissection. To accomplish this, the lungs are submerged in water, while the trachea is held above the surface. Using a large-volume syringe, air is injected into the tracheal lumen while occluding a more proximal aspect of trachea, and the water is monitored for the appearance of air bubbles indicative of focal pleural rupture. These lesions in dogs may result from spontaneous rupture of preexistent idiopathic pulmonary blebs and bullae [18],

whereas ruptured bullae in cats are often associated with underlying pulmonary disease [19, 20]. After opening along the length of the larynx and trachea, the mucosa is examined for evidence of edema, hemorrhage, erosion or ulceration, and laceration or rupture. Tracheal diameter and contour are evaluated for lesions suggestive of tracheal hypoplasia or tracheal collapse.

Examination of the heart includes gross evaluation of relative and absolute chamber size and ventricular wall thickness, valves, and myocardium, as well as documentation of heart chamber weights and calculation of heart weight: body weight and ventricular weight ratios, with comparison to reference values [21]. Assessment for the presence of congenital anomalies such as septal defects and subaortic stenosis should be included in the exam.

Examination of all other organs is carried out as in a routine necropsy, with particular attention to structures involved in the surgical or diagnostic procedure for which the animal was anesthetized. Evaluation of the brain and skeletal muscle should be included in all anesthesia-related deaths. Detailed examination of the limbs and spinal column is necessary for cases in which these sites were targeted by the surgical or diagnostic procedures. Samples of all organs and lesions should be collected for histologic examination as well as for microbiologic testing, if warranted based on gross findings and clinical history. As part of the histologic exam, the use of a histochemical stain for iron such as Perl's stain is recommended in all cases to identify hemosiderophages in the lung, potentially indicative of preexistent left-sided heart failure.

Toxicologic testing is not routinely included in the necropsy of perianesthetic mortality cases, and evaluation of blood or tissue concentrations of anesthetic drugs is not usually available in veterinary species [2]. Toxicologic assays may be useful to confirm accidental administration of a known drug, if this information is provided in the clinical history. In these cases, heart blood and urine should be collected during the exam and used for subsequent evaluation.

The necropsy report includes objective findings of the gross and histologic exams and subjective interpretation and comments that place morphologic lesions in the context of the clinical scenario described for the specific case. The importance of obtaining a complete and accurate clinical history becomes obvious when correlating lesions with clinical events. The pathologist should address the confirmed or potential relationship of lesions identified to the known clinical circumstances. Lesions may be considered the sole COD (such as severe blood loss) or contributing to the COD (such as endocardiosis). Lesions may be identified that have no or questionable relationship to the COD but are important to discuss on an individual or population level, such as gastrointestinal parasitism. The subjective section of the report offers an opinion as to the COD and to factors leading to death. In many cases, the COD may not be obvious based on necropsy findings, and this should also be communicated in the report.

In human medicine, conclusions in cases of perianesthetic mortality may be divided into the following categories: death caused by the disease or injury for which the procedure was carried out, death due to preexistent disease or condition other than that for which the procedure was carried out, death resulting from surgical complication, and death due to complication of the administration of an anesthetic [22] (Table 6.1). Consideration of this classification scheme provides a framework for interpreting the significance of various lesions identified during the necropsy. Investigation of human perianesthetic death cases may include review by experts in multiple disciplines including pathologists, anesthesiologists, and surgeons, but this approach is not common in veterinary medicine. In some situations, review of the case with a board-certified veterinary anesthesiologist may provide insight into events potentially contributing to death, in the context of necropsy findings. In cases for which there is no necropsy evidence of preexistent disease or surgical complication as the cause of death, including the condition for which a procedure under anesthesia was required, death attributable to the administration of an anesthetic should be considered. Potential contributing factors include accidental overdose of anesthetic drugs, misplacement or obstruction of the ET tube, malfunction of the anesthetic apparatus (for inhalant anesthetics), and suboptimal monitoring of the animal and assessment of the plane of anesthesia [22]. Mechanical irritation of the respiratory tract during intubation or surgical manipulation during the head, neck, and abdominal procedures may lead to stimulation of vagal pathways [22–24]. Such neural reflexes occur most commonly in patients under a light plane of anesthesia and may lead to bradycardia, cardiac dysrhythmia, hypotension, apnea, or cardiac arrest. Although clinically significant, these factors do not produce morphologic lesions detectable at necropsy. Importantly, comment on the anesthetic protocol or management or on clinical aspects of the case is not the role of the veterinary pathologist. The conclusion that a death is directly caused by anesthesia requires significant input from clinical specialists and is beyond the purview of a typical necropsy report.

6.4 Necropsy Lesions in Perianesthetic Death

A wide range of lesions may be identified by gross and/or histologic examination in cases of perianesthetic mortality. Recent studies of necropsy findings in perianesthetic deaths in veterinary species determined that lesions were absent in 43% of dogs and in 34–63% of cats [1, 2]. When present, lesions in both studies predominately involved the URT, lung, and heart. Lesions involving the respiratory system included URT obstruction due to various causes such as the mucous plug, laryngeal edema, tracheal collapse

Table 6.1 Categories of perianesthetic mortality[a]

| 1. Death caused by disease or injury for which the procedure was carried out |
| 2. Death caused by preexistent disease or condition other than that for which the procedure was carried out |
| 3. Death due to complication of the surgical or diagnostic procedure |
| 4. Death due to complication of the administration of an anesthetic |

[a]From Saukko and Knight [22]

syndrome, brachycephalic syndrome, or laryngo-spasm; aspiration, interstitial, embolic, or parasitic (*Aelurostrongylus abstrusus*) pneumonia; pneumothorax; or severe acute pulmonary hemorrhage or edema. Cardiac lesions included cardiomyopathy; congenital anomaly; myocarditis, myocardial fibrosis, or myocardial necrosis or infarct. Significant lesions involving CNS or gastrointestinal (GI) systems were identified in relatively fewer animals, as were neoplasia and lesions indicative of systemic disease.

Resuscitation is attempted in many animals that arrest during or after anesthesia. A range of lesions have been attributed to these efforts in both prospective and retrospective studies, including pulmonary or multiorgan congestion or hemorrhage; pulmonary edema; pulmonary atelectasis or emphysema; liver or diaphragm laceration; hemothorax; and hemoperitoneum [1, 25]. Pneumothorax identified during the necropsy is often attributed by pathologists to resuscitation efforts [1]; however, results of a prospective clinical study did not identify pneumothorax as a complication of resuscitation in dogs and cats [25]. This suggests that detection of pneumothorax during the necropsy should prompt careful investigation for conditions other than resuscitation that could have led to development of the lesion.

Anaphylaxis may be a contributing factor to death in some perianesthetic mortality cases. In humans, anaphylaxis in the perioperative period is most frequently associated with neuromuscular blocking agents, antibiotics, and latex [26]. Anaphylaxis is less commonly attributed to anesthetic induction agents such as propofol and thiopental, nonsteroidal anti-inflammatory drugs, contrast agents, opioids, antiseptics, and local anesthetics [26]. In veterinary species, there are fewer reports of anaphylaxis associated with anesthetic drugs and procedures, although the range of compounds potentially leading to anaphylactic reactions is similar and includes antibiotics, thiopental, narcotics, gadolinium-based contrast agents, acepromazine, and vaccines [27, 28]. Anaphylaxis has not been documented in association with inhalant anesthetics [26, 27].

Allergic (IgE-mediated or non-IgE-mediated) and nonallergic mechanisms may contribute to the clinical signs of anaphylaxis [29, 30]. Anaphylaxis may manifest clinically as a variety of clinical signs including hypotension, bronchospasm, pharyngeal and laryngeal edema, gastrointestinal signs such as vomiting, and cutaneous signs including urticaria, erythema, and pruritis [28]. Species differences and the route of drug exposure influence the clinical manifestation of anaphylaxis in animals [31]. Cutaneous and gastrointestinal signs are prominent in dogs, and the liver is considered the shock organ in this species, leading to hepatic vein congestion and portal hypertension [28, 31]. In cats, the lung is the shock organ, and respiratory and gastrointestinal signs are typical [28, 31]. In anesthetized animals, clinical signs most likely to be noted in association with anaphylaxis include hypotension, tachycardia or bradycardia, respiratory distress, or fulminant cardiovascular collapse. Postmortem evidence of laryngeal or pharyngeal edema, and hepatic and gastrointestinal congestion may support this diagnosis but are not pathognomonic for anaphylaxis. Anaphylaxis may be easily overlooked during the necropsy as a cause of death, as gross lesions may be minimal or nonexistent. In a retrospective study of clinically confirmed fatal anaphylaxis in humans, no morphologic lesions were identified in 41% of deaths [32]. The clinical history may support a diagnosis of anaphylaxis if there is a temporal association between drug administration and onset of respiratory or cardiovascular signs. Postmortem serum tryptase analysis is used in humans to support a diagnosis of anaphylaxis, although elevated tryptase levels are not specific for this condition and may occur with other causes of death, and may vary with the anatomic site sampled [33]. This test has not yet been optimized for used in animals.

Conclusion

The goal of the necropsy in cases of anesthesia-related death is to exclude preexistent disease conditions, or complications of the surgical or diagnostic procedure, as the COD or as contributing factors to the COD. In most cases, death caused solely by anesthesia does not result in morphologic lesions that can be identified during the necropsy, and this conclusion requires the input of clinical specialists. Necropsy in cases of perianesthetic mortality should begin with a review of a complete, detailed clinical history. The exam method should concentrate on the URT, lungs, and heart while also being thorough in inclusion of other body systems. Pathologists must be cognizant of potential complications inherent to the surgical or diagnostic procedure for which the animal was anesthetized. Special techniques may be used to identify pneumothorax or venous air embolism, especially if indicated by the clinical history. No morphologic lesions are detected in a substantial proportion of anesthesia-associated death cases.

References

1. DeLay J. Perianesthetic mortality in domestic animals: a retrospective study of postmortem lesions and review of autopsy procedures. Vet Pathol. 2016;53:1078–86. https://doi.org/10.1177/0300985816655853.
2. Gerdin JA, Slater MR, Makolinski KV, et al. Postmortem findings in 54 cases of anesthetic associated death in cats from two spay-neuter programs in New York State. J Feline Med Surg. 2011;13:959–66. https://doi.org/10.1016/j.jfms.2011.07.021.
3. Brodbelt DC, Blissitt KJ, Hammond RA, et al. The risk of death: the confidential enquiry into perioperative small animal fatalities. Vet Anaesth Analg. 2008;35:365–73. https://doi.org/10.1111/j.1467-2995.2008.00397.x.
4. Brodbelt DC, Flaherty D, Pettifer G. Anesthetic risk and informed consent. In: Grimm KA, Lamont LA, Tranquilli WJ, et al., editors. Veterinary anesthesia and analgesia. Ames, IA: Wiley; 2015. p. 11–22.
5. Dodman NH, Lamb LA. Survey of small animal anesthetic practice in Vermont. J Am Anim Hosp Assoc. 1992;28:439–44.
6. Dyson DH, Maxie MG, Schnurr D. Morbidity and mortality associated with anesthetic management in small animal veterinary practice in Ontario. J Am Anim Hosp Assoc. 1998;34:325–35.
7. Bainbridge D, Martin J, Arango M, Cheng D. Perioperative and anaesthetic-related mortality in developed and developing countries: a systematic review and meta-analysis. Lancet. 2012;380:1075–81. https://doi.org/10.1016/S0140-6736(12)60990-8.
8. Bidwell LA, Bramlage LR, Rood WA. Equine perioperative fatalities associated with general anaesthesia at a private practice—a retrospective case series.

Vet Anaesth Analg. 2007;34:23–30. https://doi.org/10.1111/j.1467-2995.2005.00283.x.
9. Bille C, Auvigne V, Libermann S, et al. Risk of anaesthetic mortality in dogs and cats: an observational cohort study of 3546 cases. Vet Anaesth Analg. 2012;39:59–68. https://doi.org/10.1111/j.1467-2995.2011.00686.x.
10. Gil L, Redondo JI. Canine anaesthetic death in Spain: a multicentre prospective cohort study of 2012 cases. Vet Anaesth Analg. 2013;40:57–67. https://doi.org/10.1111/vaa.12059.
11. Johnston GM, Taylor PM, Ma a H, Wood JL. Confidential enquiry of perioperative equine fatalities (CEPEF-1): preliminary results. Equine Vet J. 1995;27:193–200. https://doi.org/10.1111/j.2042-3306.1995.tb03062.x.
12. Kennedy KC, Tamburello KR, Hardie RJ. Perioperative morbidity associated with ovariohysterectomy performed as part of a third-year veterinary surgical-training program. J Vet Med Educ. 2011;38:408–13. https://doi.org/10.3138/jvme.38.4.408.
13. Carter J, Story D. Veterinary and human anaesthesia: An overview of some parallels and contrasts. Anaesth Intensive Care. 2013;41:710–8.
14. Lienhart A, Auroy Y, Pequignot F, et al. Survey of anesthesia-related mortality in France. Anesthesiology. 2006;105:1087–97. https://doi.org/10.1097/01.sa.0000267083.27551.f4.
15. Dolinak D, Dowling G, Matshes E. Select autopsy topics. In: Dolinak D, Matshes EW, Lew EO, editors. Forensic pathology. Amsterdam: Elsevier Academic Press; 2005. p. 637–60.
16. Mouser PJ, Wilson JD. Fatal venous air embolism during anesthesia in an apparently healthy adult Chihuahua*. J Am Anim Hosp Assoc. 2015;51:176–9. https://doi.org/10.5326/JAAHA-MS-6118.
17. Walsh VP, Machon RG, Munday JS, Broome CJ. Suspected fatal venous air embolism during anaesthesia in a Pomeranian dog with pulmonary calcification. N Z Vet J. 2005;53:37–41. https://doi.org/10.1080/00480169.2005.36576.
18. Puerto DA, Brockman DJ, Lindquist C, Drobatz K. Surgical and nonsurgical management of and selected risk factors for spontaneous pneumothorax in dogs: 64 cases (1986–1999). J Am Vet Med Assoc. 2002;220:1670–4. https://doi.org/10.2460/javma.2002.220.1670.
19. Liu DT, Silverstein DC. Feline secondary spontaneous pneumothorax: a retrospective study of 16 cases (2000–2012). J Vet Emerg Crit Care. 2014;24:316–25. https://doi.org/10.1111/vec.12150.
20. Mooney ET, Rozanski EA, King RG, Sharp CR. Spontaneous pneumothorax in 35 cats (2001–2010). J Feline Med Surg. 2012;14:384–91. https://doi.org/10.1177/1098612X12439947.
21. Robinson WF, Robinson N. Cardiovascular System. In: Maxie MG, editor. Jubb, Kennedy, Palmer's pathology of domestic animals. St. Louis, MO: Elsevier; 2016. p. 62.

22. Saukko P, Knight B (2004) Deaths associated with surgical procedures. In: Knight's forensic pathology, 3rd. Taylor and Francis, Boca Raton, pp 480–487.

23. Doyle DJ, Mark PWS. Reflex bradycardia during surgery. Can J Aneaesthesia. 1990;37:219–22.

24. Schaller B. REVIEW Trigeminocardiac reflex A clinical phenomenon or a new. J Neurol. 2004;251:658–65. https://doi.org/10.1007/s00415-004-0458-4.

25. McIntyre RL, Hopper K, Epstein SE. Assessment of cardiopulmonary resuscitation in 121 dogs and 30 cats at a university teaching hospital (2009-2012). J Vet Emerg Crit Care. 2014;24:693–704.

26. Harper NJN, Dixon T, Dugue P, et al. Suspected Anaphylactic Reactions Associated with Anaesthesia. Anaesthesia. 2009;64:199–211. https://doi.org/10.1111/j.1365-2044.2008.05733.x.

27. Armitage-Chan E. Anaphylaxis and anaesthesia. Vet Anaesth Analg. 2010;37:306–10. https://doi.org/10.1111/j.1467-2995.2010.00551.x.

28. Waddell LS (2005) Systemic anaphylaxis. In: Ettinger SJ, Feldman EC (eds) Textbook of veterinary internal medicine, 6th ed. Elsevier Saunders, St. Louis, MO, pp 458–460.

29. Kroigaard M, Garvey LH, Gillberg L, et al. Scandinavian Clinical Practice Guidelines on the diagnosis, management and follow-up of anaphylaxis during anaesthesia. Acta Anaesthesiol Scand. 2007;51:655–70. https://doi.org/10.1111/j.1399-6576.2007.01313.x.

30. Shmuel DL, Cortes Y. Anaphylaxis in dogs and cats. J Vet Emerg Crit Care. 2013;23:377–94. https://doi.org/10.1111/vec.12066.

31. Dowling PM (2015) Anaphylaxis. In: Silverstein DC, Hopper K (eds) Small animal critical care medicine, 2nd ed. St. Louis, MO: Elsevier, pp 807–814.

32. Pumphrey RS, Roberts IS. Postmortem findings after fatal anaphylactic reactions. J Clin Pathol. 2000;53:273–6. https://doi.org/10.1136/jcp.53.4.273.

33. McLean-Tooke A, Goulding M, Bundell C, et al. Postmortem serum tryptase levels in anaphylactic and non-anaphylactic deaths. J Clin Pathol. 2013:1–5. https://doi.org/10.1136/jclinpath-2013-201769.

Animal Fighting

Rachel Touroo and Robert Reisman

7.1 Dogfighting

The origins of modern dogfighting date back to the mid-1800s in England [2]. Dogfighting supplanted bullbaiting which was outlawed in 1886 under the Humane Act [2]. Over the years, bulldogs were selectively bred to perform better in the "pit," producing the pit bull terrier.

Dogfighting can be divided into three main categories: street fighting, hobbyist fighting, and higher level, "professionals" [2, 3]. Street fighters are typically individuals engaged in impromptu matches. There are typically no rules and the dogs are not typically fought in a pit. These individuals may be involved in gang activities and tend to have no regard for the dogs. Whereas hobbyists may own one or more dogs and tend to participate in several organized fights a year. They may make a small

amount of money but are typically involved for the entertainment value. Professionals are dogfighters who make a substantial income breeding, selling, and fighting dogs as part of organized dogfighting. They tend to maintain a larger number of dogs or a larger "yard" than hobbyists. Professionals are well connected and may function on a national or even international level [2, 3].

7.1.1 The Dogs

In the USA, higher level (professional and hobbyist) fighting dogs are almost exclusively American Pit bull Terriers [2]. These dogs are known for their strength, courage, tenacity, intelligence, and loyalty; characteristics which have been exploited for the purposes of organized fighting. Additionally, these dogs have been selectively bred by dogfighters for strength in relation to size, specific bite style, agility and athleticism, aggression toward animals, lack of bite inhibition, display of no warning of attack, and gameness (the most desirable trait of a fighting dog). *Gameness* refers to a dog's willingness or desire to fight and continue to fight despite injury, pain, and fatigue [1, 2, 4–6]. Dogfighters at higher levels (professionals and hobbyists), typically utilize smaller more agile pit bulls rather than larger or bulkier pit bulls, which may guard their yard or serve as a pet (Fig. 7.1).

R. Touroo, D.V.M.
Forensic Sciences and Anti-Cruelty Projects, American Society for the Prevention of Cruelty to Animals, New York, NY, USA

Department of Small Animal Clinical Sciences, College of Veterinary Medicine, University of Florida, Gainesville, FL, USA
e-mail: Rachel.touroo@aspca.org

R. Reisman, D.V.M. (⊠)
Forensic Sciences and Anti-Cruelty Projects, American Society for the Prevention of Cruelty to Animals, New York, NY, USA
e-mail: robert.reisman@aspca.org

© Springer International Publishing AG 2018
J.W. Brooks (ed.), *Veterinary Forensic Pathology, Volume 2*,
https://doi.org/10.1007/978-3-319-67175-8_7

Fig. 7.1 On the left is a smaller more agile pit bull-type dog, which is commonly utilized by professional or hobbyist dogfighters as opposed to the larger and bulkier pit bull-type dog on the right

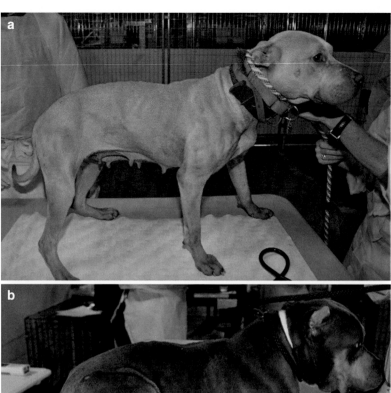
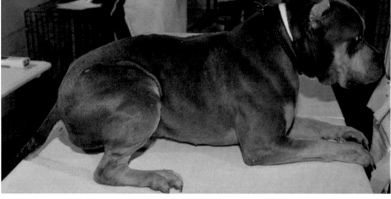

7.1.2 Housing

In rural environments, fighting dogs typically live their lives, from a few months of age at the end of a heavy chain in isolation, just out of the reach of neighboring dogs (done purposefully to increase aggression) (Fig. 7.2). Additional weights may be added to the dog's chain or around its neck, in an effort to increase muscle mass. These dogs typically have minimal shelter and are commonly not fed or watered daily, unless they are being prepared for a fight. These dogs do not have the opportunity to socialize with other animals or people and are only let off the chain to train or fight. At necropsy, alopecia and erythema of the ventral aspect of the neck may be observed on dogs that were previously tethered for prolonged periods of time.

In urban environments, dogs are frequently warehoused in crates stacked 3 high 24 h a day, in darkened basement rooms (Fig. 7.3), only leaving their crates to train or fight.

7.1.3 Training and Conditioning

Dogfighters at higher levels (professional and some hobbyist) typically will test and train their dogs as they develop, which is referred to as *schooling* [3]. Those not suitable for the pit will be culled. Typically around a year of age, a dog will begin being *rolled* [2, 3]. A roll should not cause severe injury, rather it is a short controlled fight utilized to weed out dogs that are unsuitable for fighting [1–4]. Around 2 years of age or younger, a dog will be subjected to a *game test* [2]. In a game test the dog

Fig. 7.2 Fighting dog in a rural environment

Fig. 7.3 In urban environments, dogs are frequently warehoused in stacked cages

is pitted against an older, more experienced, and sometimes larger opponent. The fight is interrupted at various points to observe how willing the dog is to continue [2]. A game test may also consist of rolling or fighting a dog until the point of complete exhaustion and then pitting it against a fresh or rested dog [3]. Dogfighters at lower levels (street fighters and some hobbyists) may not follow these protocols and may even take shortcuts. They may roll or test dogs at a younger age or may not roll or test dogs at all prior to a fight.

Dogfighters at higher levels (professional and some hobbyist) condition their dogs prior to a contracted fight, which also may be referred to as a *match*. This conditioning process is called a *keep* [1–7]. The keep is a rigorous diet and exercise program, which typically occurs approximately 4–6 weeks prior to a fight [2, 3]. Keeps are highly individualized and vary among dogfighters. The goals of the keep are to get the dog to their conditioned weight, as well as to increase the dogs' strength and endurance. The *conditioned weight* is the dogs' lowest possible weight without loss of muscle mass. The conditioned weight may also be referred to as the dogs pit weight or match weight [3]. Typically the weight at which a dog will be fought is agreed upon prior to the fight. Dogs in a keep will appear thin to underweight yet well-muscled. These dogs will typically be a three to four out of nine on the Purina Body Condition System. This is one reason the forensic veterinarian or pathologist should assign the dog a body condition score (BCS) at the time of necropsy.

A wide array of equipment and techniques are used to increase a dog's strength and endurance during a keep. These may be present at the crime scene. Various treadmills are often utilized such as slat mills, carpet mills, and converted or modified electric treadmills. Dogs are run for hours on treadmills often abrading their paw pads (Fig. 7.4). Therefore, the dogs' feet should be thoroughly examined for wear. However, paw protectors or salves may be used in an attempt to keep dogs' paw pads from becoming abraded. Additionally, the dogs may wear vests, to which weights may be added in increasing increments. Vests may result in axillary abrasions (Fig. 7.5).

Crime scene investigation may include swabs of blood spatter on training/conditioning equipment such as treadmills or a fighting pit. These samples are analyzed for DNA and can be compared to an individual dog(s)' DNA in order to potentially place the dog(s) on the treadmill or in a pit. Therefore, DNA samples should be obtained during the forensic necropsy. These can be buccal swabs, blood sample, or tissue sample such as muscle.

A variety of other devices are used during the keep to assist with the dog's prefight conditioning. These may be present at the crime scene. A *jenny or cat-mill* is a device that consists of a rotating central shaft with a long spoke to which the dog is attached [2, 3]. This is similar to a hot walker for horses but smaller in size. Weights and chains may be added to the jenny in order to increase resistance and a small animal such as a chicken may be hung in front of the dog in order to entice it to run [2, 3]. Other equipment that is commonly used includes *spring poles* or *jump poles* and *flirt poles*. A spring pole or jump pole will typically have a hide or other material suspended from a heavy spring or flexible pole [2]. This apparatus strengthens the dogs' hind

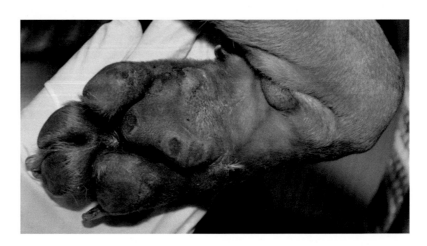

Fig. 7.4 Abraded paw pads from treadmill work

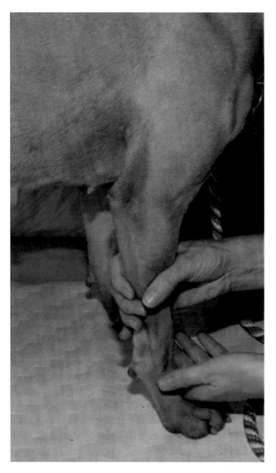

Fig. 7.5 Abrasion in right axillary region. The surrounding purple discoloration is likely due to the application of an antiseptic spray which was present at the scene

legs and jaws as it jumps up and hangs. Flirt poles consist of a pole with a lure attached to it [2, 3]. These are essentially giant "cat toys." The lure is run along the ground to entice the dog to chase it, increasing prey drive while providing exercise. Conditioning may also include *roadwork* or *waterwork*. Roadwork is where the dog is run alongside of a car, ATV, bicycle, or other vehicle [2]. Weights or drags may be attached to the dog to increase resistance. Waterwork consists of swimming dogs in various bodies of water, such as swimming in pools, rivers, or lakes [2].

Fighting dogs are commonly given dietary supplements and drugs [2, 3]. These may be present at the crime scene. Dietary supplements used during a keep commonly include, but are not limited to, vitamin B12, creatine, vitamin K, iron, liver extract, and amino acid supplements.

Dogs may also be given various drugs during the keep, just prior to a fight, or following a fight [2, 3]. Commonly utilized drugs include, but are not limited to, dexamethasone, anabolic steroids, epinephrine, furosemide, methamphetamines, antibiotics, and nonsteroidal anti-inflammatory drugs. The forensic veterinarian or pathologist should collect samples for toxicological analysis if a dog is thought to be in a keep or recently fought.

7.1.4 The Fight

Dogfighters at higher levels (professional and some hobbyist) tend to fight their dogs in a pit, which typically measures 14–20 feet square [2, 3]. The pit walls can be constructed out of a variety of materials but are more commonly plywood walls and the floor is typically covered with carpet to improve the dogs' traction. A pit that has been used will often have blood spatter on the carpet and walls. Crime scene investigation should include swabs of blood spatter on the pit walls and carpet, or collection of pieces of these items. These samples can be analyzed for DNA and compared to the DNA of an individual dog(s) to potentially place them in a fighting pit. Therefore, again the forensic veterinarian or pathologist should obtain DNA samples at the time of forensic necropsy.

At opposite ends of the pit on the floor are two diagonal lines. These lines are referred to as *scratch lines* [2, 3]. Dogs are placed behind these lines and released by their handlers, which is referred to as *scratching* [3]. There are various rules by which a dogfight maybe conducted. However, the most commonly utilized are the 19 Cajun rules. Typically males are only fought against other males and likewise, females are only fought against other females. Just prior to a fight, the dogs are weighed and washed, depending on the particular rules of the fight. The dogs must make weight, similar to a wrestling match, as they are to be fought at a previously agreed upon weight. Dogs are weighed by placing them on a hanging scale by using their harness or collar. The handlers then swap dogs and wash their opponent's dog under the supervision of the referee. Dogs maybe washed with water, milk, vinegar and baking soda, or other preparations. This is done in an effort to remove any potentially poisonous or caustic substance that may have been applied to the dogs' coat in order to harm their opponent.

During a fight, a dog may get its lip caught on its own canine tooth or its opponent's canine tooth. This is referred to as *fanged* [2, 3]. A pencil or antler is commonly used to *unfang* a dog during a fight typically resulting in a torn lip (Fig. 7.14). If two dogs need to be separated during a fight, a wedge-shaped stick, called a *break stick*, is used to pry a dog's mouth open [3]. It is inserted in the mouth at the level of the premolars and forcefully rotated. It is not uncommon to observe slab fractures on the buccal aspect of the premolars associated with the use of a break stick. Canine teeth may become fractured during a fight as dogs contact with each other with a great deal of force often head on. The forensic veterinarian or pathologist should thoroughly examine a dog's mouth and teeth during a forensic necropsy to identify trauma to the lips and dental fractures.

Fights can last for several hours. A fight ends when a handler concedes, a dog quits, or a dog dies. Typically dogs are not fought to the death. Losing a fight is often taken as a personal failure and an embarrassment by the owner causing the owner or a designated individual to kill the dog in a brutal manner. Following a fight, dogfighters may care for their dogs themselves or there may be a lay individual to whom dogs are sent for care. Dogfighters do not typically seek professional veterinary care, for fear of being reported to law enforcement. However, the authors have observed on occasion that veterinary care maybe sought out, especially if the dog is of high value. Dogfighters tend to have medical supplies on hand in order to provide care for dogs following a fight. These may include intravenous fluids and lines, suture, surgical staples, surgical glue or simply super glue, antiseptics, and other items. These items may be found at the crime scene. The forensic veterinarian or pathologist should document evidence of medical intervention, noting specifically, if possible, if it appears to have been done by a lay individual and not a veterinarian.

7.1.5 Wound Patterns

It was previously thought that the wound distribution from spontaneous dogfights mainly targeted the scruff, shoulder, and hocks of the dog. A study has demonstrated that this hypothesis may be inaccurate. Intarapanich et al. designed a study looking at the pattern of injuries associated with both spontaneous and organized dogfighting [7]. Spontaneous dogfights were selected for the study that best simulated organized dogfighting. Only dogs that were medium-sized, over 6 months of age, of the same sex, and similar weight, who engaged in a spontaneous dogfight with one other dog, were utilized and compared to a population of dogs seized by law enforcement in conjunction with a dogfighting criminal case [7]. This study found that the five most commonly injured areas associated with organized dogfighting, in decreasing order of frequency, were the front legs, dorsal and lateral aspects of the head, muzzle and oral mucosa, dorsal and lateral neck, and ventral neck and chest [7]. The most commonly injured areas associated with the selected spontaneous dogfights, in decreasing order of frequency, were the pinna followed by the dorsal and lateral neck as well as the front legs [7]. Looking closely at the percentage of dogs in each group that sustain injury, a clear difference was appreciated, as dogs engaged in organized dogfighting were much more likely to present with multiple injuries in these areas as opposed to those engaged in spontaneous dogfights where there were only single or limited injuries to these areas [7]. Therefore, when prevalence was taken into account along with the most commonly injured areas, there was a distinct difference in the pattern of injury between spontaneous and organized dogfighting [7]. The distinct distribution of organized dogfighting injuries was further validated by Miller et al., who found that scarring and wounds associated with organized dogfighting were primarily concentrated on the front legs, dorsal and lateral head, and muzzle and oral mucosa [8].

All wounds and scars and lack thereof should be thoroughly documented and photographed by the forensic veterinarian or pathologist at the time of necropsy. A "scar chart" or wound and scar diagram should be completed in order to demonstrate the distribution of the scars and/or wounds (Fig. 7.6 and 7.7). Different colors (red for wounds, blue for scars) should be utilized to differentiate scars from wounds, in order to infer repetitive injuries. Additionally, wounds may be in different stages of healing. Histopathology can be used to make

Skin (Wounds and Scars), Hair coat

Veterinarian: _Reisman_   Date: _6/24/12_

Law Enforcement Agency: NYPD   Case #: 437-11

Dog ID #: _A7L2 #4_   Distinguishing Marks/Comments: _____

Recent wounds – Red marks
Scars - Blue marks

Note: Ears removed from lateral views so that
wounds/scars under ears can be diagrammed.

ASPCA
WE ARE THEIR VOICE®

Fig. 7.6   This is the wound/scar chart for the dog on preceding page

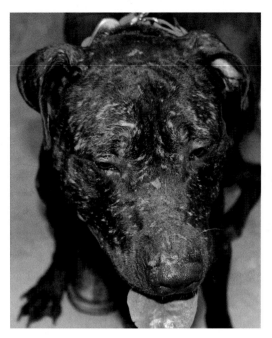

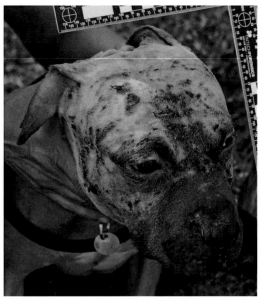

Fig. 7.9 Dog previously pictured in Fig. 7.8 after shaving

Fig. 7.7 Each white mark on the dog's face represents a bite wound injury. This dog has been bitten hundreds of times. Bite wound scars are easier to see on a dark-coated dog than a light-coated dog. This dog was part of a dog-fighting case from the Bronx New York where 50 dogs were kept in a small basement room. This dog's wound and scar diagram is depicted in Fig. 7.6

dog bite wounds, but rather that they are the result of some accidental injury such as the dog going through a window or being tangled in barbwire. The forensic veterinarian or pathologist conducting the necropsy must be confident in their recognition of dog bite wounds. Griffin (2001) described four classes of dog bite wounds [9].

Class 1	Partial-thickness laceration (without penetration of the dermis)
Class 2	Full-thickness laceration (with penetration of the dermis)
Class 3	Full-thickness puncture wound
Class 4	Full-thickness puncture or laceration with avulsion of underlying tissues and dead space

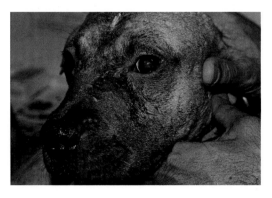

Fig. 7.8 Another dog from the Bronx dogfighting case. This photograph compared to the photograph in Fig. 7.9 shows the benefit of shaving the dog to see the full extent of wounds and scars

estimates of the age of particular lesions. It may also be helpful to shave affected areas in order to better visualize and photograph wounds (Fig. 7.8 and 7.9).

Alternative explanations are frequently offered by owners who deny that the wounds and scars are

In Munro and Munro (2008), dog bite wounds are described as penetrating injuries with a mixture of crushing and tearing [10]. Dog bite wounds often result in a classic "hole and tear" pattern, with the "hole" due to penetration of a canine tooth followed by "tearing" produced by headshaking [11]. On the surface relatively minor skin lesions, observed as individual or paired circular impressions or puncture wounds with or without bruising, may mask severe underlying tissue damage to muscle, vasculature, and possibly internal organs (Fig. 7.10) [10, 12]. Additionally, body walls may be breached

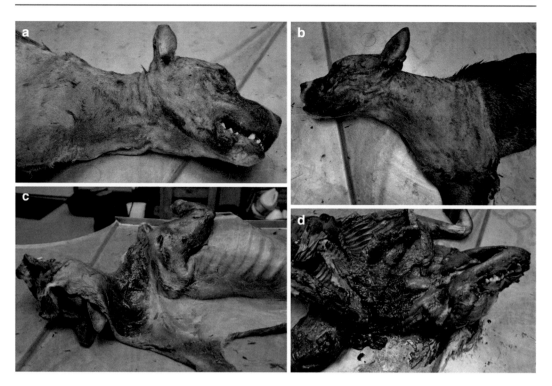

Fig. 7.10 This pit bull-type dog was known to have been killed by a housemate of similar breed and size

[10]. Since the superficial lesions may be difficult to detect, it is recommended that the body be shaved and then skinned at the time of necropsy. Furthermore, the distances between the impressions or puncture wounds can be measured and compared to that of known domestic canine intercanine distances [13]. Underlying bone fractures may also be present [10]. In the author's experience, fractures or puncture wounds may be observed more commonly on the radius and ulna as well as the skull (Fig. 7.11, 7.12 and 7.13). With this in mind, full body radiographs should be taken prior to commencing a forensic necropsy. Maceration may also be warranted following a necropsy, in order to further assess the skeleton for trauma.

As many fighting dogs tend to target the muzzle and buccal mucosa, it is not uncommon to observe thickening of the lips associated with the accumulation of scar tissue. Occasionally a portion of the lip or lips may be absent (Fig. 7.14). It is also not uncommon to observe traumatically avulsed gingiva.

In the past, it was common to observe fighting dogs with their ears cropped extremely short in an effort to decease the surface area on the head,

thereby, providing an opponent with less to grab onto and injure during a fight. However, this no longer appears to be as common as it once was.

Typically not all dogs in a dogfighting yard will have wounds and/or scars present. Some dogs may simply just be too young to have yet been rolled or fought. Others may have been rolled once or twice and then utilized for breeding purposes. Some may be maintained to act as a guard dog or may serve as a pet. Younger dogs or dogs that have just been rolled once or twice tend to have very little scarring or few wounds present. The wounds or scarring present on inexperienced or poor fighting dogs maybe be located on the hind legs or ventral abdomen, demonstrating that they either submitted or turned their back on their opponent. Additionally, it is common to find dogs at a dogfighting location with scars but without current or severe wounds. That does not mean that they were not badly injured previously (Fig. 7.15 and 7.16).

Another common finding among fighting dogs is infection with *Babesia gibsoni* a type of Babeisosis that is endemic in the American Pit

Fig. 7.11 Bite wound injuries that involved the left radius bone. Photo on the right is a close up showing fractures

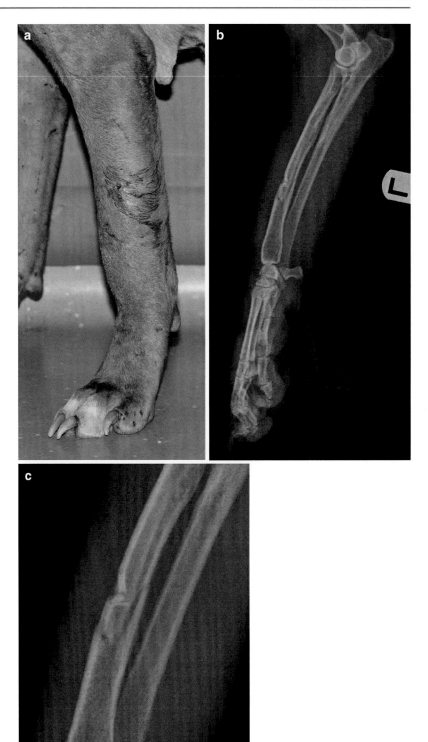

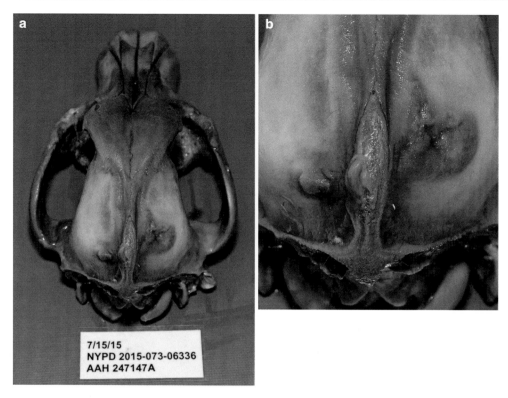

Fig. 7.12 Parietal bone bite wound injuries on either side of the sagittal crest. There is scar tissue formation. This indicates that these injuries have had time to heal and are at least weeks old and occurred at a time previous to the bite wound injuries that occurred during the fatal attack

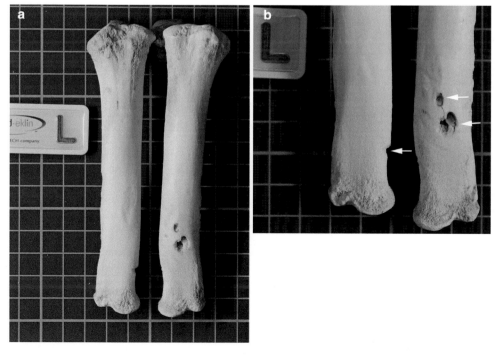

Fig. 7.13 This is the same dog as in previous photographs with skull bite wound injuries. Multiple bone punctures from bite wounds in lower right radius bone. A small defect in the left lower radius bone is also present

Fig. 7.14 This is a dog from the Missouri 500 dogfighting case. The dog has no lower lip and is missing portion on the upper lip

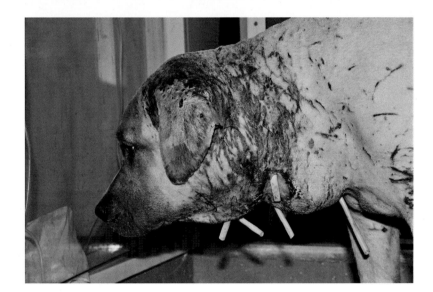

Fig. 7.15 Photo of a dog at the time shortly after the bite wounds occurred

bull population [14–16]. This protozoal, hemoparasitic disease can cause varying degrees of hemolytic anemia, splenomegaly, thrombocytopenia, lymphadenomegaly, anorexia, lethargy, fever, and vomiting [14]. Babesiosis can cause severe, life-threatening disease in some dogs, while others show few or no outward clinical signs [14]. Babesiosis is common among fighting pit bulls and seems to be more common among pit bulls in general [14–16]. *Babesiosis gibsoni* appears to be more commonly transmitted via dog bites but may also be transmitted via ticks, blood transfusions, and shared needles and

transmitted vertically from mothers to puppies [14]. Forensic veterinarians or pathologists should test for *Babesia* spp. at the time of necropsy.

7.2 Cockfighting

Cockfighting has existed for thousands of years and in many parts of the world. Dating back to ancient times in India, China, Persia, and other Eastern Countries [4, 17]. Cockfighting was introduced to Greece around 524 to 460 B.C [17].

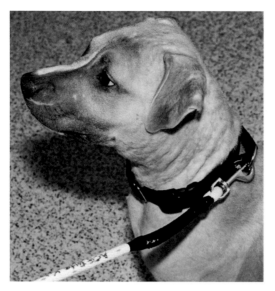

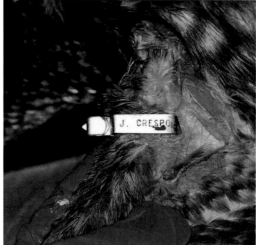

Fig. 7.17 Wing band

Fig. 7.16 The same dog 3 weeks later. Medical treatment was provided. It is common to find dogs at a dogfighting location with scars but without current or severe wounds. That does not mean that they were not badly injured previously

7.2.1 The Birds

There are many strains of game fowl utilized for cockfighting around the world. Hybrid strains related to Old English Game and sometimes Oriental Game fowl, such as the American Game (a breed not recognized by the American Poultry Association), are most commonly utilized in the USA.

Only roosters (male birds) are fought. Typically mature roosters (cocks) are fought. *Cock* refers to a male, 2 years of age or older, that has completed its first molt, [3]. Occasionally *stags* may be fought in what is referred to as a *stag derby*. A *stag* is a young rooster, who has not yet completed its first molt and is typically 18 months of age or younger [3]. Immature roosters (*cockerels*), less than a year of age, are not fought as they instinctively do not begin to fight until reaching sexual maturity. Female birds (hens) are also not fought but rather maintained for breeding purposes. Correspondingly, cockfighting operations tend to have more males than females present, as opposed to most breeding operations.

Fig. 7.18 Toe punch

Birds may be permanently or temporarily identified. Forms of identification may include leg bands, wing bands, toe punches, and removal of interdigital webbing (Fig. 7.17, 7.18 and 7.19).

7.2.2 Housing

Fighting roosters are typically either tethered out of reach of one another with access to a shelter, such as an A-frame or plastic barrel, or are individually

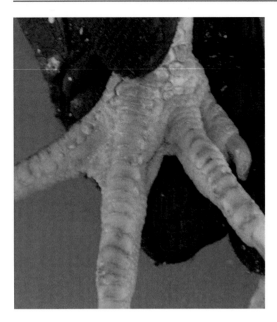

Fig. 7.19 Removal of webbing

housed in a variety of enclosures (Fig. 7.20). Additionally, if being utilized for breeding purposes a single male may be housed with one or more hens in a larger enclosure or *fly pen*.

7.2.3 Preparation for a Fight: Conditioning

Prior to a fight, most cocks and occasionally stags undergo a conditioning process, referred to as a *keep*. The keep is a rigorous diet and exercise program usually occurring 2 to 4 weeks prior to a fight. During the keep, roosters are frequently removed from the yard and placed in a separate coop or stall, called a *keep stall*, near the area where the training will take place (Fig. 7.21). *Fly pens* may also be utilized to exercise cocks during a keep (Fig.7.22). A fly pen may also contain a swing or trapeze used to build muscle strength and improve balance.

A variety of exercises such as running, flirting, flying, and leg pulls are used to condition roosters during a keep. Running involves running a cock back and forth on a bench or wheel, covered with carpet or other materials for trac-

tion, in an effort to build endurance [3]. Flirting involves tossing the bird into the air from one hand to the other continuously, causing the bird to continually flap its wings [3]. A deviation of this is referred to as forward flirts, where the bird is tossed into the air with both hands in a forward motion [3]. These exercises are done to enhance wing strength and balance. The flying exercise involves two cocks, one held on the ground, while the other is held approximately 5 feet away, off the ground and facing the other bird. The bird on the ground is released and flies toward the other bird. Before the birds come into contact, the bird being held up is raised. This process is repeated several times [3]. Leg pulls are performed by holding the cock by its tail feathers and body. The bird is moved toward a flat padded surface, reaching out and grabbing the surface, while the tail feathers are held creating resistance. The purpose of this exercise is to strengthen the leg muscles [3].

Sparring matches may also be conducted during or preceding the keep in order to determine how the rooster is progressing with their training and provide insight into the bird's fighting style. In order to prevent serious injuries, covers referred to as "sparring muffs" are placed over the cock's natural spurs. Hand sparring is a variation of this where a cull cock or dummy is held and used as a moving target. Stags will also be sparred in order to determine which stags will be culled and which will be tested further.

Roosters maybe put on a special diet during a keep and may also be given supplements or drugs during this period. Commonly utilized supplements include but are not limited to vitamin and mineral supplements, more commonly vitamin B-12, vitamin C, vitamin K, and iron. Amino acid supplements are also commonly utilized. Drugs commonly utilized include but are not limited to antibiotics, caffeine, strychnine (nux vomica), anabolic steroids, and methamphetamines. Therefore, the forensic veterinarian or pathologist should consider collecting samples for toxicological analysis if a bird was thought to be in a keep or recently fought.

Fig. 7.20 Roosters tethered to plastic barrels (**a**) and housed in individual wire enclosures (**b**)

Fig. 7.21 Keep stalls

7.2.4 Preparation for a Fight: Alterations

Game cocks will typically have their comb, wattles, and earlobes removed (Fig. 7.23 and 7.24). This is done to prevent injury during the fight as well as reduce the bird's overall weight. Excessive bleeding of the head may impair the bird's sight, putting it at a disadvantage in the pit. Similarly birds are matched by weight; therefore, any

decease in weight without loss of muscle mass may put the bird at an advantage in the pit.

Game cocks will also have one or both of their natural spurs cut down to approximately 1 cm in length (Fig. 7.25, 7.26 and 7.27). This is done so that a gaff or knife can be attached to the bird's leg. If gaffs are being utilized both spurs will be cut down prior to a fight. However, if knives are being utilized, only one spur will be cut down. To cut a spur to this length, the bone must be cut

Fig. 7.22 Fly pens

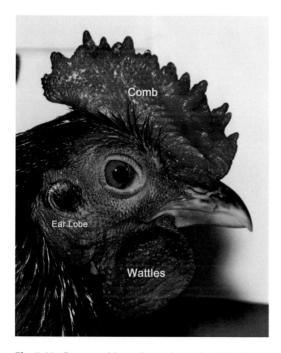

Fig. 7.23 Rooster with comb, wattles, and earlobes intact

Fig. 7.24 Rooster with comb, wattles, and earlobes removed

(Fig. 7.27). These implements are attached to the bird's leg, anchored by the remaining portion of the natural spur. Occasionally, this remaining portion of the spur may be further altered to allow for a specific implement to be attached. Therefore,

Fig. 7.25 Natural, unaltered mature spur

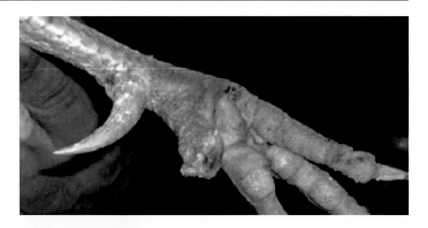

Fig. 7.26 Undeveloped spur—Cockerel or stag

narrowing of the tip of the remaining spur may be observed in correlation with the specific implement being utilized (Fig. 7.28). Game cocks may also be fought with their natural spurs, which is referred to as *naked heeled* fighting. On occasion, the natural spurs may even be sharpened (Fig. 7.29).

Knives and gaffs (Fig. 7.30, 7.31 and 7.32) are attached to a bird just prior to a fight, in a process referred to as *heeling*. Commonly the remaining spur is wrapped in moleskin, and the gaff or knife is attached with leather straps and wax string. If an acrylic gaff is being utilized, wax and bandage tape may be used to attach the gaff (Fig. 7.33).

Prior to a fight, roosters may also have certain feathers removed or trimmed, referred to

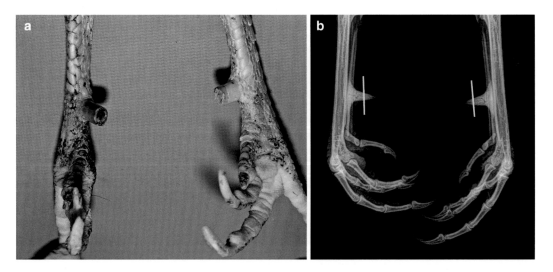

Fig. 7.27 Spurs cut short for the use with a gaff. This removes bone as well

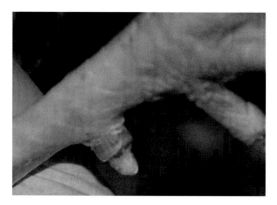

Fig. 7.28 Spur cut short with tip narrowed

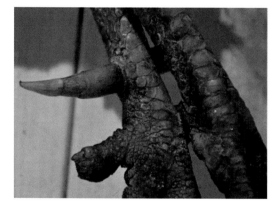

Fig. 7.29 Sharpened spurs

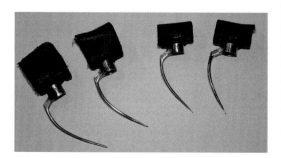

Fig. 7.30 Metal gaff

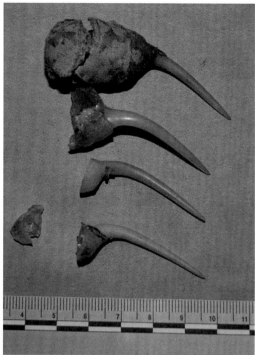

Fig. 7.31 Acrylic gaff

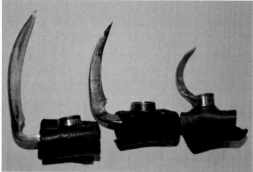

Fig. 7.32 Knives

7.2.5 The Fight

as *trimming out*. This is done with the intent to decrease the bird's weight as well as reduce the likelihood of a bird overheating during a fight. This may involve shortening the long tail feathers and primary wing feathers and removal or shortening of feathers on the body and thighs (Fig. 7.34).

The cockfighting season usually runs from late November through the beginning of July as birds are not fought during molting, which occurs between late July and mid-November. There are four main types of cockfights: The Main, Battle Royal, Welsh Main, and Derby. The Main consists of two parties who agree to fight a number of cocks, matched by weight, in an odd number of

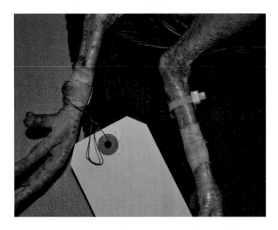

Fig. 7.33 Remaining spurs wrapped in bandage tape, following a fight with acrylic gaffs

battles with the majority of victories deciding the winner [3]. The Battle Royal involves a number of birds fighting at the same time, with the winner being the last bird standing [3]. The Welsh Main is comprised of eight pairs of cocks with the winners being fought repeatedly until there is one bird remaining [3]. A Derby is one of the most common type of fights in the USA. A Derby is a large event, where a number of individuals pay an entry fee to enter a number of birds [3]. The individual winning the most fights is the winner, collecting the purse comprised of the entry fees [3]. The purse may also be divided among those placing the highest [3].

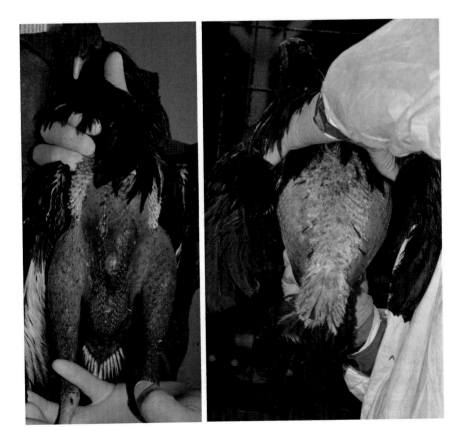

Fig. 7.34 Cock trimmed out

Fig. 7.35 Containers utilized to transport birds to a fight

Birds are transported to fights in a variety of containers, such as bags, single wooden carriers, or wooden boxes with multiple compartments (Fig. 7.35). Prior to a fight, birds are weighed and matched against a bird of equal (within a few ounces) weight. A game cock typically weighs between 4 and 6 pounds. Birds are fought in a pit which varies in shape from round to rectangular to square and can be constructed out of a variety of materials. The pit floor will vary as well, from dirt to carpet to shavings.

The rules of a fight are complex and vary from pit to pit. Before birds are fought, they are examined by the referee who will determine if the bird is eligible to fight. The fight is initiated with *billing*. Billing is done with the intention of provoking the birds. The handlers will restrain their birds while allowing them to peck at each other. The birds are then separated by a distance and simultaneously released. A fight is over when a bird either leaves the pit, dies, a handler concedes, or a bird fails to attack. If a fight has gone on for too long or if both birds fail to attack, the fight may be moved to a *drag pit*, which is a smaller pit in addition to the main pit.

7.2.6 Wound Patterns

Roosters that have been fought have wounds that are primarily located on the head [18]. Injured tissue can be edematous and contused, especially periorbitally [18]. Wounds can also be present on the lateral and ventral aspects of the body and the legs (Fig. 7.36 and 7.37).

Wounds are due to either blunt trauma or sharp trauma. Blunt force injury can be caused by a bird's beak, as it pecks and pulls. Such injuries have been reported to create "hour-glass-like" lesion [19]. Abrasions maybe caused by a bird's claws, natural spurs or acrylic gaffs (Figs. 7.37 and 7.38). Natural spurs and acrylic gaffs may also cause puncture wounds. Sharp force injuries, such as stab or incised wounds are caused by gaffs or knives.

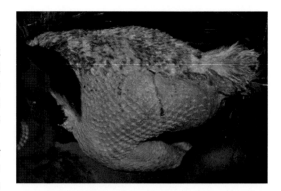

Fig. 7.38 Abrasions on the left dorsolateral back/saddle. This bird was fought with acrylic gaffs

Fig. 7.36 Fighting wounds on the head

Fig. 7.39 Scarring and recent wounds on the head

Occasionally, if a bird survives a fight, healing wounds or scarring maybe observed (Fig. 7.39). This is dependent on the style of fighting as the use of steel gaffs or knives increases the lethality of the fight [4].

It is the author's experience that birds maintained for fighting purposes are often infected with a variety of respiratory diseases including but not limited to mycoplasma, infectious laryngotracheitis, infectious bronchitis virus, and the pox virus. It may be necessary for the forensic veterinarian or pathologist to test for such disease processes at the time of necropsy.

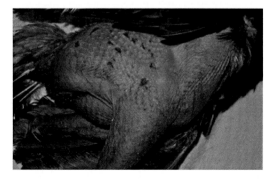

Fig. 7.37 Abrasions on lateral aspect of the right thigh. This bird was fought with acrylic gaffs

Conclusions

Animal fighting, such as organized dogfighting and cockfighting, represent intentional, severe abuse of animals. Although, dogfighting and cockfighting are illegal in all 50 states and the federal Animal Welfare Act prohibits animal fighting ventures (section 2156), they are still pervasive throughout the USA. It is critical for forensic veterinarians and pathologists to have a well-rounded understanding of dogfighting and cockfighting in order to properly recognize, document, and interpret evidence found at the scene as well as on the animal.

It is not uncommon for animals involved in animal fighting to die. Therefore the forensic veterinarian or pathologist may be called upon to perform a forensic necropsy in order to determine and document injuries and cause of death. They may also be required to provide testimony at trial regarding whether or not the pattern of injuries is consistent with or suggestive of organized animal fighting and address the non-animal medical evidence that may be present on scene.

References

1. Sinclair L, Merck M, Lockwood R. Dogfighting and cockfighting. In: Forensic investigation of animal cruelty: a guide for veterinary and law enforcement professionals. Washington, DC: Humane Society Press; 2006. p. 189–95.
2. Lockwood R. Dogfighting Toolkit for law enforcement; 2011.
3. Christiansen S, Dantzler F, Goodwin J, et al. The Final Round, A Law Enforcement Primer for the Investigation of Cockfighting and Dogfighting: The Humane Society of the United States.
4. Lockwood R. Animal fighting. In: Miller L, Zawistowski S, editors. Shelter medicine for veterinarians and staff. 2nd ed. Ames, IA: Wiley-Blackwell; 2013. p. 441–52.
5. Merck M. Animal fighting. In: Merck M, editor. Veterinary forensics: animal cruelty investigations. 2nd ed. Ames, IA: Wiley-Blackwell; 2013. p. 243–54.
6. Gibson H. Detailed discussion of dog fighting. Michigan State University College of Law: Animal Legal and Historical Center; 2005.
7. Intarapanich N, Touroo R, Rozanski E, et al. Characterization and comparison of injuries caused by spontaneous versus organized dogfighting. J Am Vet Med Assoc. 2016. https://doi.org/10.1111/1556-4029.13074.
8. Miller K, Touroo R, Spain C, et al. Relationship between scarring and dog aggression in pit bull-type dogs involved in organized dogfighting. Animals. 2016;6:72.
9. Griffin GM, Holt DE. Dog-bite wounds: bacteriology and treatment outcome in 37 cases. J Am An Hosp Assoc. 2001;37:453–60.
10. Munro HM, Munro R. Animal abuse and unlawful killing: forensic veterinary pathology. Elsevier Health Sciences: London; 2008.
11. Bury D, Langlois N, Byard RW. Animal-related fatalities—Part I: Characteristic autopsy findings and variable causes of death associated with blunt and sharp trauma. J Forensic Sci. 2012;57:370–4.
12. Ressel L, Hetzel U, Ricci E. Blunt force trauma in veterinary forensic pathology. Vet Pathol. 2016;53:941–61.
13. Murmann DC, Brumit PC, Schrader BA, et al. A comparison of animal jaws and bite mark patterns. J Forensic Sci. 2006;51:846–60.
14. Yeagley TJ, Reichard MV, Hempstead JE, et al. Detection of Babesia gibsoni and the canine small Babesia 'Spanish isolate' in blood samples obtained from dogs confiscated from dogfighting operations. J Am Vet Med Assoc. 2009;235:535–9.
15. Birkenheuer AJ, Correa MT, Levy MG, et al. Geographic distribution of babesiosis among dogs in the United States and association with dog bites: 150 cases (2000–2003). J Am Vet Med Assoc. 2005;227:942–7.
16. Cannon SH, Levy JK, Kirk SK, et al. Infectious diseases in dogs rescued during dogfighting investigations. Vet J. 2016;211:64–9.
17. Britannica TEoE. cockfighting: Encyclopædia Britannica, Inc., 2016.
18. Dinnage J, Bollen K, Giacoppo S. Animal fighting. In: Miller L, Zawistowski S, editors. Shelter medicine for veterinarians and staff. 1st ed. Blackwell Pub.: Ames, IA; 2004.
19. Roll P, Rous F. Injuries by chicken bills: characteristic wound morphology. Forensic Sci Int. 1991;52:5.

Animal Sexual Abuse Investigations

8

Adam W. Stern

8.1   Introduction

The legal definition of animal sexual abuse (ASA) will vary between jurisdictions. For the purpose of this chapter, we will consider all forms of ASA as ASA is not limited to the penetration of an animal by the human penis. Some examples of ASA include fondling of an animal's genitalia, penetration of the vagina or anus of an animal by a human penis, penetration of the vagina or anus of an animal with a foreign object, oral-genital contact (either human to animal or animal to human), masturbation of an animal by a human, and human masturbation and/or ejaculation on an animal [1]. Other types of traumatic injuries such as burns, incised wounds, or blunt force trauma to the genitalia or injuries to the nipples may also be encountered.

In some instances, injuries due to sexual assault may be accompanied by other nonsexual injuries such as blunt force trauma, sharp force trauma, and asphyxia. These accompanying injuries may be due to restraining the animal, may be part of the assailant's sexual repertoire, or may be unrelated non-accidental injuries (Fig. 8.1). The veterinarian may be asked to review a video depicting the sexual acts performed on the animal.

If such a video depicts an animal victim to be minimally responsive or non-responsive during these actions, this is suggestive that the animal may have been restrained by other non-forceful methods of restraint such as the use of sedatives/tranquilizers or may have been behaviorally conditioned to accept this behavior [1].

ASA is known in the scientific literature by other terms such as bestiality and zoophilia. These terms are used to describe the motives and actions of the human perpetrator, whereas the use of the term ASA is specific to the animal. ASA is the preferred term in veterinary forensics. There is a wide spectrum of injuries reported in animals that have been sexually abused and in some instances, animal victims of sexual abuse remain physically unharmed; therefore, even animals without physical injuries can still be the victim of sexual abuse.

There are a small number of case reports regarding ASA in the scientific literature. Due to the small number of reports, the true incidence of animal sexual abuse is not known. In a recent survey of risk factors for human penile cancer, a total of 171 out of 492 individuals reported to have had sex with animals [2]. Numerous animal species have been reported to be sexually abused including the dog, cat, horse, bovid, sheep, goat, rabbit, and chicken [1–9]. The dog is the most commonly reported victim of ASA [10], whereas in the report by Zequi et al., sex with a mare was most commonly reported [2].

A.W. Stern, DVM, CMI-IV, CFC, DACVP (✉)
Veterinary Diagnostic Laboratory,
University of Illinois, Urbana, IL 61802, USA
e-mail: awstern@illinois.edu

© Springer International Publishing AG 2018
J.W. Brooks (ed.), *Veterinary Forensic Pathology, Volume 2*,
https://doi.org/10.1007/978-3-319-67175-8_8

Fig. 8.1 Bruising of the
ventral abdomen from
possible restraint of the
dog during insertion of a
foreign body in the anus
(Photo courtesy of Dr.
Nancy Bradley,
Midwestern University)

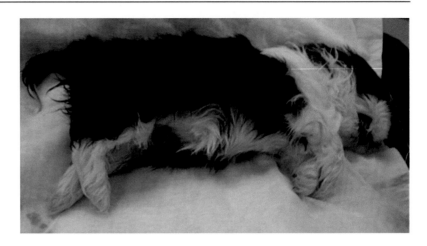

8.2 The Sexual Assault Examination

Similar to other cases of animal abuse, a detailed history should be taken and reviewed prior to beginning the forensic examination. Unlike human sexual assault cases where law enforcement will take a detailed history, cases histories are often taken by the veterinarian. Additionally, in cases of animal sexual assault, the victim is unable to provide a verbal report of the event, and the investigator must rely on the testimony of human witnesses. After obtaining a detailed history, a sexual assault examination should be performed including an alternate light source (ALS) examination, trace evidence collection, radiological imaging studies, and a forensic clinical examination or forensic necropsy. Collection of trace evidence should be performed whenever a sexual component is suspected.

The sexual assault examination of the animal should be detailed and thorough similar to other forensic examinations as injuries and trace evidence may be found anywhere on or in the animal's body. Examination findings should be recorded in the forensic report. Additional documentation including photographs and video recordings may be warranted and recommended. Examination findings including negative findings may be used at a later date such as in the defense of a suspected perpetrator.

The examining veterinarian and veterinary technical staff should wear powder-free gloves during the examination in order to avoid introducing contaminating materials. Additionally, given that human material may be encountered during the examination, the use of personal protective equipment such as safety eyewear, mask, gloves, and lab coat are required as exposure to sexually transmitted diseases and human blood-borne pathogens are a potential risk.

Many of the steps taken during the forensic necropsy in cases of ASA are similar to those performed during the forensic clinical examination. Examination of the sexual abuse victim should be begin with an alternate light source (ALS) examination in order to identify trace evidence such as human biological material. When performing an ALS examination, it should be performed in a systematic pattern covering the entire body. The use of an ALS during the forensic examination can enhance the contrast of biologic evidence against the background or cause the evidence to fluoresce. In order to clearly observe the photoluminescence effect of biologic substances, the examiner may need to wear appropriate filters or goggles which will filter out strong excitation wavelengths [11]. The accuracy of the Wood's lamp (a type of ALS) for identification of semen is questionable and other types of ALS have been reported to be more useful during sexual assault examinations of humans [12, 13]. In veterinary medicine, a Wood's lamp is the most commonly available ALS, and although there are concerns regarding accuracy and sensitivity, the use of a Wood's lamp in the absence of any other available ALS is recommended. The author knows of a single case in which a Wood's lamp was successful in identifying human semen on a dog. Regardless of the ALS utilized, identification of a positive stain should prompt further laboratory analysis on the sample of interest.

Biological evidence may be found anywhere on the animal, not only around the anus and vagina. For example, semen may be found at areas distant from the site of sexual contact because an assailant may transfer evidence to a distant site on the animal's body by touching themselves and subsequently touching the animal. Biologic evidence can be lost during normal grooming behavior by the animal. If suspect biological evidence is identified on the fur, the suspect material should be photographed and collected by snipping fur with sterile scissors or swabbing the sample. These samples should be documented (including the use of chain of custody forms), labeled and turned over to the investigating law enforcement agency. The use of sexual assault evidence collection kits for evidence collection is recommended, and these kits can be purchased from commercial sources or may be obtained from a human hospital emergency department. The general sexual assault evidence collection procedure will be subsequently described.

After the collection of trace evidence samples, full-body radiographs or a computerized tomography scan (CT) can be performed. When reviewing the radiographs or CT images, abnormalities that might be encountered in ASA victims include cavity gas accumulation, retained foreign bodies, and fractures (such as base of the tail).

8.2.1 The Perianal Examination

Regardless of the sex of the animal victim, examination of the anus and perianal region for evidence of trauma should be performed. A diagram using the face of a clock should be used as a frame of reference when describing any abnormalities to the anus. Points of reference for the anus include the anal glands located at the 4 o'clock and 8 o'clock positions. The distance between the identified lesion(s) and anus should be measured.

Documented injuries to the anus, rectum, and perianal region include insertion of foreign objects, colonic perforation, stab wounds, bruising (Fig. 8.2), and anal tears. Anal dilation has been reported in animal victims of sexually abuse [8, 14, 15]. The anal dilation is the result of trauma to the anal sphincter. Dilation of the anus is commonly observed during the postmortem examination in nonsexually abused animals, and this should not be confused with anal dilation as an antemortem finding. Rectal prolapse can occur secondary to rectal and colonic injuries as a result of anal penetration. In humans, radiating perianal lacerations without rectal mucosa trauma rule out the passage of hard fecal material and are supportive of an object being pushed into the anus from outside.

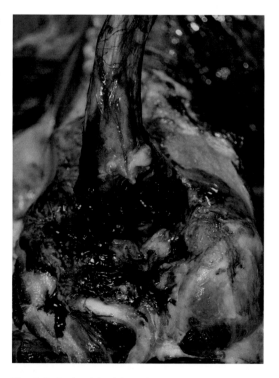

Fig. 8.2 Perianal bruising of a dog that was sexually abused (Photo courtesy of Dr. Doris Miller, University of Georgia)

Table 8.1 Steps used to perform a vaginal and anal wash

1. Insert a vaginal speculum into the vagina or anoscope into the anus
2. Infuse approximately 10–15 mL of sterile saline using a disposable plastic pipette
3. Aspirate the infuse fluid
4. Reinfuse the fluid
5. Re-aspirate the fluid
6. Place the aspirated fluid into a clean glass tube

In additional to gross examination of the anus and perianal region, a rectal wash should be performed (Table 8.1), and the fluid should be collected from both male and female animals [1]. The sample of fluid collected can be submitted for further analysis to a human forensic laboratory for microscopic examination for the presence of spermatozoa and other forensic testing for seminal fluid and spermicides [1, 7]. If the rectum contains feces, a fecal sample should be collected and can be analyzed for blood and gastrointestinal parasites [7]. Fecal analysis and perianal examination are important to rule out or contextualize the perineal trauma as the defense may suggest self-trauma due to parasitism, the presence of a rectal mass, impacted anal sacs, or anal sacculitis.

8.2.2 The Vaginal Examination

A diagram using the face of a clock should be used as a frame of reference when describing any trauma to the vagina. As points of reference, the dorsal-most aspect of the vagina would be at the 12 o'clock position, the ventral-most aspect of the vagina would be at the 6 o'clock position.

Injuries of the female reproductive tract directly related to sexual abuse include vaginal prolapse, uterine and cervical tears, vaginal stricture, scarring of the reproductive tract, uterine hemorrhage, and the presence of foreign bodies (intrauterine, intracervical, or vaginal). Vaginitis has been reported in cases of repeated sexual abuse [7]. Objects inserted in the vaginal vault may be forced through the uterine stump into the peritoneal cavity in animals that have previously been spayed. Foreign objects have

been recovered from the female reproductive tract including candles and sticks. In humans, trauma to the vagina including abrasions and lacerations occur between the 3 o'clock and 9 o'clock positions resulting from digital and attempted penile penetration. Similar lesions have been observed in the dog.

In additional to gross examination of the vagina, a vaginal wash should be performed and the fluid should be collected as previously described in Table 8.1 [1]. Testing performed is similar to that for rectal washes.

8.2.3 The Penile and Scrotal Examination

The penis and external genitalia of male victims of sexual abuse should be examined. Examination of the penis and genitalia may identify evidence of traumatic injury in the form of hemorrhage and/or abrasions. If oral sex is performed on the male animal, it is theoretically possible that teeth marks may be identified on the penis.

In male dogs that have been castrated using rubber bands (band castration), the scrotum may be swollen and painful or infarcted depending on the time frame for placement of the band (Fig. 8.3). The elastic band or other material (such as a string) used to perform the procedure may be recovered from the victim and should be collected as evidence (Fig. 8.4). Injuries that may be observed in cases of traumatic castrations (such as cutting of

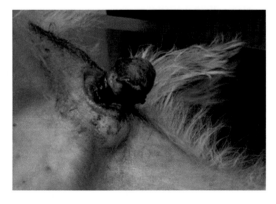

Fig. 8.3 Dog at home castration with testicular infarction

Fig. 8.4 Rubber band used to perform at home castration in Fig. 8.3

the scrotum with a knife) can result in massive hemorrhage [8].

Swabs of the penis should be obtained as human DNA may be recovered from these samples. DNA recovery may be useful if oral sex was performed on the animal or if the animal had been used to penetrate a human.

8.2.4 The Negative Examination

In cases of examination of a potential victim of animal sexual assault, the veterinarian has a number of roles including examination of the animal, collection of evidence from the animal victim, documentation of the injuries, and if the animal is alive, treatment of the animal.

Regardless of whether or not there is evidence of any significant findings, a complete sexual assault examination including trace evidence collection should be performed if a sexual component is reported or suspected. In some cases, the examination of a sexually abused animal will result in "negative" findings, as some sexually abused animals will have a lack of physical injuries. It should be noted that the collection of evidence can not only be useful to prosecute a potential suspect; it can also be used to exonerate a wrongly accused person. When presented with a potential sexually abused animal, it is also important to consider nonsexual causes for the observed injuries/lesions. Some urogenital and

perianal lesions that may mimic lesions of ASA include transmissible venereal tumors, perianal fistulas, bite wounds, and vaginal tears from copulation with a larger animal.

8.3 Trace Evidence Collection

In many instances spermatozoa may not recovered in cases of ASA. Reasons for lack of recovery include the use of a condom by the perpetrator, aspermia due to testicular disease, aspermia due to vasectomy, lack of ejaculation by the perpetrator, actions by a female perpetrator, or the use of a foreign object [1].

As previously discussed, specimens should be collected whenever ASA was suspected to have occurred. Failure to collect appropriate samples can severely hinder the possibility of prosecuting the case in court. It is important to remember that in some instances, sexual assault may have occurred in the absence of physical injuries. Sample collection should be performed for both female and male victims.

Swabs should always be collected in pairs and in duplicates. This duplicate sampling will provide for sufficient material to allow the defense to send samples to another laboratory for testing if necessary. After collection of swabs from any part of the body, swabs should be placed in a paper envelope where they can aerate and dry. Do not store swabs within plastic containers or bags. Swabs should be taken from standard locations such as the oral cavity, anus, vagina, perianal region, and penis. Swabs should also be taken from any suspicious area that is identified during the ALS examination.

If the animal is standing, vaginal swabs should be taken before anal swabs in order to prevent contamination of the vagina. Swabs can be rolled across clean microscope slides to evaluate for spermatozoa. If spermatozoa are observed, additional staining (Baecchi stain, Kernechtrot-Picroindigocarmine stain) of the sample can be performed to further characterize the spermatozoa (Fig. 8.5). For example, spermatozoa of dog and human have different morphology [16]. Currently, the use of field test kits for compounds identified

Fig. 8.5 (**a**) Human
spermatozoa
(Kernechtrot-
Picroindigocarmine
Stain). Note the dark
staining of the post-
acrosomal region (Photo
courtesy of Kevin Zeeb,
Illinois State Police).
(**b**) Canine spermatozoa.
Note the subtle pale ban
within the head of the
spermatozoa. (Photo
courtesy of Dr. Reena
Roy and Dr. Jason
Brooks, The
Pennsylvania State
University)

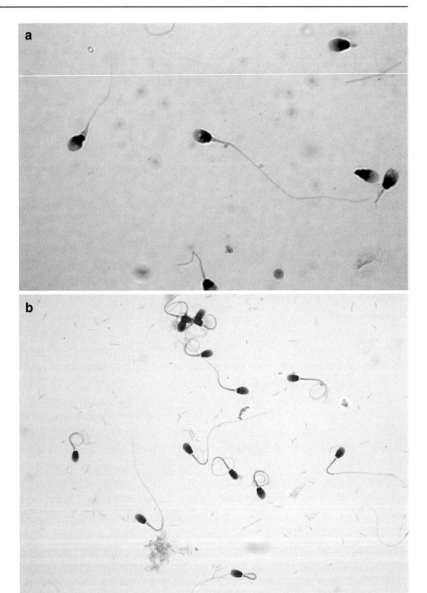

within human seminal fluid (such as semenogelin, prostatic acid phosphatase) should not be performed as they are not validated for use in animals. Identification of semenogelin shows promise as it has not been identified with canine seminal fluid [17]. After collection of anal and vaginal swabs, a rectal and vaginal wash can be performed as previously described. The wash samples can be saved in clean glass or plastic tubes.

Conclusion

ASA is uncommonly encountered in everyday practice; however, the forensic veterinarian should be aware of the steps needed to perform a sexual assault examination on an animal and be aware of possible lesions that may be encountered. Data collected from the forensic examination including interpretation of the injuries must be adequately documented

Table 8.2 List of evaluation techniques to be used during the sexual assault examination of an animal

Sexual assault examination
Alternative light source examination
Swab fluorescent areas for biologic evidence
Trace evidence collection
Male and female
• Perianal region swabs
• Oral cavity swabs
• Anal swabs
• Anal flush
Female
• Vaginal swabs
• Vaginal wash
Male
• Penile swabs
Complete forensic examination
• Imaging studies are recommended

and are critical for producing evidence that is admissible in court. A list of evaluation techniques to be used during the sexual assault examination of an animal is provided (Table 8.2). A sexual assault examination should be performed in any case in which sexual assault of an animal is suspected. In addition, during the sexual assault examination, the forensic veterinarian should evaluate the animal for other types of trauma. Throughout the examination, it is important to also evaluate for other causes of the observed injuries/lesions such as natural disease.

In some instances, information collected from the scene of the crime may be available and should be considered along with any facts received from witness statements. The investigator is advised to consider all the facts before rendering a diagnosis of ASA as several other disease processes can mimic some of the findings similar to those found in an animal that was sexually abused.

References

1. Stern AW, Smith-Blackmore M. Veterinary forensic pathology of animal sexual abuse. Vet Pathol. 2016;53:1057–66.
2. Zequi S, Guimaraes G, da Fonseca F, et al. Sex with animals (SWA): behavioral characteristics and possible association with penile cancer. A multicenter study. J Sex Med. 2012;9:1860–7.
3. Blevins RO. A case of severe anal injury in an adolescent male due to bestial sexual experimentation. J Forensic Legal Med. 2009;16:403–6.
4. DeGiorio F, Polacco M, Rossi R, Lodise M, Rainio J. Fatal blunt injuries possibly resulting from sexual abuse of a calf: a case report. Med Sci Law. 2009;49:307–10.
5. Earls C, Lalumiere ML. A case study of preferential bestiality. Arch Sex Bahav. 2009;38:605–9.
6. Imbschweiler I, Kummerfield M, Gerhard M, Pfeiffer I, Wohlsein P. Animal sexual abuse in a female sheep. Vet J. 2009;182:481–3.
7. Merck M, Miller DM. Veterinary forensics: animal cruelty investigations. 2nd ed. Wiley: Ames; 2013.
8. Munro HMC, Thursfield MV. 'Battered pets': sexual abuse. J Small Anim Pract. 2001;42:333–7.
9. Munro R, Munro HMC. Animal abuse and unlawful killing: forensic veterinary pathology. Edinburgh: Elsevier; 2008.
10. Beetz AM. Bestiality and zoophilia: a discussion of sexual contact with animals. In: Ascione FR, editor. The international handbook of animal abuse and cruelty: theory, research, and application. West Lafayette, IN: Purdue University Press; 2008. p. 201–20.
11. Stoilovic M. Detection of semen and blood stains using polilight as a light source. Forensic Sci Int. 1991;51:289–96.
12. Eldredge K, Huggins E, Pugh LC. Alternate light sources in sexual assault examinations: an evidence-based practice project. J Forensic Nurs. 2012;8:39–44.
13. Nelson DG, Santucci K. An alternate light source to detect semen. Acad Emerg Med. 2002;9:1045–8.
14. Bradley N, Rasile K. Recognition and management of animal sexual abuse. Clin Brief. 2014:73–5.
15. Bradley N, Rasile K. Addressing animal sexual abuse. Clin Brief. 2014;4:77.
16. Schudel D. Screening for canine spermatozoa. Sci Justice. 2001;41:117–9.
17. Stern AW, Lanka S. Evaluation of human semenogelin membrane strop test for species cross-reactivity in dogs. Vet Pathol. 2016;53:1095–8.

Ritualistic Animal Killing

9

Sean P. McDonough and Brian Holoyda

9.1 Introduction

Necropsy of mutilated, dismembered, or decapitated remains presents the veterinary pathologist with a unique challenge. First, such cases are often attributed to "occult" or "satanic" animal sacrifice, but these terms have no standard definition, and their use may obscure the true motivation of the perpetrator [1–3]. Second, ritualistic animal slaughter and sacrifice are legally protected components of worship and daily life for practitioners of many major and minor belief systems [4]. Third, predation and postmortem scavenging can be mistaken for animal sacrifice [5]. Improper disposal of viscera from legally taken game animals can also raise concern. Hence, the veterinary pathologist performing a necropsy on an animal with unusual injuries must interpret the postmortem findings in light of the circumstances surrounding the animal's death, have knowledge of practices around religious animal slaughter and animal sacrifice, and have some insight into the psychological and potential criminal motives for these acts.

The lack of standardized definitions of ritualistic animal sacrifice and slaughter has hindered the evaluation of these cases. A ritual is a series of actions performed in a prescribed order. Rituals may involve the systematic use of symbols, rites, emblems, insignia, or sacred objects. Most religions incorporate rituals in the process of worship and other activities, such that ritualistic animal killing may represent a sacrifice to a deity or some other component of one's belief system. Alternatively, some animal killing that occurs in a ritualistic manner, such as various forms of patterned animal mutilation, may occur for nonreligious purposes, such as teenage "prankster" behavior, sadistic animal cruelty, and childhood animal abuse by conduct disordered youth, among many others [6, 7]. To further complicate matters, members of organizations that engage in unconventional practices, such as cults, may abuse or kill animals for reasons that some may view as religious, and others may view as criminal. Not surprisingly, then, the outcome of these evaluations commonly depends on the perspective of the person investigating the crime scene and the necropsy results.

S.P. McDonough, D.V.M., Ph.D., D.A.C.V.P. (✉)
Department of Biomedical Sciences,
Cornell University, Veterinary Research Tower,
Ithaca, NY 14853, USA
e-mail: spm13@cornell.edu

B. Holoyda, M.D., M.P.H., M.B.A.
Division of Forensic Psychiatry, Department of
Psychiatry and Behavioral Neuroscience,
St. Louis University, Monteleone Hall, St. Louis,
MO 63104, USA
e-mail: holoyda@gmail.com

9.2 The Right to Practice Religious Animal Slaughter and Animal Sacrifice

One must distinguish between criminal ritualistic animal killings and constitutionally protected religious practices. In the United States, religious slaughter and religious animal sacrifice are

© Springer International Publishing AG 2018
J.W. Brooks (ed.), *Veterinary Forensic Pathology, Volume 2*,
https://doi.org/10.1007/978-3-319-67175-8_9

protected by the First Amendment's guarantee of the free exercise of religion. In the case of *Church of Lukumi Babalu Aye v. City of Hialeah* (1993), the Supreme Court was unable to distinguish animal sacrifice from legally permissible secular animal killing. The court ruled that laws banning ritualistic animal slaughter and/or sacrifice are unconstitutional if the goal is the suppression of religion. However, laws regulating animal husbandry, zoning, humane killing, and the sanitary disposal of carcasses are constitutional, even if the laws make a religious practice difficult or even impossible as long are they are "neutral" and of "general applicability."

The situation regarding religious animal killing is more complex in Europe. Article 9 of the European Convention on Human Rights provides for a right to freedom of thought, conscience, and religion, which includes the freedom to practice religion subject only to restrictions that are "in accordance with law" and "necessary in a democratic society." The European Union directive, "European Convention for the Protection of Animals for Slaughter," generally requires stunning before slaughter but allows member states to permit exemptions for religious slaughter: "Each Contracting Party may authorize derogations from the provisions concerning prior stunning in the following cases: slaughtering in accordance with religious rituals...." Denmark has banned all religious slaughter without stunning since 2014. To critics that complain the ban infringes on religious freedom, Dan Jorgensen, Denmark's Food and Agriculture minister, observed that "nothing stops people buying ritually-slaughtered meat from abroad."

9.3 Religious Animal Slaughter for Consumption

Religious laws of several major religions around the world dictate the appropriate methods by which animals may be slaughtered for consumption. Various forms of religious animal slaughter are widely practiced. When evaluating an animal subjected to religious slaughter, three basic issues regarding humaneness need to be assessed:

(1) stressfulness of the restraint method, (2) pain perception during the procedure, and (3) the time to unconsciousness (latency of insensibility). Abusive abattoir workers will cause suffering regardless of the method of slaughter employed [8]. Abusive practices include rough handling, constant prodding, slamming gates on animals, overcrowding, striking animals with sticks or whips, kicking, dragging "downer" animals, or picking animals up by the ears or tail. Failure to maintain clean pens and chutes and the presence of sharp protrusions are additional causes of injury and emotional distress of animals at slaughter.

Kashrut is a set of Jewish dietary laws that delineate what can (kosher) and cannot (treif) be eaten by an observant Jew [9]. The animals must be alive, healthy, treated humanely, and killed without pain or emotional distress. Shechitah (ritual slaughter) is performed by the shochet, a pious man well-trained in Jewish law. Preslaughter stunning is not allowed. The shochet makes a quick, deep stroke across the neck with a chalaf to sever the trachea, esophagus, jugular veins, and carotid arteries. The animal dies due to exsanguination. The chalaf must be razor sharp and free of nicks and must be at least twice the width of the animal's neck. The cut must be made without hesitation or delay. The incision must not close back over the knife during the cut ("halagramah" or digging) in order to reduce the animal's reaction to the cut. Sheep lose consciousness within 2–15 s after the carotid arteries are cut. The time to insensibility in cattle is more variable.

Dhabihah in Islamic law prescribes the method of religious slaughter of permissible (halal) animals as opposed to forbidden (haram) animals that may not be slaughtered. The slaughter can be done by any mentally competent adult Muslim. Some Muslims will use the meat slaughtered by Jews or Christians, since the latter are "people of the Book," though some Islamic jurists do not consider Christians who follow Pauline Christianity to be "people of the Book." Women can perform the slaughter if necessary. The person performing the slaughter must say "Bismillah" or more commonly "Bismillah Allah

Akbar" ("in the name of God, God is great") separately for each animal slaughtered. Saying the name of Allah at the time of slaughter is meant to be an act of piousness affirming that life is sacred and to be valued. Similar to Jewish shechitah, a swift, deep incision using a very sharp knife is used to cut the trachea, esophagus, jugular veins, and carotid arteries, but leaves the spinal cord intact. Death is by exsanguination.

Since Muslims who perform animal slaughter do not typically receive the same level of specialized training in slaughter techniques as compared to Jewish shochtim, Temple Grandin has strongly recommended that Muslim clerics mandate pre-slaughter stunning. The permissibility of pre-slaughter stunning for halal is debated. In some jurisdictions, stunning is permitted if it is possible to revive the animal afterwards. At one point it was estimated that 88% of halal animals in Great Britain were stunned prior to slaughter. More recently, the proportion of animals slaughtered in the United Kingdom for halal without pre-stunning has risen because of a campaign by Muslims promoting traditional slaughter and the mistaken belief that stunning kills the animal [10]. For the stunning to ensure the halal status of the slaughter, the stunning equipment must be under the control of a Muslim supervisor or slaughter man at all times, the stunning can neither kill nor cause permanent injury to the animal, and the equipment must not be used to stun pigs.

In Hinduism, the Jhatka method of ritual slaughter requires that the animal be killed instantly with a single decapitating blow with an axe or sword. Animals that make noise are seen as a bad omen and indicates that the animal is suffering [11].

9.4 Religious Animal Sacrifice

Although no rituals for the slaughter or sacrifice of animals are broadly accepted or used by Christian religions, such practices are held sacred and widely practiced by some other major religions of the world including Judaism, Islam, and others. Ancient Jewish tradition only permitted animal sacrifices in the temple in Jerusalem (Deut. 12:13–14). Because the temple was destroyed by the Roman army in 70 CE, Jews do not currently practice animal sacrifice. Jews now obtain forgiveness through repentance, prayer, and tzedakah (charity or other good deeds). Orthodox Jewish teaching states that when the messiah comes, animal sacrifice will resume because God will provide a place for the practice.

The Hajj is an annual pilgrimage to Mecca required of all Muslims at least once in their lifetime if they are physically and financially capable of making the journey [12]. After performing Ramy al-Jamarat (symbolic stoning of the devil), the fifth in a numbered series of obligations for the pilgrim is to slaughter a camel, cow, or sheep of appropriate age in commemoration of the story of Ibrahim (Abraham) and Ishmael (the older brother of Isaac). Pilgrims do not need to sacrifice the animal themselves, and many buy a sacrifice voucher that allows the sacrifice to be made in their name without having to be physically present. The abattoirs process the meat and work with the government of the Kingdom of Saudi Arabia and nongovernmental organizations to send the meat as charity to poor people around the world. Similar sacrifices are performed worldwide during the 3-day feast of Eid al-Adha. The sacrifice is meant to be a submission to Allah as opposed to a means of atoning for one's sins, as in Judaism.

Although most Hindus do not participate, animal sacrifice is practiced in all parts of India. Most sacrifice is performed to pacify local deities or to celebrate the birth of a child. During the festivals of Navaratri dedicated to the nine forms of Shakti (Mother Goddess), goats, chickens, and sometimes male water buffalos are sacrificed. In some areas, a priest recites the Gayatri Mantra in the ear of the animal to release it from the cycle of life and death. The Ashvamedha ritual in the Rigveda describes the sacrifice of a horse, but this practice no longer seems to be followed [11].

The teachings of Buddha decry animal cruelty in all forms because the destruction of any living creature represents a disturbance of the Universal Order. Thus, Buddhists do not practice animal sacrifice. Although some Buddhist sects oppose eating meat, other sects have varying opinions. Buddhist monks are forbidden from eating meat from certain animals (elephants, horses, dogs, snakes, lions, tigers, panthers, bears, and hyenas) and may not eat the meat of an animal that was killed specifically for them [13].

Syncretic belief systems combine two or more different cultural and spiritual beliefs into a new faith. Several million people in the United States practice the Afro-Caribbean syncretic faiths of Voodoo, Santeria, Hoodoo, Palo Mayombe, Candomble, and Shango [14].

Voodoo is the best known Afro-Caribbean syncretic faith because of widespread but highly inaccurate and racist depictions in film. Voodoo emerged among Haitian slaves and is practiced by as many as 60 million people worldwide. Voodoo first came to the United States in 1803 when the prohibition against importing slaves from the West Indies was lifted. Voodoo eventually evolved into Hoodoo, which has substituted many of the religious aspects of Voodoo with more cultural and medical features. Houngans (male priests) and mambos (female priests) limit their practices to white magic, whereas bokors practice black magic or evil sorcery. The Haitian form of Voodoo has many deities, known collectively as Loa. Rituals are held to invoke a particular god who best fits the need of the moment. Rada spirits are revered for their wisdom and benevolence, while Petro spirits are known for their power. Each Loa has its own attributes, form of worship and symbolic drawings (veves). A veve is most often drawn during ceremonies to worship a particular spirit. Animal sacrifice occurs most often at large ceremonies since the houngan or mambo is responsible for providing a sacred meal to the participants.

Santeria is probably the most widely practiced Afro-Caribbean syncretic religion, but accurate figures are lacking. Santeria combines the cultural and spiritual beliefs of the Yoruba tribe from Nigeria with the religious practices of Catholicism. The gods and goddesses of Santeria, orishas, are the repositories of ashe (divine power) that can solve problems, vanquish enemies, and acquire love and money. An offering (ebbo) is made to an orisha so that they will give their ashe. Ebbo can be an offering of fruits, flowers, candles, or a favorite food. Santeria rituals also require the use of sacrificial birds and other animals. The blood of roosters and goats is the most common sacrificial offering. Birds (pigeons, canaries, hens) are used in rubbing rituals where negative feelings caused by evil are passed into the birds. Ancestor worship is central to the practice of Santeria. The dead must be fed periodically, just as the orishas are given offerings.

Palo Mayombe practitioners use magical rituals to manipulate, captivate, and/or control another person, most often for the practitioners' malevolent purposes. Palo Mayombe, derived from the Spanish word "palo" meaning "wooden stick" or "branch," refers to the pieces of wood practitioners use in their magic spells. While the rituals of Santeria usually focus on positive actions designed to improve one's personal position or please an orisha, Palo Mayombe centers its rituals on inflicting misfortune or even death upon an enemy by invoking the evil spirit of a specific patron who resides in the nganga, the sacred cauldron used during most rituals. Items typically found in the nganga include a human skull, bones, graveyard dust, crossroads dust, branches, herbs, insects, animal and bird carcasses, coins, spices, and blood. When the spirit of the nganga carries out its owner's wishes, he or she gives it blood as an expression of gratitude. Rituals may include leaving animal carcasses (decapitated roosters, dead goats, etc.) at the entrance of a business or home. Palo Mayombe rituals require the use of human bones, which entails the theft of human remains. Animals sacrificed for Palo include domesticated pets such as dogs and other larger animals.

Many neo-pagan groups attempt to recreate ancient European pre-Christian religions (e.g., druids). These groups have a reverence for nature (animism and pantheism), belief in polytheism and the practice of white magic. Many neo-pagan religions practice Wicca, a form of witchcraft. Neo-pagan principles do not entail illegal activities and, significantly, "witches," as they refer to themselves, do not engage in animal sacrifice or other blood rituals.

9.5 "Occult" and "Satanic" Animal Sacrifice

Derived from the Latin word occultus, meaning concealed, occult refers to beliefs, practices, or phenomena that are supernatural, mystical, or magical. Occult practices are typically kept secret and communicated only to the initiated. Adherents to these unconventional ideologies do not publicize their beliefs and rites because of the social stigma associated with "occult" practices. Cults, extremist offshoots of major religions, and satanic societies are examples of minor religions that are often classified as "occult" religions.

The line between mainstream religions and the "occult" is blurry. The distinction between "major" and "minor" religions is also unclear. The ease with which organizations can establish themselves as religions in the eyes of the law further confuses definitional issues [15]. State and federal case law involving such organizations' beliefs and practices that have led to individuals' physical, psychological, or financial ruin demonstrate differential treatment in varying settings [16]. Regardless, such organizations have long been associated with ritualistic animal cruelty and killing and therefore deserve mention here.

Many people believe that occult and satanic animal sacrifice is widespread in the United States. This belief reached a peak during the "satanic panic" of the 1980s. It was during this time that allegations of "satanic ritual abuse (SRA)" began to appear. Numerous social changes and conditions, such as a growing national fear of cults and other minor religious organizations, the development of the child protection field, and recognition of the psychological sequelae of trauma, fostered an environment in which claims of SRA found support among psychotherapists, police investigators, and children's advocates, among others [17]. One component of many SRA claims was the ritualistic abuse or killing of animals, including children and others being forced to abuse and kill animals against their will. For example, in the Faith Chapel Church ritual abuse case, a mentally handicapped abuser was alleged to have killed a giraffe, rabbit, and elephant and consumed their blood in front of a group of abducted children. Additionally, he was accused of forcing children to eat their own excrement and of sexually assaulting them. In this case there was no forensic evidence that supported the SRA claims [18].

During the satanic panic, self-styled experts on "occult crime" wrote books and published videos that were touted as "training" materials for law enforcement officials. One such text [19] described how it is "relatively common for law enforcement officers to find dead animal carcasses at outdoor ritual sites and in abandoned buildings" (pp. 103) and related different patterns of animal killing associated with various delineated groups of Satanists, including "clandestine Satanists," "self-styled Satanists," and "independent Satanists." Dubois went on to offer a profile of the typical self-styled Satanist, whom he asserted committed the vast majority of satanic animal sacrifice, as a white male, 12–17 years old, and coming from a middle-class family. He further claimed that these perpetrators have a sense of inferiority, vulnerability, and loneliness despite their claims of superiority. Without any description of actual cases or citations from official criminal records or empirical literature to support their claims, however, these sensationalist materials are more likely a phenomenon of the satanic panic than a useful source for understanding ritualistic animal killing.

Anton LaVey, the founder of a branch of Satanism, authored the *Satanic Bible* in 1969. The text is a collection of essays, observations, and rituals and is meant to describe core principles of Satanism. LaVey's followers consider it to be an authoritative, scriptural text. In the chapter entitled "On the Choice of a Human Sacrifice," LaVey writes the following regarding animal sacrifice:

> Under no circumstances would a Satanist sacrifice any animal or baby! ... The purest form of carnal existence reposes in the bodies of animals and human children who have not grown old enough to deny themselves their natural desires ... The Satanist does not hate himself, nor the gods he might choose, and has no desire to destroy himself or anything for which he stands! It is for this reason he could never willfully harm an animal or child.

According to this one "official" text of Satanism, then, the ritualistic harming and killing of animals are not condoned among at least some sects of Satanists [20].

The incidence of "occult" or "satanic" ritualistic animal killing remains uncertain. Some cases bearing odd or bizarre details may suggest an occult, ritualistic intent behind the killing. For example, in a graveyard in Ephraim, Utah in 2003 eight decapitated cat heads were aligned atop a grave and surrounded by severed paws and legs arranged in a pentagram. Grocery bags filled with dried blood were suspended from an arch over another grave [21]. Whether or not such cases represent true occult ritualistic practices or violent pranks, however, cannot be determined without apprehending and evaluating the offender(s).

9.6   Criminal Ritualistic Animal Killing

Ritualistic animal slaughter and ritualistic animal sacrifice, as previously described, are culturally condoned aspects of many major and minor world religious traditions. Governments have responded differently to such practices throughout time and in the context of varying social climates. For example, the Nazi government banned shechitah early during the Third Reich, presumably as a component of general anti-Semitic religious suppression. Alternatively, in *Church of the Lukumi Babalu Aye, Inc. v. Hialeah* (1993), the United States Supreme Court found a local Floridian ordinance that prohibited the unnecessary killing of "an animal in a public or private ritual or ceremony not for the primary purpose of food consumption" to be unconstitutional.

Legal standards regulating the treatment of animals and the behavior of religious organizations continue to evolve through case and statutory law. This makes it difficult to know whether or not a group's animal-related activities would be considered criminal or not in a given context. It is therefore a challenge to differentiate between individuals who engage in legally sanctioned animal sacrifice and slaughter and those who illegally abuse or kill animals in a ritualistic manner.

9.7   Perpetrators of Ritualistic Animal Abuse and Killing

Given inconsistent and evolving legal standards, the lack of scientific research on ritualistic animal abuse and killing, and popular misconceptions about organizations purported to support such behavior, it is not surprising that little is known about the characteristics and motivations of those engaged in ritualistic animal abuse and killing. In addition, there is a dearth of research and knowledge about these individuals. Searches in academic databases including PubMed, PsychINFO, and Ovid using terms including "ritualistic animal abuse," "satanic animal abuse," "ritualistic animal killing," "satanic animal killing," "ritualistic animal sacrifice," and "satanic animal sacrifice" yield no scientific articles on the topic. It is perhaps most useful, then, to describe specific cases in which ritualistic animal abuse and killing have occurred or been purported to occur.

Case 1

Michael Ryan led a cult that lived on a farm in rural Nebraska in the mid-1980s [22]. The organization operated under a belief system based on Anglo-Saxon supremacy, the unconstitutionality of income taxes, and a predicted forthcoming Battle of Armageddon. Over time, Ryan became progressively more paranoid, warning his followers that "Yahweh" had instructed him to build a base camp at a farm outside the town of Rulo, where they would stockpile weapons and machinery in preparation for the upcoming battle. He told his followers that they would not be safe unless they complied with requests for items needed at the base camp. Over a period of a few years, Ryan obtained over 75 thousand rounds of ammunition and dozens of weapons.

Like most cult leaders, Ryan consolidated his control over his cult members' day-to-day lives. He married multiple followers, including a mother and her daughter. At one point he announced that one of his wives had become the queen of Israel. During a religious meeting, one cult member, James Thimm, expressed doubts regarding the existence of Yahweh and of Ryan's reported abilities. Another member, 5-year-old Luke Stice, also expressed doubts about Yahweh's existence. In response, Ryan demoted James Thimm, Luke Stice, and Luke's father Rick Stice to the status of "slaves" who were in charge of guard duty, washing dishes, and caring for the compound's animals. He forced Luke and his father to orally copulate each other, and killed Luke by slamming his head against a cabinet. After Luke's death, Ryan made Rick Stice copulate with a goat three times. After Stice escaped from the compound, Ryan made Thimm have sex with a goat, as well. Ryan told Thimm that he had not done a good enough job with the goat and required him to be "probed." He subjected Thimm to torture including having a shovel handle inserted up his rectum, shooting off his fingers, and ultimately killing him by stomping on his chest (*State v. Ryan*, 1989). Once the farm and the murders were discovered, Ryan was prosecuted and sentenced to death.

This case demonstrates the sexual abuse of an animal in the setting of a cult. The sexual abuse of an animal was forced upon two followers as punishment for their expressions of doubt of their charismatic leader's proclamations. Though the sexual abuse did not occur expressly in the setting of a "ritual," it could be considered ritualistic as it was a component of the cult's methods of maintaining order and adherence to cult doctrine. The use of animal sexual abuse as a form of punishment suggests that the focus was on the discomfort and disgust of the person being punished, as opposed to the infliction of pain and suffering on the animal.

Case 2

In 2013 a 2-month-old foal was found dead on Yennadon Down, a popular family picnic spot in Dartmoor National Park in southwestern England. Early media reports described the foal in gruesome detail, noting that its genitals and right ear had been cut off, and its tongue and eyes were cut out. In addition, it was reportedly surrounded by a circle of scorch marks, which led initial investigators into identifying the horse's death as a "ritual" conducted by "devil worshippers." [23] Local villagers from Yelverton insisted that the foal was killed as the result of cult behavior due to the southwest's "long association with Satanic groups." A local animal welfare officer described the positioning of the dead animal as "sinister" and noted, "We have not jumped to any conclusions but it certainly seems that it could have been ritualistic."

Investigations into the cause of the foal's death revealed that the animal had died from natural causes. Forensic analysis revealed that the pattern of tissue removal was consistent with normal predation by birds and other scavengers [24]. Clearly, the description of Satanic, pagan, or cult involvement in this animal's death was a sensationalist media strategy to attract readership. Notably, however, local villagers and the local animal welfare officer were swept into the media hype. This case demonstrates the fascination that "occult" behavior, whether it be attributed to Satanists, cults, or other groups, holds in the popular imagination. In addition, it offers a cautionary tale about how the natural death and dismemberment of an animal can become national news when it is alleged to be the result of an occult ritual.

Case 3

Pazuzu Algarad was a self-identified worshipper of "evil Gods" who lived in Clemmons, North Carolina. Originally named John Lawson, news reports variously claim that Algarad or his mother changed his name to Pazuzu after the mythological king of demons of the wind, supposedly from the book *The Exorcist* [25]. Algarad's body and face were covered in tattoos including "666," "Lucifer," "Villain," "Pazuzu," a black Nazi sign, and a black dragon, among many others. He also had his teeth filed into spikes and his tongue split down the middle [26]. At age 36 Algarad was charged with first-degree murder and accessory after the fact to first-degree murder after he and his 24-year-old girlfriend, Amber Nicole Burch, were accused of fatally shooting and burying Joshua Wetzler and Tommy Welch in their backyard in 2009. Algarad had reportedly boasted to a former girlfriend about the skeletal remains in his backyard and having consumed parts of his victims before burying them, as well as about having previously picked up, killed, and eaten two prostitutes [27].

After his arrest, officials condemned Algarad's house, which was noted to be covered in graffiti and filth. A report documented that the house contained "decayed animal parts and remains," "animal cages with carcasses," "broken glass and sharp instruments everywhere," and a "dried blood-like substance" on the walls [28]. Acquaintances claimed that Algarad had previously boasted about getting high from eating the "still-beating heart" of sacrificial animals. While in custody, Algarad told psychiatrists that he practiced a "Sumerian religion" that required him to conduct a monthly sacrifice of a small animal during a specified time that he called the "black moon." Algarad's mother reportedly expressed concern that Algarad might kill himself if he was not released from custody to engage in his ritualistic animal killing. He ultimately died in prison after sustaining blood loss from a deep wound he cut into his left arm [29].

The case of Pazuzu Algarad demonstrates the types of ritualistic animal abuse and killing that self-styled "devil worshipers" may perform. Though information on Algarad's behavior is limited to brief, sensational news reports, his reported "black moon" sacrifices and the presence of the animal parts and full carcasses in his house suggest that animals played a role in his "spiritual" activities. Algarad's acquaintances described him as a drug-abusing, hypersexual individual. His criminal history and reported statements are certainly suggestive of someone with severe, underlying personality dysfunction. There are no reports that others participated in the gruesome, "ritualistic" killing and eating of animal and human remains, suggesting that Algarad's religious activities were limited to him and perhaps his significant other. Algarad's own report of his "Sumerian religion" is dubious, and, had he not been arrested for first-degree murder, it is quite likely that his animal abuse and sacrifice would not have been protected under the law.

This series of cases demonstrates the various settings in which ritualistic animal abuse and sacrifice can occur, specifically as part of an individual's self-identified spiritual practices or within religious sects. In addition, it delineates two different motivations for the behavior, including as a form of ritualized punishment and as a means of worshiping "evil gods." Case 2 demonstrates the widespread sensationalistic media hype that even natural animal deaths can receive when there is someone willing to accuse a cult or Satanic group for the death. As mentioned previously, little is known about individuals and groups that engage in ritualistic animal abuse and sacrifice, and there is little discussion of these behaviors in the scientific literature. With further study of this topic, however, the motivations for engaging in ritualistic animal abuse and sacrifice will become clearer.

9.8   The Necropsy

No peer reviewed case series or even single case reports detailing the forensic pathology findings in cases of ritualistic animal abuse can be found in the literature. A further complication is the need to distinguish constitutionally protected ritualistic animal slaughter and animal sacrifice from illegal activity. In addition to determining the cause, manner, and mechanism of death, the pathologist should document evidence of pain and suffering, since animal cruelty is not a constitutionally protected religious practice.

The pathologist can only offer a valid opinion on the manner of death when all the evidence is evaluated in light of the necropsy findings. The scene in which the body is found is important in all forensic death investigations but takes on added importance when suspected ritualistic abuse is being investigated. The symbolic objects found at the crime scene or accompany the body can indicate which belief system is practiced. Other relevant information includes who offered the sacrifice, what was offered, where and when the sacrifice was offered, to whom the sacrifice was offered, and the reason for the sacrifice. Some practitioners use animals of opportunity (e.g., stray cats or neighborhood pets), while others maintain an inventory of animals. The husbandry and nutrition of this livestock should be determined, since housing livestock in an urban setting may violate zoning restrictions and sacrificial animals must receive adequate food, water, and shelter. Answers to these questions are not only relevant to the current death investigation but are necessary in order to develop a typology that can contribute to solving and preventing ritualistic animal abuse.

The use of blood in ritualistic crimes is common. The physical pattern of blood stains (i.e., blood stain analysis) is not as important as the symbolic meaning of blood. The level of experience of the perpetrator can be deduced by the cleanliness of the crime scene and the victim. Highly experienced practitioners can exsanguinate an animal without spilling blood at the scene or soiling the carcass. A "dabbler" will not have the same level of proficiency.

Humane animal sacrifice is usually performed by quickly slitting the animal's throat, but birds are typically sacrificed by disarticulating the neck. In these cases there will be no other injuries. The carcass will usually be drained of blood, since blood is an essential feature in most animal sacrifice. Headless birds may be discarded in doorways and on the steps of courthouses and government buildings as part of a spell to protect the believer from being convicted. Although animal sacrifice is protected by the First Amendment to the Constitution, disposing of the carcass in a public space is a violation of health codes and is not legally sanctioned.

Mutilation of the carcass is common and includes cutting out eyes, tongue, genitalia, or heart. Field dressing wild game typically involves removing the viscera and hide, which can be mistaken for mutilation by those not familiar with wild game processing. Dismemberment, decapitation, and skinning can represent a religious ritual in the context of a specific belief system. Disturbingly, in some traditions, prolonged pain is thought to release more life energy that can be used by the perpetrator to achieve specific goals. Evidence of a vital reaction should be sought to determine if the injuries were inflicted while the animal was still alive. Vital reaction can include hemorrhage along incisions and traces of blood spattering from severed arteries. Pallor to the mucous membranes and muscles may indicate external blood loss. In cases of decapitation, blood aspiration would indicate antemortem removal of the head.

Care should be taken to rule out postmortem depredation. Broad soft tissue defects with irregular, partially curved wound margins and tooth punctures indicate scavenging. Parallel skin scratches may represent claw marks. Gnaw marks on bones, best viewed on macerated specimens, support postmortem scavenging.

Evidence of a struggle should be sought. If the animal scratched or bit the perpetrator, it may have epidermal cells or blood under the claws or around the teeth. Evidence that the animal was bound should be sought. Ligature marks from cords, ropes, or tape may be present around the extremities. The mouth may have been taped shut by the perpetrator to prevent the animal from biting.

Conclusions

An abundance of opinion surrounds the ritualistic abuse and killing of animals, but virtually no objective evidence is available. In the United States, animal sacrifice for religious purposes is protected by the First Amendment to the Constitution. Evidence of pain and suffering must be meticulously documented since animal cruelty is illegal, even if that means the religious rite cannot be performed according to the tenets of a particular belief system. The pathologist must interpret the necropsy findings in light of the evidence from the scene and have some knowledge of religious practices and the psychology of perpetrators of ritualistic animal abuse.

References

1. Grauel, T. Occult expert finds the black magic in animal killings. The (Westchester County, NY) Journal News. 6 October 2014 (np).
2. Rudick T. Pet serial killer on the loose. Houston culturemap.com news. 23 January 2014 (np).
3. Demasters T. Cats found dead, mutilated in southern Utah. Fox channel 13, Salt Lake City Utah 23 September 2013.
4. Talensi, IT. Animal sacrifice and its archaeological implications. World Heritage Encyclopedia.
5. Tsia, C. Animals killed Denver Cats. Deseret News Utah. 2 August 2003 (np).
6. Pescaro M. Teen accused of mutilating cats behind abandoned house. Massachusetts: the latest news from around the state. 13 May 2015 (np).
7. Gleyzer R, Felthous AR, Hozer CE. Animal cruelty and psychiatric disorders. J Am Acad Psychiatry Law. 2002;30:257–65.
8. Grandin T. Making slaughterhouses more humane for cattle, pigs, and sheep. Annu Rev Anim Biosci. 2013;1:491–512.
9. Velarde A, Rodriguez P, Dalmua A, et al. Religious slaughter: evaluation of current practices in selected countries. Meat Sci. 2014;96:278–87.
10. Barclay C. Religious slaughter. UK Parliament Standard Note SN/SC/1314 June 11, 2012.
11. Das V.. The Oxford India companion to sociology and social anthropology, volume 1, 2003.
12. Anonymous. Hajj. Wikepedia, 29 August 2016.
13. Horner IB. Book of the discipline, vol. 4. London: Luzac and Co; 1954.
14. Perlmutter D. Investigating religious terrorism and ritualistic crimes. Boca Raton, FL: CRC Press; 2003.
15. Internal Revenue Service. Tax guide for Churches and religious organizations. Washington, DC: International Revenue Services; 2015.
16. Holoyda B, Newman W. Between belief and delusion: Cult members and the Insanity Plea. J Am Acad Psychiatry Law. 2016;44:53–62.
17. Richardson, James T.; Best, Joel; Bromley, David G. The Satanism Scare. Hawthorne, NY: Aldine Transaction; 1991.
18. Soesz D, Costin LB, Karger HJ. The politics of child abuse in America (child welfare). Oxford, UK: Oxford University Press; 1996.
19. Dubois WEL. Occult crime: detection, investigation, and verification. Las Vegas: San Miguel Press; 1992.
20. LaVey A. The satanic bible. Avon; 1969.
21. Jensen DP. Mutilated cats found in Ephraim cemetery. The Salt Lake Tribune 23 September 2003, p. B2.
22. *State v. Ryan.* (1989). 444 N.W. 2d 610.
23. Rowley T, Hedges-Stocks Z. Pony mutilated in suspected satanic act in Dartmoor. The Telegraph. 26 July 2013 (np).
24. Radford, B. Real Cause of 'Satanic Sacrifice' Pony Found. Live Science. 23 August 2013 (np).
25. Gillman O. Devil worshiper 'who ate parts of his murder victims before burying them in shallow graves in his backyard' found dead in his prison cell in apparent suicide. Daily Mail UK. 28 October 2015 (np).
26. Murdock, Sebastian. Pazuzu Algarad arrested; skeletal remains found in yard of 'Evil Gods' worshiper." Huffington Post 6 October 2014.
27. Anonymous. Inside home of 'devil worshiper' accused of murder, sacrificing animals. PIX11 News 6 November 2014.
28. Truesdell, J. Inside the 'Satanist' house in North Carolina murder case: animal remains, 'blood-like' markings. People 8 November 2014.
29. Hewlett M. Pazuzu Algarad, charged with killing and burying 2 in Clemmons yard, died from blood loss. Winston-Salem J 17 December 2015.

Writing the Necropsy Report

10

Gregory J. Davis and Sean P. McDonough

10.1 Importance of the Necropsy Report

As important as the necropsy may be to an understanding of the cause of death and circumstances surrounding death, the report will be irrelevant if it does not address the needs of the court. The findings and opinions of the forensic veterinary pathologist must be communicated in a clear and understandable fashion. The report should be given utmost care and receive as close attention as any physical procedure in the necropsy room.

The necropsy report should accurately record factual information discovered during the necropsy itself while also synthesizing information gleaned by the investigation of death. In addition, a cause of death opinion should be included, incorporating information from the investigation as well as necropsy gross and microscopic findings. While some traditional pathologists believe that the report should only contain objective anatomic findings (and in some jurisdictions, the report may be limited to same), such limited reports may do a disservice to the numerous constituents reading the report as they attempt to understand the circumstances surrounding death, especially in potentially criminal deaths in which the pathologist's conclusions may be critical to investigative officials, attorneys, and courts. By including historical and investigative information, the pathologist may justify his or her eventual cause of death findings in those cases with minimal to nonexistent anatomic findings (e.g., in some asphyxia and toxicological cases).

The necropsy report is a permanent record of the pathologist's findings and plays a critical role in medicolegal proceedings in which every word may be scrutinized in a deposition or court months to years afterward, when all memory of the examination will have faded from the pathologist's mind. Therefore, the medicolegal document should be as useful as possible in answering questions regarding the cause of death.

10.2 Content and Format of the Forensic Necropsy Report

The necropsy report should contain separate sections in logical order for organization and reference, including but not necessarily limited to:

G.J. Davis, M.D., F.C.A.P.
Department of Pathology and Laboratory Medicine,
University of Kentucky College of Medicine,
800 Rose Street, Lexington, 40536 Kentucky, USA

S.P. McDonough, D.V.M., Ph.D., D.A.C.V.P. (✉)
Department of Biomedical Sciences, Cornell
University College of Veterinary Medicine, Upper
Tower Road, Ithaca, NY 14853, USA
e-mail: spm13@cornell.edu

© Springer International Publishing AG 2018
J.W. Brooks (ed.), *Veterinary Forensic Pathology, Volume 2*,
https://doi.org/10.1007/978-3-319-67175-8_10

- Demographic information of the decedent with date and time of necropsy and a list of those in attendance and their role
- Who authorized the necropsy
- External physical examination, including but not limited to:
  - Demographic data (species, age, breed, gender, coat color, weight, and body condition score)
  - Unique identifying characteristics such as tattoos, brands, congenital and acquired deformities, microchips, etc.
  - Evidence of postmortem changes such as livor mortis, rigor mortis, discoloration, and decomposition
  - Evidence of medical/surgical therapy, keeping in mind that some therapies, if not known from the medical record, may artifactually appear to be injury (e.g., a chest tube insertion site after removal of the tube)
  - Evidence of injury
  - Internal examination, including but not limited to:
    Cardiovascular system
    Respiratory system
    Gastrointestinal system
    Genitourinary system
    Reticuloendothelial system
    Endocrine system
    Musculoskeletal system
    Central nervous system
- Microscopic examination
- Toxicological findings
- Ancillary studies (e.g., radiography, DNA)
- Summary of findings
- Statement regarding cause, manner, and mechanism of death
- Disposition of remains

Templates can be useful for collecting necropsy information as well as providing a uniform report format. A word of caution: do not over-rely on the template. Any irrelevant information that is not depleted from the template will create confusion and potentially impugn the perceptions of the quality of the examiner. A sample format used at Cornell University is provided in Appendix 1 as one example of an acceptable template format. Sample body diagrams for a dog and cat are shown in Appendix 2 and Appendix 3 respectively.

After the descriptions noted above, a short paragraph listing all pertinent positive and pertinent negative findings and their relation to the pathologist's opinion as to the cause of death may be included. In many cases, the cause of death may be obvious (e.g., a gunshot wound of the head), but in many cases, the findings are nebulous or multiple, and when appropriate, a differential diagnosis should be discussed with a possible ranking of the probability of differing causes of death. One should offer such opinions as coherently as possible, citing references if necessary, all the while refraining from pure speculation. Unfortunately, popular television shows portray the forensic pathologist as omniscient, and some pathologists may be tempted to "give the public what it wants" by speculating and coming to conclusions based on minimal data. As Saukko and Knight state:

> What is really required is as full an interpretation as possible, without venturing into the undesirable fields of unwarranted speculation or "Sherlock Holmes" style of over interpretation, which was the bane of forensic pathology in former years and is still practiced too much even today, to the detriment of the good reputation of the specialty.

10.3   Pitfalls of Report Writing

Some advocate the issuance of a "Preliminary Anatomic Diagnosis" within a day or two of the necropsy, allowing interested parties to be informed of initial thoughts regarding the possible cause of death. Of course, such impressions can radically change as the microscopic sections become available, the toxicology report is finalized, or as other investigative evidence is received. Whether one adheres to this practice or waits until all necessary information is collected before a report is issued, the descriptive facts must be written, dictated, or transcribed during or immediately after the necropsy. The necropsy must not be relegated to the prosector's memory, as circumstances, new cases, and other events will cause the fresh recollection of findings to quickly fade. The use of pre-printed body sketches and notes may help (and should be kept clean, as they or copies thereof may be entered into evidence), but it is imperative to not let the report linger more than a few hours before it is committed to paper or digital media. Some pathologists choose to incorporate photographs into the body of the report; others prefer to keep the photographs separate. Such decisions are left to individual discretion and/or office custom.

Clear wording free of unnecessary jargon is important, as many lay persons, including but not limited to law enforcement officials, attorneys, and judges, may rely upon the report. If the prosector is not affiliated with an institution that has a standard operating procedure for the necropsy technique, one should reference the technique used. This presupposes the prosector adheres to the procedure referenced. One should avoid describing standard necropsy procedures such as "serial parallel incisions are made in the liver" or "the left kidney is incised along the long axis." Unique procedures, such as layer-by-layer musculoskeletal dissection, may be pertinent to describe. Superfluous wording adding nothing pertinent to the necropsy report should be avoided, especially such common redundancies as "there is," "is located," "measures," and "is noted." Avoid unnecessary redundancies such as "red in color" or "soft in consistency." For example, in lieu of the painful sentence, "Inspection of the right lower leg shows that there is a firm in consistency mass that measures 4 × 3 × 2 cm in dimension and is red in color," one might more succinctly state, "a firm, red, 4 × 3 × 2 cm mass is on the right lower leg."

A few words of caution are in order. Many times, individuals will ask the forensic pathologist if they may attend the necropsy. The pathologist should note the presence of any person at necropsy and be ready to justify their presence to an attorney or court. Many such requests are legitimate, such as for educational purposes by students or postgraduates or for medicolegal purposes by law enforcement officials. The pathologist should be careful not to allow persons to attend for curiosity reasons alone.

It is important to proofread one's necropsy report or have a colleague do so. The final report should be free of all substantive errors and all typographic, spelling, punctuation, and other clerical errors must be corrected. Cross-examining attorneys, in exercising their due diligence, will critically study every word of the report and call the pathologist to account for errors large and small. One only has to hear once the question: "Doctor, if you can't be counted upon to spell correctly or tell your patient's left from right, how can the court trust that your observations and interpretations are correct?" before the importance of proofreading becomes manifest. As such, there are no meaningless or minor mistakes in a necropsy report.

And finally, the forensic necropsy is performed for the well-being of the public, as society, public health, and the law demand answers and explanations of the cause and circumstances of unusual, suspicious, or violent animal deaths. Animal cruelty is not only a moral concern but also a crime that may indicate other forms of interpersonal violence that threaten public health. The necropsy report should reflect in readable form the quest for such answers.

10.4 The Cause, Manner, and Mechanism of Death

10.4.1 The Cause of Death (COD)

The cause of death (COD) is usually the principal question to be answered by the necropsy exam. The primary, proximate, or underlying COD is the etiologically specific disease or injury that initiated the train of events leading to death. Importantly, cardiopulmonary arrest is never the COD, since heart and lung failure is the final, common pathway in all deaths regardless of cause. In some cases, there is also an immediate COD, the last, final etiologically specific disease or injury resulting from the primary COD. The immediate cause of death in animals is often euthanasia necessitated by the severity of the

injury an animal received. The method of euthanasia must meet local, national, and/or species-
specific standards, such as the American
Veterinary Medical Association (AVMA) guidelines on euthanasia. Distinguishing between
approved methods of euthanasia and the unlawful
killing of animals, no matter how purportedly
painless or rapid, can be critical in cases of
alleged animal abuse. The defendant may claim
that they were simply "euthanizing" an animal.
Courts unfamiliar with standards may accept this
argument, and so the difference should be highlighted in the written report.

Whether an animal survived, died, or was
euthanized as a result of abuse or neglect is often
irrelevant in the eyes of the law. What is relevant
is whether abuse or neglect was committed, not
the outcome of events. A clear statement as to the
primary COD with euthanasia listed as the immediate COD necessitated by the primary COD will
aid the court in their deliberations.

In criminal cases "to a reasonable degree of
medical certainty" is required of the expert to
offer an opinion, even though there is no precise
definition of what the phrase means. In civil
actions, "to a reasonable degree of medical probability" is the standard, i.e., more likely than not.
Some have argued that the degree of certainty in
the cause of death should be stated. The following categories of certainty have been offered:

- Undetermined: less than 50% certainty
- Reasonable medical certainty (or investigative
  probability): 50–70% certainty
- Clear and convincing medical certainty (or
  investigative probability): 70–90% certainty
- Beyond any reasonable doubt: 99% certainty
- Beyond any doubt: 100% certainty

For the time being, "to a reasonable degree of
medical certainty" is the generally accepted standard and should be used in the report.

10.4.2 The Mechanism of Death

In contrast to the COD, the mechanism of death
is the altered physiology and/or biochemistry set
in motion by a COD. Mechanisms of death are,
by definition, etiologically nonspecific and
include pathophysiologic events that precede cardiopulmonary failure and/or loss of brain activity
(e.g., septicemia, disseminated intravascular
coagulopathy, brainstem trauma). Although it is
not necessary to discuss the mechanism of death
in the final report, elucidating it will help clarify
one's understanding of a case. In some instances,
the COD may be known with certainty but the
mechanism unknown (e.g., starvation).

10.4.3 The Manner of Death

All human deaths are placed into one of five categories: accident, homicide, suicide, natural, or
undetermined. The manner of human death is a
classification scheme that exists almost exclusively for epidemiological purposes, and the
compiled data are used to track trends and guide
public health recommendations. Application of
this scheme varies by jurisdiction and is governed
more by precedent than statute. Drunken driving
deaths in most states are classified as accidents,
but in others they are called homicides. Regardless
of the manner of death ascribed by the pathologist, the District Attorney has absolute discretion
on whether or not to take a case to a grand jury or
to prosecute the accused. The pathologist's opinion that a human death is a suicide does not
preclude the district attorney from filing murder
charges.

The Federal Bureau of Investigation's National
Incident-Based Reporting System now collects
data on animal cruelty including gross neglect,
torture, organized abuse, and sexual abuse. Thus,
some consideration should be given to ascribing
a manner of death for the purposes of increasing
the value of databases that attempt to track cases
of animal abuse and neglect.

Significant differences between human and
veterinary medicine necessitate adaptation of the
concept of manner of death. Suicide and homicide are not applicable to animal deaths. One
scheme suggests classifying animal deaths as (1)
accidental injury, (2) non-accidental injury, (3)
natural, or (4) undetermined. Brownlie and

Munro suggest the manner of animal death be described as natural or unnatural and the unnatural category subdivided (e.g., blunt force trauma, starvation due to exogenous causes, incised wound, etc.) The court may expect a manner of death, but the ambiguities surrounding the issue should be carefully explained when proffering a manner of death.

10.5   The Opinion

The opinion as to the cause, manner, and mechanism of death is the most important part of the report. In criminal cases, the opinion will be used by prosecutors, defense attorneys, the judge and jury, news media, and other interested parties in an attempt to determine if a crime was committed and, if so, ascertain an appropriate punishment. The opinion may also be used in civil actions. Because the audience for the necropsy report will likely have little medical or scientific training, the opinion should be written in lay language as much as possible. If technical terms are used, they should be briefly explained. In complex cases, it may be useful to provide a glossary that explains medical terms.

The veterinary forensic pathologist, like all experts that provide evidence in legal matters, must bear in mind that their overriding duty is to the court. The pathologist is not an advocate, and their role is to neither convict a guilty party nor is it to save an innocent person. Thus, the report should state the facts or assumptions used to reach an opinion and avoid bias. A common mistake is to extract negative information from the record without putting it into context. Facts that do not support the opinion should be acknowledged and research provided that shows why these facts do not alter the opinion. No expert should comment on issues that fall outside their area of expertise. Due to the nature of their training, veterinary pathologists are not qualified to comment on the quality of surgical or medical care an animal may have received. Clinicians who perform forensic necropsies are advised to adhere to the same standard.

The duty of the pathologist is to distinguish between natural disease on the one hand and accidental trauma versus non-accidental abuse or neglect on the other. It is impossible to know with certainty the intention of someone who caused an injury to an animal. Thus, avoid terms that speculate on the mindset of the person of interest such as "intentional" or "deliberate."

The organization of the opinion will vary depending on judgment and personal preferences. We advocate a structured opinion that starts with the identity of the deceased animal including the name (if known), species, breed, age, and sex. Next, briefly summarize the circumstances surrounding the death investigation. For example, "Mitzi, a 5-year-old female spayed Dachshund, was found dead in an abandoned, locked apartment with no food or water." All evidence reviewed in arriving at the opinion should then be listed. This evidence may include crime scene photographs, police reports, witness statements, statements made by the person of interest, and the medical record. Circumstances at the scene (e.g., ambient temperature, availability of shelter, location and amount of food and water, other animals, urine and fecal soiling, and the presence of hazardous debris) may be crucial to interpreting changes noted at necropsy and establishing a pathophysiologically valid and likely COD. Human forensic pathologists routinely determine a COD based on evidence from the scene when the autopsy does not reveal one but rules out other competing, possible CODs. It is for these reasons, and the frequency of autopsies without significant findings, that the police investigation and crime scene analysis are often as important as the necropsy.

Some animal cruelty investigators mistakenly withhold information with the illogical justification that they "do not want to prejudice the pathologist." If all the evidence is not evaluated, the cross-examining attorney is likely to ask "Doctor, if you are unaware of all the circumstances in this case, how can you possibly arrive at a valid conclusion?" One should insist on being provided all relevant information before issuing a final opinion. Sometimes the necropsy is performed during an active investigation, and not all the evidence will be available. In these cases, it is prudent to indicate the opinion is based on the evidence available at the time of writing and could be modified if new facts come to light.

The next section of the opinion should discuss the necropsy findings. If multiple injuries are present, attempt to organize them in chronological order. For example, "Approximately 40% of the skin over the back is scarred and hairless, which corresponds to the incident of scalding reported by the owner to have occurred 3 months ago. At postmortem, six, partially healed, broken ribs are found, compatible with the report of the veterinarian who treated the dog 3 weeks ago for the sudden onset of chest pain. At necropsy, the abdomen is filled with blood that came from a ruptured liver due to blunt force trauma. The lack of a cellular reaction indicates the liver fracture is recent (less than 8 hours old)."

A concise discussion of the mechanism of death may follow the summary of the necropsy findings. This section must be well researched but should not be encumbered with excessive detail. We find it useful to include references from both standard textbooks as well as current peer-reviewed scientific literature. If only current literature is cited, the cross-examining attorney may ask why you ignored time-honored classics in the field. If only standard reference texts are consulted, that very same attorney will want to know why your opinion rests on books that are out of date in lieu of cutting edge research!

The final section should address any areas of uncertainty. It is often not possible to establish a precise time since death. The exact order of injuries may not be clear since they occurred in rapid succession. Several competing causes of death may be present that preclude ascribing death to a single cause. The degree of pain and suffering are often difficult to establish as is the amount of force needed to inflict an injury. Finally, if the relevance of a specific finding is uncertain, state so explicitly. It is a rare case indeed that is free of any confounding issues.

Appendix 1: Cornell University Forensic Necropsy Report Form

Date:
Time:
Location:
The necropsy was authorized by
Indicate the name of the individual or agency that authorized the necropsy. The authorizing agent is the only one who receives a copy of the results. All other requests for copies of the report should only be honored if accompanied by a subpoena.

The purpose of the examination is to establish, if possible, the cause of death.
The purpose of the examination is modified based on questions that the submitting agency would like answered. For example, the degree of pain and suffering, chronicity of wounds, etc.

The standard Cornell University method of necropsy is performed, with the body in left lateral recumbency and the organs removed en masse, including the pluck, gastrointestinal tract, genitourinary system, eyes, and brain.
For small animals, reference Necropsy Guide for Dogs, Cats, and Small Animals, First Edition. Edited by Sean P. McDonough and Teresa Southard. John Wiley & Sons, Inc, 2017.

For large animals, reference The Necropsy Book, Fourth Edition. Edited by John M. King, Lois Roth-Johnson, David C. Dodd and Marion E. Newson. Charles Louis Davis, DVM Foundation, 2005.

Those in attendance and their role

Pathologist-in-charge:
Assistant:
Observer/representative:

Gross Description:
1. Presentation
    (a) How the body was protected (*e.g.*, plastic bag) and stored prior to necropsy (e.g., refrigerated, frozen, etc.):
    (b) Carcass weight:
    (c) Items accompanying the body (blankets, food bowls, toys):

2. Postmortem changes
   (a) Postmortem interval (indicate if estimated):
   (b) Rigor mortis
   (c) Livor mortis:
   (d) Degree of corneal clouding and collapse:
   (e) Discolorations:
   (f) Drying of the tongue:
   (g) Other (skin slippage, loss of hair, insects, etc.):
3. External exam
   The body is documented with at least five pictures: dorsum, ventrum, left side, right side, and face

   (a) Identifying features
       i. Species:
       ii. Breed:
       iii. Sex:
       iv. Coat color:
       v. Age (indicate if estimated):
       vi. Special markings/tattoos:
       vii. Scanned for microchip (Y/N)

   (If a microchip is found, record the ID number and save as evidence)

   (b) Body condition score (indicate scale) or general condition:
   (c) Items on the body (collars, harnesses, etc.):
   (d) Evidence of medical intervention (intravenous catheters, bandages, etc.):
   (e) Hair coat
       i. General quality:
       ii. Abnormalities/lesions (alopecia, ectoparasites, etc.):
   (f) External exam findings by body region (note WNL if within normal limits or NE if not examined):
       i. Head and neck:
       ii. Thorax:
       iii. Abdomen:
       iv. Thoracic limbs, including nails/hooves:
       v. Pelvic limbs, including nails/hooves:
       vi. Genitalia, perineum, and tail:

4. Internal exam (note WNL if within normal limits or NE if not examined):
   (a) Integument (including mammary glands):
   (b) Head
       i. Subcuticular surface of scalp:
       ii. Skull:
       iii. Brain and meninges:
       iv. Nasal cavity/nasal sinuses:
       v. Atlanto-occipital junction:
       vi. Pinnae:
       vii. External ear canal:
       viii. Middle and inner ears:
   (c) Neck and pharynx
       i. Oral cavity (teeth and gums, hard and soft palate):
       ii. Tongue:
       iii. Pharynx:
       iv. Larynx, hyoid apparatus, and trachea:
       v. Neck vessels and strap muscles:
   (d) Thoracic wall and pleural space:
   (e) Abdominal wall and peritoneal space:
   (f) Vertebral column and spinal cord:
   (g) Cardiovascular system:
   (h) Respiratory system:
   (i) Digestive system:
   (j) Hepatobiliary system and pancreas:
   (k) Reticuloendothelial system:
   (l) Urogenital system:
   (m) Endocrine system:
   (n) Musculoskeletal system:
       i. Joints opened:
   (o) Additional dissection (Placenta, etc.):
5. Evidence of trauma:
   Since projectiles often pass through multiple organs and body regions, it is best to describe them in a single, coherent manner rather than separating the projectile path across multiple sections of the report. In the event of multiple wounds, each should be numbered and referred to by number in the report. Diagrams showing the location of entrance and exit wounds are also useful.

Ancillary Procedures and Laboratory Tests:

Histologic Description:
1. Block Listing
2. List slide number and tissues.

Significant changes were found in the following tissues:

Pathologic Diagnoses

Cause of Death:

To a reasonable degree of medical certainty, the primary cause of death is …..

List the primary (proximate/underlying) cause of death first, and then list the immediate cause of death (e.g., euthanasia). The primary (underlying, proximate) cause of death is the etiologically specific first, earliest injury or disease that set in motion the sequence of events that led to death (if not for X, the animal would still be alive). **Cardiopulmonary arrest is NEVER the underlying cause of death (heart and lungs fail in all animals that die).** The immediate cause of death is the last, final, etiologically specific injury or disease, different from but the consequence of the underlying cause of death. This includes euthanasia.

Opinion

Appendix 2

CONDITION OF SKIN, HAIRCOAT, AND NAILS

Date_____ Investigating Agency_____
Case#_____ Officer_____ Veterinarian_____
Animal ID_____ Breed_____ Color_____ Male___ Female___
Physical Care Scale: Haircoat and Nails (1) (2) (3) (4) (5)
Record skin lesions or wounds. Describe on diagram or comments section.

COMMENTS:

Physical Care Scale
(1) Adequate – clean, hair can be easily brushed or combed; nails ok
(2) Lapsed – haircoat may be somewhat dirty or have a few mats present that are easily removed; remainder of coat can be easily brushed or combed; nails need a trim
(3) Borderline – numerous mats but can still be groomed without a total clip down; no significant fecal or urine soiling; nails overgrown which may alter gait
(4) Poor – substantial matting of haircoat; large sections of hair matted together; occasional foreign material embedded in mats; much of the hair will need to be clipped; fecal and urine soiling of hind end and legs; long nails that interfere with normal gait
(5) Terrible – haircoat is single mat that prevents normal movement and interferes with vision; soiling of hind end and legs with trapped urine and feces; complete clipdown required; nails extremely overgrown into circles and may be penetrating pads causing pain and infection; nails interfering with normal gait
(www.tufts.edu/vet/hoarding/pubs/tacc.pdf)

Used with permission by Dr. Melinda Merck

Appendix 3

CONDITION OF SKIN, HAIRCOAT, AND NAILS

Date_____ Investigating Agency_____

Case#_____ Officer_____ Veterinarian_____

Animal ID_____ Breed_____ Color_____ Male___ Female___

Physical Care Scale: Haircoat and Nails (1) (2) (3) (4) (5)

Record skin lesions or wounds. Describe on diagram or comments section.

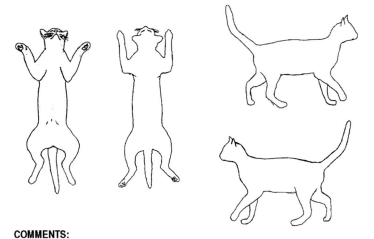

COMMENTS:

Physical Care Scale

(1) Adequate – clean, hair can be easily brushed or combed; nails ok

(2) Lapsed – haircoat may be somewhat dirty or have a few mats present that are easily removed; remainder of coat can be easily brushed or combed; nails need a trim

(3) Borderline – numerous mats but can still be groomed without a total clip down; no significant fecal or urine soiling; nails overgrown which may alter gait

(4) Poor – substantial matting of haircoat; large sections of hair matted together; occasional foreign material embedded in mats; much of the hair will need to be clipped; fecal and urine soiling of hind end and legs; long nails that interfere with normal gait

(5) Terrible – haircoat is single mat that prevents normal movement and interferes with vision; soiling of hind end and legs with trapped urine and feces; complete clipdown required; nails extremely overgrown into circles and may be penetrating pads causing pain and infection; nails interfering with normal gait (www.tufts.edu/vet/hoarding/pubs/tacc.pdf)

Used with permission by Dr. Melinda Merck

Bibliography

1. Adelson L. The pathology of homicide: a vade mecum for pathologist, prosecutor and defense counsel. Springfield, IL: Charles C. Thomas; 1974.
2. Dolinak D, Matshes E, Lew E. Forensic pathology: principles and practice. Boston, MA: Elsevier Academic Press; 2005.
3. Froede RC, editor. Handbook of forensic pathology. 2nd ed. Northfield, IL: College of American Pathologists; 2003.
4. Prahlow JA, editor. Basic competencies in forensic pathology. Northfield, IL: College of American Pathologists; 2006.
5. Saukko P, Knight B. Knight's forensic pathology. 4th ed. Boca Raton, FL: CRC Press; 2016.
6. McDonough SP and Southard T, eds. Necropsy guide for dogs, cats, and small animals, 1st ed. Ames, IA: Wiley, 2017.
7. King JM, Roth-Johnson L, Dodd DC, Newson ME. The necropsy book. 4th ed: Gurney, IL, Charles Louis Davis, DVM Foundation; 2005.

Age Determination in Dogs and Cats

11

Lerah K. Sutton, Jason H. Byrd, and Jason W. Brooks

11.1 Introduction

Veterinary forensic science is a growing field within the forensic sciences that applies principles of both veterinary medicine and forensic science to investigate crimes against animals including cruelty, neglect, and death. As with any criminal investigation, it is paramount to know as much information about the victim as possible. In a an investigation with a human victim, the investigators seek to establish the "biological profile" wherein age, sex, ancestry/race, stature, unique pathology, and any trauma present are determined via osteological analysis when only skeletal remains are present. The same aspects of a biological profile are desired in an animal investigation with the main difference being species and breed instead of ancestry/race. In veterinary practice, age is traditionally estimated by visual examination of the dentition, assessing for completeness of dental eruption and extent of tooth wear. The technique, however, is known to be imprecise and its greatest utility limited to the first several months of life, prior to the eruption of the full adult dentition. In human forensic science, the main technique for age determination in the biological profile is by physeal and ossification center appearance and closure rates. This is useful in humans from birth to approximately 24–26 years and is well documented in radiographic atlases which show the progressive development of various bones as individuals age [1]. Similar radiographic atlases have been published documenting the normal growth and development rates of canines and felines according to anatomical region that can be used, with some modification, to assess age [2–9]. The anatomical processes of bone development proceeds in the same ways in humans and animals; therefore, the same techniques for determination of various aspects of the biological profile can be ascertained using common research protocols.

This manuscript represents a portion of a thesis written by Lerah Sutton at the University of Florida based on research conducted in partial fulfillment of the requirements for a Master of Science degree.

L.K. Sutton, M.S. (✉)
Departments of Pathology, Immunology and Laboratory Medicine, College of Medicine, University of Florida, Gainesville, FL 32608, USA

William R. Maples Center for Forensic Medicine, College of Medicine, University of Florida, 4800 SW 35th Dr., Gainesville, FL 32608, USA
e-mail: lerahsutton@ufl.edu

J.H. Byrd, Ph.D.
Departments of Pathology, Immunology and Laboratory Medicine, College of Medicine, University of Florida, Gainesville, FL 32608, USA

J.W. Brooks, VMD, PhD, DACVP
Department of Veterinary and Biomedical Sciences, Animal Diagnostic Laboratory, The Pennsylvania State University, University Park, PA 16802, USA
e-mail: jwb21@psu.edu

© Springer International Publishing AG 2018
J.W. Brooks (ed.), *Veterinary Forensic Pathology, Volume 2*,
https://doi.org/10.1007/978-3-319-67175-8_11

It is fundamental to the analysis of bone for forensic investigation, specifically age determination, to first understand bone growth and development, and the components of bone that are responsible for bone growth. Anatomically speaking, there are four major areas of bone development: the epiphysis, the growth plate, the metaphysis, and the diaphysis. The diaphysis is the shaft portion of long bones which develops in utero and contains the primary ossification center. The epiphysis is the portion on the distal and proximal ends which contains the secondary ossification center. The portion of bone between the epiphysis and the diaphysis and the metaphysis is considered to be the growing end of the bone. The growth plate (also sometimes called the epiphyseal plate) is the radiolucent (not opaque in radiographs) linear portion between the epiphysis and the metaphysis that is responsible for growth along the long axis of the bone. These features are the same in the long bones of both animals and humans [10].

Ossification occurs in both the diaphysis and the epiphysis and continues until only a small amount of cartilage is left which forms a thin line—the epiphyseal plate—which separates the two parts. This process continues until the osteoblasts no longer multiply, and as a result the epiphyseal plate becomes ossified meaning the epiphysis and diaphysis fuse, at which time growth ceases. This occurs throughout the human skeleton in a known order, and, by comparison of the "normal" published standards to an unknown specimen, skeletal age can be determined [1].

The idea of what is "normal" in both animals and humans is an important aspect to the application of studies of this nature in forensic casework and clinical work. There are a number of factors that can affect bone growth and cause abnormal radiographic findings. Clinically, an understanding of what is normal is necessary to identify disorders that affect growth and the orthopedic system as a whole, including mobility, joint pain, etc. Many factors including genetics, nutrition, activity, disease, and trauma can affect the development rates of the skeleton causing deviation from the norm. In a veterinary context, differences between breeds must be considered,

whereas in a forensic context, trauma plays a more important role than other factors since it can be an indicator of animal cruelty.

11.2 Methods for Age Determination

In the veterinary community, age of specimens has been traditionally assessed using dentition, rather than physeal closure, since it is assessed rather easily. A chart indicating the typical eruption times of teeth in canines and felines is shown in Table 11.1. The difficulty with utilizing dentition, particularly in a forensic context, is that there is a good deal of variation in the eruption times depending on breed, nutrition, and the quality of dental care an animal has received. Often, neglected animals are not given proper diets or proper veterinary care; thus, their teeth are in poor condition. The teeth may be missing, decayed, or have stunted growth as a result of substandard diet and improper care. Because dental eruption time are useful only until all teeth have erupted, age estimation after the appearance of the full adult dentition is problematic. In this case, practitioners attempt to estimate age based on wear patterns of incisor, premolar, and molar teeth. Such wear, however, is highly variable and subject to diet, nutritional status, and other factors. It is therefore prudent to utilize a secondary method to estimate age, if age estimation based on dentition is not possible or if it is insufficient for the age determination desired (i.e., specifically age beyond 6 months) [8]. Age estimation from physeal and ossification center appearance and closure rates provide another method which can be utilized in both clinical and forensic cases.

This research addressed age determination in domestic small animals (i.e., cats and dogs) through assessment of rates of physeal and ossification center appearance and closure rates across all breeds of canines and felines. The main method used for accumulating the data was an extensive review of the published literature on physeal and ossification center formation and closure rates for cats and dogs. The primary source utilized in this study was the *Atlas of*

Table 11.1 Typical dental eruption times for canines and felines (Modified with permission from Atlas of Normal Radiographic Anatomy and Anatomic Variants in the Dog and Cat by Thrall and Robertson 2011)

Site	Canine	Feline
Scapula		
• Body	Birth	Birth
• Supraglenoid tubercle	6–7 weeks	7–9 weeks
Humerus		
• Proximal epiphysis (head and tubercles)	1–2 weeks	1–2 weeks
• Diaphysis	Birth	Birth
• Condyle	2–3 weeks	2–4 weeks
• Medial epicondyle	6–8 weeks	6–8 weeks
Radius		
• Proximal epiphysis	3–5 weeks	2–4 weeks
• Diaphysis	Birth	Birth
• Distal epiphysis	2–4 weeks	2–4 weeks
Ulna		
• Olecranon tubercle	6–8 weeks	4–5 weeks
• Diaphysis	Birth	Birth
• Anconeal process	6–8 weeks	
• Distal epiphysis	5–6 weeks	3–4 weeks
Carpus		
• Radial carpal (three centers)	3–6 weeks	3–8 weeks
• Other carpal bones	2 weeks	3–8 weeks
• Accessory carpal—diaphysis	2 weeks	3–8 weeks
• Accessory carpal—epiphysis	6–7 weeks	3–8 weeks
• Sesamoid bone in abductor pollicis longus	4 months	
Metacarpus/metatarsus		
• Diaphysis of 1–5	Birth	Birth
• Proximal epiphysis of MC1	5–7 weeks	
• Distal epiphysis of MC2–5	3–4 weeks	3 weeks
• Palmar sesamoid bones	2 months	2–2.5 months
• Dorsal sesamoid bones	4 months	
Phalanges (fore and hind)		
• P1—Diaphysis of digits 1–5	Birth	Birth
• P1—Proximal epiphysis digit 1	5–7 weeks	3–4 weeks
• P1—Distal epiphysis digits 2–5	4–6 weeks	3–4 weeks
• P2—Diaphysis of digits 2–5	Birth	Birth

(continued)

Table 11.1 (continued)

Site	Canine	Feline
• P2—Proximal epiphysis of digits 2–5	4–6 weeks	4 weeks
• P3 (one ossification center)	Birth	Birth

Normal Radiographic Anatomy and Anatomic Variants in the Dog and Cat [8]. This study utilized 12 of the major publications in veterinary clinical radiology published regarding physeal and ossification center appearance and closure rates, 5 of which were independently assessed for this study in addition to 2 others not utilized by the primary source for a total of 7 sources utilized for the compilation of data found in Tables 11.1, 11.2, 11.3, 11.4, 11.5, 11.6, 11.7, 11.8 and 11.9 [8]. All of the published literature was based upon "normal" subjects—that is, subjects who had undergone lifelong assessment by researchers to ensure that no medical conditions (genetic or otherwise), trauma, activity or inactivity, or dietary conditions would affect the progression of typical bone growth for study purposes.

Additionally, this study validated the compiled published literature data based on an independent evaluation of radiographs obtained from the University of Florida College of Veterinary Medicine: Department of Diagnostic Imaging. For this study, only "normal" subjects were assessed for validation. Criteria for a "normal" subject in the validation portion of this study included: known age documented with the greatest degree of accuracy known by the owner, no known medical conditions (genetic or otherwise) that affect bone growth and development, and no trauma to the area of assessment. Several of the radiographs viewed for the validation portion of this study had trauma present since they were taken as part of a veterinary exam at the University of Florida's Small Animal Hospital. "No trauma to the area of assessment" does not mean that there was no soft tissue trauma present; it is rather intended to mean that the radiograph was utilized if it showed other anatomical regions suitable for analysis that were unaffected by identified localized trauma.

Table 11.2 Approximate ages at which physeal and ossification centers appear for canines and felines (Modified with permission from Atlas of Normal Radiographic Anatomy and Anatomic Variants in the Dog and Cat by Thrall and Robertson 2011)

Pelvis		
• Ilium/ischium/pubis	Birth	Birth
• Acetabular bone	2–3 months	
• Iliac crest	4–5 months	
• Ischial tuberosity	3–4 months	
• Ischial arch	6 months	
Femur		
• Greater trochanter	7–9 weeks	5–6 weeks
• Lesser trochanter	7–9 weeks	6–7 weeks
• Head	1–2 weeks	2 weeks
• Diaphysis	Birth	Birth
• Distal epiphysis	3–4 weeks	1–2 weeks
Stifle sesamoid bones		
• Patella	6–9 weeks	8–9 weeks
• Fabellae	3 months	10 weeks
• Popliteal sesamoid	3–4 months	
Tibia		
• Tibial tuberosity	7–8 weeks	6–7 weeks
• Proximal epiphysis	2–4 weeks	2 weeks
• Diaphysis	Birth	Birth
• Distal epiphysis	2–4 weeks	2 weeks
• Medial malleolus	3 months	
Fibula		
• Proximal epiphysis	8–10 weeks	6–7 weeks
• Diaphysis	Birth	Birth
• Distal epiphysis	4–7 weeks	3–4 weeks
Tarsus		
• Talus	Birth	Birth
• Calcaneus—tuber calcanei	6 weeks	4 weeks
• Calcaneus—diaphysis	Birth	Birth
• Central tarsal bone	3 weeks	4–7 weeks
• First and second tarsal bones	4 weeks	4–7 weeks
• Third tarsal bone	3 weeks	4–7 weeks
• Fourth tarsal bone	2 weeks	4–7 weeks

Table 11.3 Approximate age when physeal and ossification center closure occurs for canines and felines (Modified with permission from Atlas of Normal Radiographic Anatomy and Anatomic Variants in the Dog and Cat by Thrall and Robertson 2011)

Site	Canine	Feline
Scapula		
• Supraglenoid tubercle	4–7 months	3.5–4 months
Humerus		
• Proximal	10–15 months	18–24 months
• Medial epicondyle	6–8 months	
• Condyle to shaft	6–8 months	3.5–4 months
• Condyle (lateral and medial parts)	6–10 weeks	3.5 months
Radius		
• Proximal	7–10 months	5–7 months
• Distal	10–12 months	14–22 months
Ulna		
• Anconeal process	< 5 months	
• Olecranon tuberosity	7–10 months	9–13 months
• Distal	9–12 months	14–25 months
Metacarpus/metatarsus		
• MC1 proximal	6–7 months	4.5–5 months
• MC2-5 distal	6–7 months	4.5–5 months
Phalanges (fore and hind)		
• P1 and P2 proximal	6–7 months	
Pelvis		
• Acetabular bone	3–5 months	
• Ischiatic tuberosity	10–12 months	
• Iliac crest	24–36 months	
• Pubic symphysis	4–5 months	
Femur		
• Head, capital physis	8–11 months	7–11 months
• Greater trochanter	9–12 months	13–19 months
• Lesser trochanter	9–12 months	
• Distal physis	9–12 months	
Tibia		

(continued)

Table 11.3 (continued)

Site	Canine	Feline
• Tibial tuberosity	10–12 months	9–10 months
• Tibial plateau	9–10 months	12–19 months
• Distal physis	12–15 months	10–12 months
• Medial malleolus	3–5 months	
Fibula		
• Proximal	10–12 months	13–18 months
• Distal (lateral malleolus)	12–13 months	10–14 months
Tarsus		
• Calcaneus tuberosity	6–7 months	

Table 11.4 Approximate age at which physeal and ossification centers appear in the spine for canines (Modified with permission from Atlas of Normal Radiographic Anatomy and Anatomic Variants in the Dog and Cat by Thrall and Robertson 2011)

Site	Canine
Atlas (three centers of ossification)	
• Neural arch (bilateral)	Birth
• Intercentrum	Birth
Axis (seven centers of ossification)	
• Centrum of proatlas	6 weeks
• Centrum 1	Birth
• Intercentrum 2	3 weeks
• Centrum 2	Birth
• Neural arch (bilateral)	Birth
• Caudal epiphysis	2 weeks
Cervical, thoracic, lumbar, sacral vertebrae	
• Paired neural arches and centrum	Birth
• Cranial and caudal epiphyses	2 weeks

Table 11.5 Approximate age when physeal and ossification center closure occurs in the spine for canines (Modified with permission from Atlas of Normal Radiographic Anatomy and Anatomic Variants in the Dog and Cat by Thrall and Robertson 2011)

Site	Canine
Atlas (three centers of ossification)	
• Arches fuse	3–4 months
• Intercentrum	3–4 months
Axis	
• Centrum of proatlas + C1	100–110 days
• Intercentrum 2, centrum 1, and centrum 2	3.3–5 months
• Neural arches (bilateral)	30 days
• Caudal physis	7–12 months
Cervical, thoracic, lumbar	
• Cranial physis	7–10 months
• Caudal physis	8–12 months
Sacrum	
• Cranial and caudal physes	7–12 months
Caudal	
• Cranial and caudal physes	7–12 months

Table 11.6 Approximate age when fusion of skull bones occurs for canines and felines (Modified with permission from Atlas of Normal Radiographic Anatomy and Anatomic Variants in the Dog and Cat by Thrall and Robertson 2011)

Site	Canine and Feline
Occipital	
• Basilar part	2.5–5 months
• Squamous part	3–4 months
• Interparietal part	Before birth
Sphenoid	
• Body/wings of presphenoid	Before birth
• Body/wings of basisphenoid	3–4 years
• Basisphenoid and presphenoid	1–2 years
• Sphenobasilar suture	8–10 months
Parietal	
• Interparietal suture	2–3 years
Frontal	
• Interfrontal suture	3–4 years
Temporal	
• Petrosquamos suture	2–3 years
Mandible	
• Intermandibular symphysis	Never or very late

Validation of the available data occurred through a sampling procedure of applicable (i.e., normal) radiographs from the 50 most recent dogs and the 50 most recent cats between May and December 2012 admitted to the University of Florida Small Animal Hospital. The studies utilized for data compilation were based on various breeds of dogs and cats; thus, the validation portion of this study was not breed specific. Within the studies utilized, many did not list the specific breeds that were assessed; however, two did—beagles and greyhounds—so an effort was made to include these breeds within the validation study.

The subjects for validation were identified using the University of Florida, College of Veterinary Medicine's Radiology Information

System (RIS), and their radiographs were viewed using the Picture Archiving and Communication Systems (PACS). All subjects were searched by accession number only. Once the record was identified as suitable through RIS, the accession number was brought up in PACS to view the radiograph. For radiographic assessment purposes, the primary source was used as a guide for interpretation of appropriate stages of physeal and ossification center appearance and closure; diagrams contained within it were used as an initial guide for the ways in which specific bones

Table 11.7 Approximate ages of physeal and ossification center appearance (*black*) and closure (*light gray*) rates for canines (Overlap indicated in dark gray)

Scapula	B	1w	2w	3w	4w	5w	6w	7w	8w	2m	3m	4m	5m	6m	7m	8m	9m	10m	11m	12m	1yr	2yr	3yr	4yr
o Body	■																							
o Supraglenoid tubercle							■	■				▓	▓	▓										

Humerus	B	1w	2w	3w	4w	5w	6w	7w	8w	2m	3m	4m	5m	6m	7m	8m	9m	10m	11m	12m	1yr	2yr	3yr	4yr
o Proximal epiphysis (head and tubercles)		■																▓	▓	▓	▓	▓		
o Diaphysis	■													▓	▓	▓								
o Condyle (medial and lateral)				■											▓	▓	▓							
o Medial epicondyle						■	■																	

Radius	B	1w	2w	3w	4w	5w	6w	7w	8w	2m	3m	4m	5m	6m	7m	8m	9m	10m	11m	12m	1yr	2yr	3yr	4yr
o Proximal epiphysis				■	■	■										▓	▓	▓	▓	▓				
o Diaphysis	■																							
o Distal epiphysis				■	■	■												▓	▓	▓	▓			

Ulna	B	1w	2w	3w	4w	5w	6w	7w	8w	2m	3m	4m	5m	6m	7m	8m	9m	10m	11m	12m	1yr	2yr	3yr	4yr
o Olecranon tubercle								■	■							▓	▓	▓	▓					
o Diaphysis	■																							
o Anconeal process							■	■					▓											
o Distal epiphysis						■	■											▓	▓	▓	▓			

Carpus	B	1w	2w	3w	4w	5w	6w	7w	8w	2m	3m	4m	5m	6m	7m	8m	9m	10m	11m	12m	1yr	2yr	3yr	4yr
o Radial carpal (3 centers)				■	■	■	■																	
o Other carpal bones				■																				
o Accessory carpal – diaphysis				■									▓	▓										
o Accessory carpal – epiphysis							■	■																
o Sesamoid bone in abductor pollicis longus												■												

Metacarpus/metatarsus	B	1w	2w	3w	4w	5w	6w	7w	8w	2m	3m	4m	5m	6m	7m	8m	9m	10m	11m	12m	1yr	2yr	3yr	4yr
o Diaphysis of 1-5	■																							
o Proximal epiphysis of MC1						■	■	■						▓	▓									
o Distal epiphysis of MC2-5				■										▓	▓									
o Palmar sesamoid bones										■														
o Dorsal sesamoid bones												■												

Phalanges (fore and hind)	B	1w	2w	3w	4w	5w	6w	7w	8w	2m	3m	4m	5m	6m	7m	8m	9m	10m	11m	12m	1yr	2yr	3yr	4yr
o P1 – Diaphysis of digits 1-5	■																							
o P1 – Proximal epiphysis digit 1						■	■	■						▓	▓									
o P1 – Distal epiphysis digits 2-5				■	■																			
o P2 – Diaphysis of digits 2-5	■																							
o P2 – Proximal epiphysis of digits 2-5					■	■	■							▓	▓									
o P3 (one ossification center)	■																							

Pelvis	B	1w	2w	3w	4w	5w	6w	7w	8w	2m	3m	4m	5m	6m	7m	8m	9m	10m	11m	12m	1yr	2yr	3yr	4yr
o Ilium/ischium/pubis	■												▓	▓										
o Acetabular bone									■	▓		▓	▓											
o Iliac crest																							▓	
o Ischial tuberosity											■						▓						▓	
o Ischial arch														■										
Femur	B	1w	2w	3w	4w	5w	6w	7w	8w	2m	3m	4m	5m	6m	7m	8m	9m	10m	11m	12m	1yr	2yr	3yr	4yr
o Greater trochanter																		▓	▓					
o Lesser trochanter								7-9 weeks										▓	▓					
o Head				■																				
o Diaphysis	■																							
o Distal epiphysis					■													▓	▓	▓				
Stifle sesamoid bones	B	1w	2w	3w	4w	5w	6w	7w	8w	2m	3m	4m	5m	6m	7m	8m	9m	10m	11m	12m	1yr	2yr	3yr	4yr
o Patella								6-9 weeks																
o Fabellae																								
o Popliteal sesamoid											■	■												
Tibia	B	1w	2w	3w	4w	5w	6w	7w	8w	2m	3m	4m	5m	6m	7m	8m	9m	10m	11m	12m	1yr	2yr	3yr	4yr
o Tibial tuberosity							■										▓							
o Proximal epiphysis				■	■																			
o Diaphysis	■																							
o Distal epiphysis				■	■	■														12-15m				
o Medial malleolus														■	▓									
Fibula	B	1w	2w	3w	4w	5w	6w	7w	8w	2m	3m	4m	5m	6m	7m	8m	9m	10m	11m	12m	1yr	2yr	3yr	4yr
o Proximal epiphysis									8-10wk											▓	▓			
o Diaphysis	■																							
o Distal epiphysis					■	■	■	■												12-13m				
Tarsus	B	1w	2w	3w	4w	5w	6w	7w	8w	2m	3m	4m	5m	6m	7m	8m	9m	10m	11m	12m	1yr	2yr	3yr	4yr
o Talus	■																							
o Calcaneus – tuber calcanei						■								▓										
o Calcaneus – diaphysis	■																							
o Central tarsal bone				■																				
o First and second tarsal bones					■																			
o Third tarsal bone				■																				
o Fourth tarsal bone				■																				

within each anatomical region grow and ossify as animals age [8]. Examples of these diagrams are shown in Figs. 11.1 and 11.2.

11.3   Data Tables for Clinical and Forensic Use

Through the compilation of data from the published literature, initial data tables (Tables 11.2, 11.3, 11.4, 11.5, and 11.6) outlining the times at which physeal and ossification center appearance and closures occur were created. The anatomical regions outlined in these tables were modified with permission from the tables found in the primary source [8]. These primary tables were then validated using the methods detailed above, and once all data had been corroborated through both the published literature and the University of Florida radiographs, final tables (Tables 11.7, 11.8, and 11.9) were created with a specific focus on forensic application and use. These final tables were arranged with a horizontal time axis ranging in weeks from birth through 8 weeks, months through 12 months, and years through 4 years and a vertical axis of anatomic regions of the body. Within these tables according to the horizontal and vertical axis system, boxes for time periods for each anatomic body region were created which could be filled in with different colors (black for appearance and light gray for closure) of the physes and ossification centers. The master's thesis published by Chapman was the first study of its kind addressing age determination from epiphyseal closure rates in a veterinary context which organized the information by anatomical region with the intended use by clinical radiologists and other veterinary practitioners [2]. It was this format that became the model followed by all other subsequent studies of this nature. By arranging the data in both a chronological and anatomical way in this study, it allows clinical and forensic application of the data.

Preliminary review of the data produced initial tables show in the appendix labeled Tables 11.2, 11.3, 11.4, 11.5, and 11.6. Table 11.2 indicates the approximate ages at which physeal and ossification centers appear for both dogs and cats. Table 11.3 indicates the approximate ages at which physeal and ossification centers close for

Table 11.8 Approximate ages of physeal and ossification center appearance (*black*) and closure (*light gray*) rates for felines

Scapula	B	1w	2w	3w	4w	5w	6w	7w	8w	2m	3m	4m	5m	6m	7m	8m	9m	10m	11m	12m	1yr	2yr	3yr	4yr
o Body	█																							
o Supraglenoid tubercle								7-9 weeks			3.5-4m													
Humerus	B	1w	2w	3w	4w	5w	6w	7w	8w	2m	3m	4m	5m	6m	7m	8m	9m	10m	11m	12m	1yr	2yr	3yr	4yr
o Proximal epiphysis (head and tubercles)		█																				18-24m		
o Diaphysis	█										3.5-4m													
o				█	█	█					3.5m													
o Medial epicondyle						█	█	█																
Radius	B	1w	2w	3w	4w	5w	6w	7w	8w	2m	3m	4m	5m	6m	7m	8m	9m	10m	11m	12m	1yr	2yr	3yr	4yr
o Proximal epiphysis				█	█									▨	▨									
o Diaphysis	█																							
o Distal epiphysis				█	█																	14-22m		
Ulna	B	1w	2w	3w	4w	5w	6w	7w	8w	2m	3m	4m	5m	6m	7m	8m	9m	10m	11m	12m	1yr	2yr	3yr	4yr
o Olecranon tubercle					█	█												9-13m						
o Diaphysis	█																							
o Anconeal process																								
o Distal epiphysis				█	█	█																14-25m		
Carpus	B	1w	2w	3w	4w	5w	6w	7w	8w	2m	3m	4m	5m	6m	7m	8m	9m	10m	11m	12m	1yr	2yr	3yr	4yr
o Radial carpal (3 centers)				█	█	█	█	█	█															
o Other carpal bones				█	█	█	█	█	█															
o Accessory carpal – diaphysis				█	█	█	█	█	█			▨												
o Accessory carpal – epiphysis				█	█	█	█	█	█			▨												
o Sesamoid bone in abductor pollicis longus																								
Metacarpus/metatarsus	B	1w	2w	3w	4w	5w	6w	7w	8w	2m	3m	4m	5m	6m	7m	8m	9m	10m	11m	12m	1yr	2yr	3yr	4yr
o Diaphysis of 1-5	█																							
o Proximal epiphysis of MC1												4.5-5m												
o Distal epiphysis of MC2-5				█								4.5-5m												
o Palmar sesamoid bones										2-2.5m														
o Dorsal sesamoid bones																								
Phalanges (fore and hind)	B	1w	2w	3w	4w	5w	6w	7w	8w	2m	3m	4m	5m	6m	7m	8m	9m	10m	11m	12m	1yr	2yr	3yr	4yr
o P1 – Diaphysis of digits 1-5	█																							
o P1 – Proximal epiphysis digit 1				█								▨												
o P1 – Distal epiphysis digits 2-5																								
o P2 – Diaphysis of digits 2-5	█																							
o P2 – Proximal epiphysis of digits 2-5					█							▨												
o P3 (one ossification center)	█																							

	B	1w	2w	3w	4w	5w	6w	7w	8w	2m	3m	4m	5m	6m	7m	8m	9m	10m	11m	12m	1yr	2yr	3yr	4yr
Pelvis																								
o Ilium/ischium/pubis	■																							
o Acetabular bone																								
o Iliac crest																								
o Ischial tuberosity																								
o Ischial arch																								
Femur																								
o Greater trochanter						■	■														13-19m			
o Lesser trochanter							■	■																
o Head				■													▒	▒	▒					
o Diaphysis	■																							
o Distal epiphysis				■																				
Stifle sesamoid bones																								
o Patella									8-9wks															
o Fabellae									10w															
o Popliteal sesamoid											▒	▒												
Tibia																								
o Tibial tuberosity							■	■									▒							
o Proximal epiphysis				■																	12-16m			
o Diaphysis	■																							
o Distal epiphysis				■													▒	▒						
o Medial malleolus																								
Fibula																								
o Proximal epiphysis							■	■													13-18m			
o Diaphysis	■																							
o Distal epiphysis				■														10-14m						
Tarsus																								
o Talus	■																							
o Calcaneus – tuber calcanei					■																			
o Calcaneus – diaphysis	■																							
o Central tarsal bone					■	■	■	■																
o First and second tarsal bones					■	■	■	■																
o Third tarsal bone					■	■	■	■																
o Fourth tarsal bone					■	■	■	■																

both dogs and cats. Both of these tables are arranged by anatomic body region on the vertical axis with the bones of the forelimb first followed by bones of the hind limb. They are listed with anatomical region headings according to the major bone within which the physes and ossification centers are present (e.g., scapula, humerus, pelvis, femur, etc.), and underneath those headings are listed the specific physes and ossification centers. Tables 11.4 and 11.5 show the approximate ages at which physeal and ossification center appearance and closure occur, respectively, for appearance and closure. These two tables only contain data for canines as there was not available data on the spinal appearance and fusion rates for felines. Table 11.6 shows a list of approximate ages at which the skull bones fuse for dogs and cats. There are not separate columns for dog and cat since these times are approximately the same for both species.

The validation of Tables 11.2, 11.3, 11.4, 11.5, and 11.6 using the methodology detailed above showed that the data were consistent and accurate across all literature reviewed. The validation was not breed specific so there was some of variation within the time frames indicated within these tables. Larger dogs, in particular, were at the longer end of the time range. "Giant breeds" such as Great Danes, Mastiffs, or Saint Bernards were sometimes beyond the published ranges for appearance and closure. This is supported by published literature that indicates giant-breed

Table 11.9 Approximate ages of physeal and ossification center appearance (*black*) and closure (*light gray*) rates in the spine for canines

Atlas (three centers of ossification)	B	1w	2w	3w	4w	5w	6w	7w	8w	2m	3m	4m	5m	6m	7m	8m	9m	10m	11m	12m	1yr	2yr	3yr	4yr
o Neural arch (bilateral)	■																							
o Intercentrum																								
Axis (seven centers of ossification)	**B**	**1w**	**2w**	**3w**	**4w**	**5w**	**6w**	**7w**	**8w**	**2m**	**3m**	**4m**	**5m**	**6m**	**7m**	**8m**	**9m**	**10m**	**11m**	**12m**	**1yr**	**2yr**	**3yr**	**4yr**
o Centrum of proatlas							■				~3.5m													
o Centrum 1	■										3.3–5m													
o Intercentrum 2				■							3.3–5m													
o Centrum 2	■										3.3–5m													
o Neural arch (bilateral)	■																							
o Caudal epiphysis			■																					
Cervical, thoracic, lumbar	**B**	**1w**	**2w**	**3w**	**4w**	**5w**	**6w**	**7w**	**8w**	**2m**	**3m**	**4m**	**5m**	**6m**	**7m**	**8m**	**9m**	**10m**	**11m**	**12m**	**1yr**	**2yr**	**3yr**	**4yr**
o Paired neural arches and centrum	■																							
o Cranial epiphysis		■																						
o Caudal epiphysis		■																						
Sacrum and caudal	**B**	**1w**	**2w**	**3w**	**4w**	**5w**	**6w**	**7w**	**8w**	**2m**	**3m**	**4m**	**5m**	**6m**	**7m**	**8m**	**9m**	**10m**	**11m**	**12m**	**1yr**	**2yr**	**3yr**	**4yr**
o Cranial and caudal physes		■																						

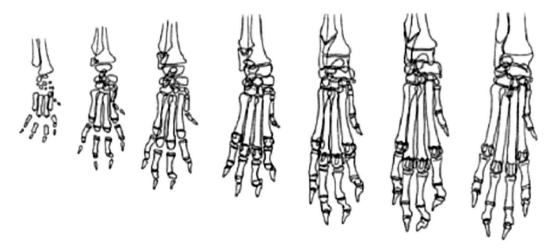

Fig. 11.1 Diagram of canine manus, dorsopalmar view (reproduced with permission from Atlas of Normal Radiographic Anatomy and Anatomic Variants in the Dog and Cat by Thrall and Robertson 2011)

dogs experience delays of closure of some of their long bones by periods of up to 3–6 months beyond typical published data. It is generally accepted that closure occurs earlier in smaller animals which was seen in the validation portion of this study where smaller animals were at the earlier range of times of closure [10].

The validated data in the initial tables were used to create a new set of tables (Tables 11.7, 11.8, and 11.9) that are presented and arranged differently from previously published literature. Table 11.7 shows the approximate age ranges at which physeal and ossification centers appear and close for canines. Table 11.8 shows the

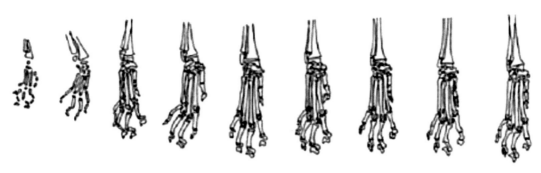

Fig. 11.2 Diagram of feline manus, dorsomedial plantarolateral oblique view (reproduced with permission from Atlas of Normal Radiographic Anatomy and Anatomic Variants in the Dog and Cat by Thrall and Robertson 2011)

approximate age ranges at which physeal and ossification centers appear and close for felines. Table 11.9 shows the approximate age ranges at which physeal and ossification centers appear and close in the spine for canines. The final tables created for this study are arranged with two axes which can be used together or independently for estimating the approximate age at which physeal and ossification center appearance and fusion occurs. The vertical axis is arranged the same way as the initial tables with headings indicating the major bone and subheadings indicating the physes and ossification. The most significant difference in these new tables is the horizontal axis which represents a timeline. This horizontal axis begins at birth and extends weekly up through 8 weeks. After 8 weeks it changes to monthlong increments ranging from 2 months through 12 months. At 12 months it switches to yearlong increments from 1 year through 4 years. After 4 years the axis ends as no normal physeal or ossification center closure occurs beyond that time. Utilizing these axes together creates a grid system within the table that has been filled in different colors representing appearance and closure of the physes and ossification centers. A black box indicates the time frame for appearance of the physis or ossification center, and a light gray box indicates the time frame for closure of the physis or ossification center. Extended boxes in either color represent an extended range of appearance or closure possibilities within the timeframe indicated on the horizontal axis. Dark gray boxes indicate an overlap between possible times of appearance and possible times of closure for certain physes and ossification centers. This overlap is uncommon. When the time frames indicated in the literature did not directly line up with the time indicated on the horizontal axis, the whole box for the next incremental time marker was filled. But, the specific time within that window was indicated in text within the box.

Some of the colored boxes in the final tables may appear in slight opposition to the text in the initial tables. This is due to differences in data that was used to compile these tables. Times were marked in days, weeks, months, or some combination of each. It became apparent in the validation portion, and supported by the literature, that as animals get older the variation in the ranges for appearance and closure (closure more so than appearance) of physes and ossification centers become greater [2]. There was not any indication in the published literature or in the validation study that sex of the animal makes a difference in appearance or closure times. There was noticeable variation between individuals of the same breed in both the published literature and in the validation study and a greater amount of variation between individuals of different breeds. In the validation this could be explained by the uncertainty about the accuracy of the age reported by the owners of the animals as well as how diet or other factors (e.g., health or activity) may have affected the animal. As a result of this uncertainty in the data, the ranges were extended slightly on either end to accommodate potential differences between time units of all studies, variations between breed, and interpretation of those units of time.

11.4 Factors for Consideration in Forensic Application

There was a stark lack of literature data for felines as compared to canines. There were no published or otherwise available data on the appearance and closure rates of physes and ossification centers in the spine for felines and very little data about the pelvis. This can be remedied with future research. Despite assessing a significant number of felines in the validation study, those specimens could not be used to fill in the gaps in the data from the published literature as the specimens used for validation were not "research subjects." That is, the exact age of the specimens was unknown; the full medical history (including genetic conditions) was unknown; and the diet, activity, and other factors that could potentially affect the bone growth rates measured in this study were also unknown. In order for this data to be useful, the specimens must be monitored from a known birth date and radiographed at known and marked intervals throughout their growth. The specimens available at the time of this study were unsuitable for this task.

Another factor that affected the data compiled within this study was the data in the published literature. Of all studies utilized that specified the number and type of specimens used, there was not a consistent number used between studies; many were not statistically significant on their own and referenced "dogs of unknown breed" rather than offering more specific information. Future research should include breed information.

The common method of using dentition for age determination in animals was considered for forensic use. As illustrated in Table 11.1, dental eruption times are only useful up through approximately 6–7 months of age in animals. Additionally, there are a number of outside factors that affect dentition. These include wear and tear on the teeth from improper diet/nutrition or improper hygiene and care of an animal's dental health. This can result in missing, decayed, or damaged teeth, which could preclude the applicability and usefulness of age determination via dentition. This is particularly significant in forensic cases as animals that are neglected often have poor diets and are malnourished, which results in poor dentition. That is not to say that age determination via physeal and ossification center appearance and closure rates are without potential pitfalls. This method can be affected by nutritional, hormonal, genetic, and traumatic factors that could make age estimation difficult. Two advantages this method provides over dental age are its usefulness beyond 6 months of age as well as the numerous options for areas of study throughout the body. If one of the forelimbs has been traumatically injured, the other forelimb is still available for study, whereas in dentition, if the teeth are adversely affected as a result of diet, it is often a large number of teeth. It is important to understand the physiology of bone growth and how it can be affected by outside factors such as nutrition and internal factors such as hormonal imbalances and hereditary disorders [11]. A thorough understanding of these can enhance the ability and usefulness of age determination through physeal and ossification center appearance and closure rates.

Another important aspect to consider is the effect of trauma on bone growth. Younger animals in particular are more susceptible to trauma that could potentially have lifelong effects because the bone still in its growing phase is softer and more prone to injury, even from minor trauma [11]. When bone trauma occurs during the growth phase, it can potentially lead to growth deformities that cause persistent symptoms of bone dysfunction. This is significant because more than half of dogs with reported long bone fractures sustained the initial trauma that caused the fracture when they were less than 1 year old. Of those, nearly a third had trauma to the growth plate, and nearly 10% of the original 50% experienced resulting growth deformities [12].

Often, animals with bone trauma in a forensic investigation are of unknown age. They undergo a series of "serial radiographs"—that is, they are x-rayed at 1 month intervals for a 2–3 month period in an effort to document healing trauma. Using these sets of radiographs with the final tables contained in this study (Tables 11.7, 11.8, and 11.9), the physes and ossification centers present in each radiograph could be documented in the charts at each stage of examination, and over the course of the 2–3-month follow-up, the changes in bone growth and development could be documented and recorded. With the current format of the chart showing anatomical regions (visible in the serial radiographs) plotted against a timeline (the data that is desired for the animal), the forensic investigator could use the available information radiographically to more effectively estimate the age of the animal with the given ranges in the chart. The reverse could be accomplished clinically with an animal of known age who is being assessed for deviations from the norm in growth patterns.

Acknowledgments Funded by the American Society for the Prevention of Cruelty to Animals through the UF-ASPCA Graduate Fellowship Program.

References[1,2]

1. Gilsanz V, Osman R. Hand bone age: a digital atlas of skeletal maturity. Berlin: Springer; 2005.
2. Chapman WL. Appearance of ossification centers and epiphyseal closures as determined by radiographic techniques. J Am Vet Med Assoc. 1965;147:138–41.
3. Newton CD, Nunamaker DM. Appendix C—Canine and feline epiphyseal plate closure and appearance of ossification centers. In: Textbook of small animal orthopaedics. Philadelphia: Lippincott; 1985.
4. Schebitz H, Wilkens H. Atlas of radiographic anatomy of the dog and cat. Berlin: Verlag P. Parey; 1978.
5. Smith RN. Radiological observations on the limbs of young greyhounds. J Small Anim Pract. 1960;1(1-4):84–90.
6. Smith R. Appearance of ossification centers in the kitten. J Small Anim Pract. 1968;9:496–511.
7. Smith R. Fusion of ossification centers in the cat. J Small Anim Pract. 1969;10:523–30.
8. Thrall DE, Robertson ID. Atlas of normal radiographic anatomy & anatomic variants in the dog and cat. St. Louis: Elsevier/Saunders; 2011.
9. Ticer JW. Radiographic technique in small animal practice. Philadelphia: Saunders; 1975.
10. Pfeil v, Dirsko JF, DeCamp CE. The epiphyseal plate: physiology, anatomy, and trauma. Compend Contin Educ Vet. 2009;31(8):E1–11.
11. Pfeil v, Dirsko JF, DeCamp CE, Abood SK. The epiphyseal plate: nutritional and hormonal influences; hereditary and other disorders. Compend Contin Educ Vet. 2009;31(8):E1–13.
12. Moore, William. Salter-Harris fracture imaging. Salter-Harris fracture imaging. Medscape reference: drugs, diseases, and procedures, 24 Jan. 2013. Web

Appendix

	Canines		Felines	
	Deciduous (weeks)	Permanent (months)	Deciduous (weeks)	Permanent (months)
Incisors	3–4	3–5	2–3	3–4
Canines	3	4–6	3–4	4–5
Premolars	4–12	4–6	3–6	4–6
Molars	n/a	5–7	n/a	4–5

[1]A number of these sources utilized additional published literature and radiographic atlases to compile their data tables. It was the data tables in these sources themselves that were used in this study. Other studies used to compile the original tables were not listed unless specifically consulted.

[2]This was the primary source for compiling the data table in this study as it utilized numerous additional studies for compiling its data table, several of which were independently consulted for this study as well.

Index